Social Justice in the Global Age

Social Justice in the Global Age

Edited by
Olaf Cramme and Patrick Diamond

polity

First published in 2009 by Polity Press

Polity Press
65 Bridge Street
Cambridge CB2 1UR, UK

Polity Press
350 Main Street
Malden, MA 02148, USA

ISBN-13: 978-0-7456-4419-6
ISBN-13: 978-0-7456-4420-2(pb)

A catalogue record for this book is available from the British Library.

Typeset in 10.5 on 13 pt Swift
by Servis Filmsetting Ltd, Stockport, Cheshire
Printed and bound in Great Britain by MPG Books Ltd, Bodmin, Cornwall

The publisher has used its best endeavours to ensure that the URLs for external websites
referred to in this book are correct and active at the time of going to press. However, the
publisher has no responsibility for the websites and can make no guarantee that a site will
remain live or that the content is or will remain appropriate.

Every effort has been made to trace all copyright holders, but if any have been inadvertently
overlooked the publishers will be pleased to include any necessary credits in any
subsequent reprint or edition.

For further information on Polity, visit our website: www.polity.co.uk

Contents

About Policy Network

Policy Network is an international think-tank dedicated to promoting progressive policies and the renewal of social democracy. Launched in 2000 to facilitate the sharing of ideas and experiences among politicians, policy-makers and experts on the centre-left, it seeks to inject new ideas into progressive politics that address the common challenges and opportunities of the global age.

Progressive governments and parties in industrialised countries are facing similar pressures. Perceived threats to economic, political and social security linked to globalisation, migration or climate change, and the limitations of traditional policy prescriptions in the light of rapid social and technological change, increasingly demand that progressives look beyond national borders to find common solutions.

Through its international programme of research, publications and events, Policy Network seeks to promote international best practice and provide innovative answers to shared problems, equipping social democrat modernisers with the intellectual tools necessary to meet the policy and political challenges of the twenty-first century.

Selected recent publications

Patrick Diamond (ed.), *Public Matters: The Renewal of the Public Realm* (London: Politicos, 2007)

Anthony Giddens, Patrick Diamond and Roger Liddle (eds), *Global Europe, Social Europe* (Cambridge: Polity, 2006)

The Hampton Court Agenda: A Social Model for Europe (London: Policy Network, 2006)

Anthony Giddens and Patrick Diamond (eds), *The New Egalitarianism* (Cambridge: Polity, 2005)

www.policy-network.net

About the Contributors

Robert Atkinson is President and founder of the Information Technology and Innovation Foundation, Washington, DC. Previously, he was Vice President of the Progressive Policy Institute and Director of PPI's Technology and New Economy Project. He is author of the *State New Economy Index* series and the book, *The Past and Future of America's Economy: Long Waves of Innovation That Power Cycles of Growth* (2005).

David Coates holds the Worrell Professorship in Anglo-American Studies at Wake Forest University in North Carolina. His current research interests focus on 'third-way politics' and on the response of organised labour in both the UK and the US to the increasingly global nature of production and trade. His most recent books include *Blair's War* (with Joel Kreiger, 2004); *Prolonged Labour: The Slow Birth of New Labour Britain* (2005); and *A Liberal Tool Kit: Progressive Answers to Conservative Arguments* (2007).

Olaf Cramme is the Director of Policy Network and a Lecturer in European Politics at London Metropolitan University. Previously, he worked as a parliamentary researcher at the Houses of Parliament. He holds a PhD in European Studies from London Metropolitan University and has studied history, politics and international relations in Heidelberg and Paris.

Patrick Diamond is the Director of Policy and Strategy for the Commission for Equality and Human Rights. He is also a senior visiting fellow at the London School of Economics and Transatlantic fellow of the German Marshall Fund of the United States. Previously, he was Director of Policy Network. His recent publications include *Shifting Alliances: Europe, America and the Future of Britain's Global Strategy* (2008); *Public Matters: The Renewal of the Public Realm* (ed. 2007); and *Global Europe, Social Europe* (ed. with Anthony Giddens and Roger Liddle, 2006).

Germano Dottori teaches Strategic Studies at the International Free University for Social Sciences, and International Security at the Link-Campus of Malta University, both in Rome. He is the author of several books and essays. In 2007, he delivered at the Colloquium on Italy's approach to international issues, promoted by the University of Cambridge, a paper entitled 'Italy and the Challenge of Mass Migration: Risks and Opportunities – A Test for Europe'.

Maurizio Ferrera is Professor of Comparative Social Policy and President of the Graduate School in Social, Economic and Political Studies at the University of Milan. He also directs the Research Unit on European Governance (URGE) at the Collegio Carlo Alberto, Turin. He is a member of the Group of Societal Policy Analysis advisers to the European Commission and writes regularly in *Il Corriere della Sera*. His recent publications in English include *The Boundaries of Welfare: European Integration and the New Spatial Politics of Social Protection* (2005); *Rescued by Europe? Social and Labour Market Reforms from Maastricht to Berlusconi* (with E. Gualmini, 2004); and *Recasting the European Welfare State* (co-edited with Martin Rhodes, 2000).

Lionel Fontagné is Professor of Economics in the Paris School of Economics, Université Paris I (Panthéon-Sorbonne). He is also a member of the Conseil d'Analyse Économique (Council of Economic Analysis to the French Prime Minister), a scientific adviser to the Centre d'Études Prospectives et d'Informations Internationales (CEPII, Paris), and an adviser to the International Trade Center (UNCTAD-WTO, Geneva). He has formerly been the director of the CEPII, a Supply Professor at the Free University of Brussels and a Professor at the University of Nantes. He is co-editor of the online think-tank Telos.

Andrew Gamble is Professor of Politics at the University of Cambridge. Before that he was Professor of Politics at the University of Sheffield, where he was a founder member and subsequently the Director of the Political Economy Research Centre. He is joint editor of *The Political Quarterly*, and a Fellow of the British Academy and the Academy of Social Sciences. His books include *Between Europe and America: The Future of British Politics* (2003) and *Politics and Fate* (2000). In 2005 he received the Sir Isaiah Berlin Prize for Lifetime Contribution to Political Studies from the UK Political Studies Association.

Anke Hassel is Professor of Public Policy at Hertie School of Governance, Berlin. Previously, she worked for the Planning Department of the Federal Ministry of Economics and Labour (BMWA). She is also an adjunct professor of the Graduate School of Social Sciences at Bremen

University and has published a range of articles and books, the most recent of which was *Wage Setting, Social Pacts and the Euro: A New Role for the State* (2006).

Roger Liddle is the vice chair of Policy Network and a visiting fellow at the European Institute, London School of Economics. He is former economic adviser to the European Commission President José Manuel Barroso, and for eight years was European adviser to Tony Blair. His publications include *The Blair Revolution: Can New Labour Deliver* (with Peter Mandelson, 1996); *The New Case for Europe* (2005); and *Economic Reform in Europe: Priorities Over the Next Five Years* (with Maria Joao Rodrigues, 2005).

Wolfgang Merkel is Professor of Political Science at the Humboldt-Universität zu Berlin, and Director of the research unit Democracy: Structures, Performance, Challenges at the Wissenschaftszentrum Berlin für Sozialforschung (Social Science Research Centre in Berlin). He was previously Managing Director of the Institute of Political Science at both the University of Heidelberg and the University of Mainz. He is the author of *Social Democracy in Power: The Capacity to Reform* (with Alexander Petring, Christian Henkes and Christoph Egle, 2007).

David Miller is an Official Fellow in Social and Political Theory at Nuffield College, University of Oxford. His current areas of research focus on theories of justice and equality; multiculturalism and justice; nationality, citizenship and deliberative democracy; and responsibilities with and between nations. He has published widely on issues in contemporary political theory and philosophy. His most recent books include *National Responsibility and Global Justice* (2007); *Political Philosophy: A Very Short Introduction* (2003); and *Citizenship and National Identity* (2000).

Diane Perrons is Director of the Gender Institute and Reader in Economic Geography and Gender Studies at the London School of Economics. Her current research projects are: new economy, work-life balance, equality and representation (financed by Leverhulme); and work life and time in the new global economy (financed by the Economic and Social Research Council). She is the author of *Globalisation and Social Change: People and Places in a Divided World* (2004).

Gene Sperling is Senior Fellow for Economic Policy at the Center for American Progress. He is also Director of the Center for Universal Education, Council on Foreign Relations, and US Chair of the Global

Campaign for Education. Previously, he served as National Economic Advisor to President Clinton from 1997–2001 and Deputy National Economic Advisor from 1993–96. He is the author of *The Pro-Growth Progressive: An Economic Strategy for Shared Prosperity* (2005).

Acknowledgements

This book is the outcome of a series of seminars and conferences organised by Policy Network in the course of 2007. The events, which took place in London, Brussels, Washington, Santiago de Chile and Melbourne, were unique opportunities to discuss and share ideas with senior international experts and policy-makers about the relationship between globalisation and social justice. We would like to thank all those who attended and co-organised these meetings, in particular the Chilean Instituto Igualdad, the Australian think-tank Per Capita, and the Center for American Progress. Above all, we are enormously grateful to the Alfred Herrhausen Society and its director Wolfgang Nowak and its deputy director Ute Weiland, who generously supported our initiative and work. They have been an invaluable source of help.

We would also like to thank the many people who have helped in the preparation of this book. During her time as researcher at Policy Network, Chelsey Wickmark thoroughly managed the seminar series, liaised with the authors and provided useful research assistance. By helping with the production of the volume and editing early drafts, Annie Bruzzone, Mark Day, Sophie Heitz and Michael McTernan greatly facilitated the process. Thanks are also due to Joanne Burton who played an instrumental role in organising the international events. We would also like to thank Sarah Lambert and all the staff at Polity Press who have been efficient and helpful throughout.

Last but not least, we owe immense gratitude to our good friend Roger Liddle, whose commitment and intellectual stimulation has been an inspiration for years.

Olaf Cramme and Patrick Diamond
London, August 2008.

INTRODUCTION

1

Rethinking Social Justice in the Global Age

Olaf Cramme and Patrick Diamond

Our argument

The aim of this volume is to articulate a modern conception of social justice that remains relevant for an era of rapid globalisation. The authors have developed a robust theoretical account of the relationship between globalisation and social justice, complemented by an underpinning policy framework that aims to promote new forms of equity and solidarity in both developing and industrialised economies.

The very definition of *social justice* has always been complex and contested. Here we use the term to refer to the relative distribution of rights, opportunities and resources within a given society, and whether it deserves to be regarded as fair and just. It is our contention that the principles of justice are under attack from two broad directions. There are those who believe that social justice is no longer a credible aspiration given the disciplines imposed by globalisation, the shift in the balance of power between labour and capital, and the extent of international economic competition. There are others who suggest that the claims of social justice in the west are now of a second order as against the new concern with *global justice*, where the focus is on defining the moral responsibilities of the world's rich towards the world's poor.

The underlying assumption of this book is that globalisation has profoundly affected both how we think about social justice and the extent to which we believe it is attainable. Our purpose is to reassess both the central principles of social justice and the radical reforms necessary to bring it about, as well as to tackle the myth that globalisation renders any strategy for social justice impotent. In essence, the contributors to this volume advance the following core arguments:

First, it is neither intellectually credible nor morally desirable to speak of social justice in one country. In other words, we cannot think of global and national social justice in separate compartments, but need to recognise that both are inextricably intertwined given the nature of globalisation in the twenty-first century. But second, this should not lead us to conflate the principles of social justice and global justice. Not only is our sense of solidarity and our shared self-interest inevitably stronger at the national than at the global level. There is also a major discrepancy in how the national and the international community can assume responsibility for the promotion and execution of distributive justice. We need to realise that there may indeed be complex trade-offs and difficult choices to be made between advancing social justice at home and promoting global justice abroad.

Third, this demands a credible reassessment of the principles required to achieve domestic social justice as well as a carefully nuanced analysis of how globalisation is actually affecting the capacity to achieve greater fairness in our own societies. The evidence suggests that secular trends in addition to globalisation may be responsible for increasing inequality in the distribution of rights, opportunities and resources, including the decline of manufacturing industry, the impact of fiscal policy, advances in technology, accelerating demographic change and the very different characteristics of family formation. Essentially, social change is often internally driven, but globalisation – in particular when considered in relation to international economic competition and migration – may accentuate the risk of polarisation.

Fourth, there is still significant space for national political choices about the extent to which social justice ought to be a central driver of domestic policy. Nonetheless, the heyday of the nation-state is irrefutably at an end. The argument is not that national governments are absolutely powerless in the face of global forces, but rather that it may be increasingly necessary to pursue a strategy of multi-tiered governance in which power is redistributed between different levels of the state in pursuit of collective action at the local, national, regional and global levels. This includes being prepared to rethink the role of the European Union, as well as to undertake reform of international financial institutions from the World Bank to the International Monetary Fund.

Finally, if we want to pursue a fairer distribution of opportunities and life chances, we also need to develop sophisticated policy approaches capable of dealing with the rise of complexity in western societies. This includes the vast range of choices and information now available to citizens; constantly rising aspirations and expectations alongside feelings of insecurity; fluid and flexible family lives; complex and demanding careers; and new global anxieties ranging from terrorism to the looming threat of climate change.

In the light of these arguments there are two central principles underlying a new kind of twenty-first-century social contract. On the one hand, it is important to consider how social justice might be advanced beyond the bounded territories of the nation-state, taking into account new forms of governance using complex, overlapping forms of jurisdiction and authority to meet progressive goals. In addition, the practical policy challenge is to refashion a set of instruments developed in the mid twentieth century that presupposed the existence of national economies and that did not take into account the concerns and aspirations of developing countries – many of them still on their way to independence after decades of colonial occupation and repression. Back then, governments could attempt to strike a balance between the power of capital, labour and the state by embedding the market within a regulatory framework that sought to reconcile economic efficiency with social justice. In the United States, this led to the concept of the New Deal; in Europe to the social market economy; and in Britain to the post-war welfare state of Attlee, Beveridge and Keynes. The most recent phase of global economic integration and financial turbulence is, however, continuing to alter significantly the context in which governments operate, while heightening tensions over the extent of inequality between 'winners' and 'losers'.

On the other hand, building on the work of the political philosopher David Miller, it is important to be able to demonstrate how the basic principles of social justice and global justice might be interwoven and mutually reinforcing rather than fundamentally incompatible. It is not a case of global justice *versus* domestic social justice, but of how different conceptions of justice might be brought into play in order to advance ethical objectives such as the dignity and the equal worth of all. The relationship between principles of social justice and global justice is of course complex, and it is important to grasp how the world order as a context for justice is both similar and different to that of the nation itself, as Miller elaborates.

For instance, a familiar notion of social justice such as the commitment to equality of opportunity cannot be easily transposed to the global level. In the domestic context, such principles are pursued through the redistributive machinery of national governments, but no such means exist on a global scale. Neither is there the same ethic of mutual self-interest and belonging globally that sustains collective risk-pooling and social insurance in bounded national territories. As a consequence, we cannot dismiss the possibility of profound and fundamental conflicts in the pursuit of both social justice and global justice. Instead, it is vital to confront the potential dilemmas and trade-offs upfront.

Social justice and global justice

This naturally leads to the question of how we can best reconcile the quest for greater social justice in our own societies with greater social justice in the world. There are no simple answers. This inevitably challenges our thinking about how to create the necessary conditions under which social justice and global justice can be simultaneously realised.

The first prerequisite is economic growth and wealth creation. If individuals and societies care about improving the living standards of people in both the developed and developing world, the pursuit of growth will remain an imperative. It matters not only because of its positive consequences for employment and the labour market, but also because economic growth helps to generate the revenues that are necessary to deal with the long-term challenges of an ageing society and demographic change – such as financing national health systems and improving income support for the elderly – and to avoid a 'generational clash' which may result from stagnant, or even worse declining per-capita incomes, in particular when coupled with widening inequalities.

There are recent critics of growth who have highlighted its apparent incompatibility with the challenge of environmental sustainability and tackling climate change. While this claim certainly requires careful exploration, practical solutions to the challenge of climate change are more likely to originate in a combination of technological progress and intelligently designed policies that curb carbon emissions through a global 'cap and trade' approach – and ultimately, this still requires rapid economic development and innovation.[1]

The mounting literature on the economics of happiness and well-being has also challenged some of the taken for granted assumptions about the virtues of growth.[2] It is suggested that despite record levels of GDP and the emergence of what Ronald Inglehart terms 'post-materialist values', people have not become happier over the last fifty years.[3] It is certainly true that relative degrees of wealth may be more important to our sense of well-being than absolute wealth, but without economic growth current levels of prosperity could simply not be sustained in the developed world. Neither would it be possible to effectively tackle poverty, in particular in developing countries where roughly two billion people still live on the equivalent of less than two dollars a day. The fact that growth rates in developing countries have accelerated during the last three decades and are now higher than in richer countries should in many respects be celebrated.

But there are many who still believe that growth in emerging economies will take place at the cost of our own living standards in the west, fuelling the seemingly inexorable drift towards protectionist trade policies in the United States and elsewhere. As a result, so it is thought, globalisation will not only create new winners and losers in industrialised nations, but also slowly shift prosperity from one region of the world to another. Such fears are fundamentally misplaced, however. Growth is not a zero-sum game whereby every dollar or euro which accrues to one country comes out of another. Instead, global economic integration often creates win–win scenarios, allowing countries to use their competitive advantage while growing their economies through increased trade. Unsurprisingly, there are a considerable number of policy-makers in the industrialised world who regard globalisation as a major opportunity for their countries and their people, not as a threat.

The debate in western Europe should be concerned with how we develop a vision of global integration and of how market forces are shaped that works in the interests of both developed and developing countries. Addressing global justice requires us to meet the collective challenges of securing decent humanitarian and environmental standards. This is best advanced through a twofold strategy. First, through international political engagement that addresses key issues such as poverty and development, energy and climate change, security and migration, and improved global governance. Second, through economic openness that permits developing countries to benefit from international trade.

We also have to accept that in industrialised democracies this approach of openness to globalisation will only be sustainable if the economic, social and cultural changes unleashed are seen to benefit the majority, not just privileged elites, and if we find a way to advance social justice that ensures a fairer distribution of life chances, tackling the insidious transmission of inter-generational disadvantage. In truth, the global economic system will not be durable unless the winners are prepared to share more of the gains with the losers.

The urgency of defining a modern conception of social justice carried forward in this volume is based precisely on that proposition. The book is divided into four main parts. First, it seeks to develop new principles of social justice appropriate to the global era. It then considers the impact of globalisation and other secular trends on patterns of social justice in the industrialised countries over the last thirty years. Third, it puts the debate in the context of political economy by focusing on the social justice challenges for modern social democracy in the global era.[4] Finally, the volume examines the variety of policy frameworks, from social policy to sustainability, that could be implemented by international institutions and national governments in pursuit of social justice principles. In particular, the concern is how to entrench progressive change, ensuring that reforms at both the domestic and the international level acquire popular support and leave a lasting legacy equivalent to Franklin D. Roosevelt's New Deal and the form of welfare capitalism that prevailed throughout much of western Europe in the mid to late twentieth century.

Social justice as a theoretical concept

As a concept, social justice cannot be defined as a set of principles that apply in all situations and contexts, as David Miller has elaborated elsewhere.[5] Nor can social justice be measured along a single metric such as human welfare or individual liberty. Of course, the basic idea of social justice is inevitably contested since it is an ethical commitment, not an empirically verifiable end-state or 'ideal-type' of society. While it often involves ensuring that people are treated equally, at the same time the demands of social justice might require that people are treated differently according to the diversity of human needs and capabilities. As the philosopher Michael Walzer has speculated, social justice is a radically plural notion, with its principles often determined by the different social goods that are available for allocation.[6] Accordingly, social justice at the domestic level will be implemented differently in the economic sphere than in the realm of public services and the welfare state, for example. Miller proposes four principles of social justice within the context of the nation-state:

- Equal Citizenship: an equal set of basic rights including the means to exercise those rights effectively.
- Social Minimum: the resources that allow all citizens to meet essential needs and to live a secure and dignified life in today's society.
- Equality of Opportunity: where life chances depend on motivation and aptitude, not on factors such as class, gender or ethnicity.
- Fair Distribution: the resources that do not form part of equal citizenship or the social minimum may be distributed unequally, but that distribution must reflect relevant factors such as personal desire and personal choice.

What is imaginative about Miller's formulation is his insistence that social justice is not merely about the distribution of income and wealth, but involves a richer appreciation of human well-being. Social justice should be defined in terms of personal autonomy, self-esteem, and the capacity to open up life opportunities and make use of them – all desirable qualities of the good life. The pursuit of social justice also requires an understanding of the underlying attitudes and values of the population at large, and how policy can work with the grain of these views. It is necessary to explore how particular conceptions of justice might reinforce or undermine strongly held public sentiments about fairness involving such issues as the legitimacy of inheritance tax and the extent of reciprocity towards new migrants, both central to contemporary political debate in the industrialised countries.

To reiterate, the central concern of this volume is that the basic context for social justice has substantially altered over the last fifty years as the traditional boundaries of the nation-state have melted away under pressure from global forces. In particular, it means that the link between social justice and the boundaries of the nation-state that was central to the formation of the welfare settlement in Europe during the late nineteenth and early twentieth centuries can no longer be taken for granted.

Globalisation and new social realities

Any discussion of globalisation implies a vast range of issues and debates linked to a rather elusive, misunderstood and heavily contested concept. It is a commonplace assertion – particularly among leading exponents of neo-liberalism – that nation-states no longer have the latitude to pursue domestic objectives such as equality of opportunity. Indeed, such myths have become the dominant theme of contemporary debate about economic policy in the west. It is asserted that countries are no longer free to pursue their own macroeconomic policy given the disciplines imposed by global financial markets.

The attempt to limit financial market liberalisation is viewed as anachronistic and positively harmful to future growth. Moreover, the tax base is apparently under threat as the result of intense competition for mobile capital and labour, and levels of public expenditure in western Europe are judged to be unsustainable given the competitive pressures unleashed by globalisation.[7]

The difficulty with these now widely accepted assumptions is that they are either half-true but plainly exaggerated, or merely just wrong. For instance, while elements of all national economies in the west have been increasingly open to international trade and competition since the 1970s, a large proportion of economic activity, particularly in the low-skilled service industries, is inherently untradeable. It is only a minority of the workforce which is in reality exposed to global competition. In certain respects, economies have become more local and less global since the late 1970s.

In this context, threats of off-shoring and outsourcing have become a populist rallying cry. For many, openness to globalisation equates with being threatened by dislocation and loss of jobs, depressing wages and living standards. Economists are still arguing about the actual scale of the phenomenon, yet those who have examined the precise levels of aggregated job losses due to international economic competition have not found any large-scale negative impact on employment patterns. In his contribution to this collection, Lionel Fontagné elaborates how standard trade theories fail to capture the precise magnitude of changes in the labour market as well as the distribution of income. The empirical evidence appears to suggest that biased technological progress has largely been responsible for widening inequality and shifts in the demand for skilled and unskilled labour. Furthermore, Fontagné uncovers a degree of international specialisation which has profound consequences for the trade relationship between developed and emerging economies. If high-wage and low-wage countries specialise in varieties within products rather than on the same bundle of goods, fears that global competition will have a large-scale impact on jobs may well be misplaced. In addition, increasing pressure on the income of blue-collar workers has to some extent been compensated by the further fall in import prices which translates into increasing purchasing power, especially among low-income households.

Finally, there is very little robust economic evidence that global tax competition has made the welfare state inherently unaffordable. Theories abound concerning an alleged 'race to the bottom' in taxes and welfare standards. It is argued that international competition severely constrains welfare-state spending as a consequence of declining rates of corporation tax. It is true that over the last two decades we have witnessed a considerable reduction in corporation tax rates across the OECD, leading to a large degree of convergence across countries. However, it is often overlooked that corporation taxes are of only limited importance for welfare finances and therefore cannot be blamed for any major retrenchment of the welfare state. The contribution of corporation taxes to overall tax revenues in OECD countries has held steady over the last two decades, primarily due to rising corporate profits. Claims that levels of social spending are under strain because of globalisation should therefore be treated cautiously. In fact, in most OECD countries social spending as a proportion of national income has increased since the late 1970s.

All too often distinct and specific events and crises in the international economy are misleadingly attributed to the hidden hand of globalisation. The collapse of central planning and the spread of markets is not the same as the increasing interdependence of the global economic system, which – as David Coates reiterates in this volume – has been brought about through the greater capital mobility following the collapse of exchange controls in the early 1980s. It is necessary to distinguish here between the international economy and the global economy, which implies the existence of a co-ordinated neo-liberal policy regime. One of the most significant developments is the increasing integration of the European economies over the last thirty years, rather different to the changes implied by the concept of globalisation.

As a matter of fact, global integration is not only limited to economic factors but also impinges on other dimensions. For instance, in the last decade alone, the volume of migration into the advanced economies has increased substantially and migrant flows have grown more complex in their scale and impact. The United Nations estimates that more than 200 million people live and work outside their country of birth – twice the level of twenty-five years ago. In 2006, according to the Migration Policy Institute, migrants worldwide sent home an estimated $206 billion in remittances – more than twice the level of official aid received by developing countries.[8] The issue of increasing levels of migration has already provoked heated debate in many European countries. All too often such increases are misleadingly attributed to the scope and role of national politics in managing the process of migration and integration. As Germano Dottori argues, mass migratory flows in today's world stem primarily from strong demographic pressures as a consequence of global population imbalances and will not significantly decrease at least in the short to mid term, regardless of a particular country's immigration-control policy.

This only serves to emphasise that it is vital to operate with a more sophisticated understanding of what is, and has been, involved in the process of globalisation – that is to say, a better understanding of the extent to which the principal facets of globalisation (capital mobility, technology transfer, outsourcing, trade adjustment, pressure on energy supplies, environmental sustainability and climate change, migration, crime and security) are impacting on our social models and welfare states. Roger Liddle exposes in his contribution how the success of Europe's social models as well as the development of the knowledge and service economy are fundamentally altering the underlying trajectory of our societies: increased life expectancy with its consequences for pensions and social care; extended life choices for women with their impact on the differing fortunes of one-earner and two-earner households; new social risks relating to the emergence of a rise in depression and mental illness, obesity and alcohol misuse; and the disappearance of the 'good working-class job' due to major occupational shifts in the labour market in the light of new demands and the widespread use of technology.

As a result, new forms of insecurity and inequality have emerged, often relating to a complex set of causal drivers. Despite the claims that globalisation has considerably widened the gap between rich and poor, Liddle shows how European states still have considerable room for manoeuvre about the choices they make over the distribution of opportunities and resources, as well as how they counter the risks of polarisation. As a precondition, we need to recognise that the needs of 'losers' from structural change are often very diverse, while fears about marginalisation and alienation can have multiple and complex roots.

Social justice and political economy

At any rate, whether or not globalisation itself has been conceptually misunderstood, it is no longer plausible to pursue a conception of social justice that assumes a closed political community, usually the nation-state. In a fundamental sense, the post-1945 era of 'golden age' Keynesianism, where many traditional instruments of social justice were developed, presupposed a particular kind of 'closed' world order based on two distinct characteristics that have now largely disappeared. As David Coates elaborates, the first was communism, which split the world in two and created hermetically sealed units shutting off vast swathes of labour and capital from integration into the world economy. Second, colonialism in the third world locked workers into subsistence agriculture and primary export production, reinforcing the separation of the world economy into discrete enclaves and limiting the flow of capital and labour.

Inevitably, social justice in the industrialised countries was associated with a national settlement between the corporate interests of labour and capital, in which 'fair shares' for all and universal welfare provision were guaranteed through national citizenship. But the conditions that underpinned this class compromise have all but evaporated, replaced by a global order whose central characteristic is the free and rapid movement of people and capital across borders. Capital mobility in particular has enabled business and governments in the industrialised countries to contain and discipline the demands of labour.

This context entails a wholly different approach to social justice and its implementation. Of particular importance to redefining social justice is consideration of the relationship between states and markets, and the role of the state itself in the production and distribution of public goods. For Coates, this means that a 'strategy of progressive competitiveness' will ultimately fail to adequately tackle the socio-economic challenges thrown up by the latest phase of capitalist development. Globalisation should not only be considered in relation to new technologies and opportunities for innovation, but also in relation to the global increase in the supply of labour. As a consequence, re-education and up-skilling alone will ultimately transfer unemployment and precariousness to different regions of the world economy. Instead, globalisation needs to be understood as a 'social relationship' which requires new forms of regulation. The progressive challenge is to pursue policies at the supranational and national level that strengthen the economic and social rights of labour around the world, and which avoid unregulated free trade between economies with vastly different wage levels but common access to modern technologies.

Robert Atkinson adopts a very different stance, arguing that raising domestic productivity through global production chains, as well as better use of information and communication technologies, ought to be the priority for those concerned with social justice. This approach seeks to defend economic openness, refuting claims that globalisation is the culprit for widening inequalities and job losses in the industrialised nations. Atkinson dismisses 'new mercantilism' and 'global Keynesianism' which would merely aim at a supposedly fairer distribution of the global economic cake, but fail to raise living standards in both developed and developing nations. The debate should instead turn to the question of how best to *manage* globalisation to ensure that the benefits of the new global economy characterised by an international division of labour between industrialised and emerging economies flow to all workers and not only the wealthy winners.

That said, none of the contributors to this volume would deny that there is a price to be paid for economic openness: to remain an integral part of the global economy, national governments must sustain the confidence of the financial markets, and this has altered the terms of trade in political debate and domestic policy-making. The rapid growth of international trade since the 1950s and the increasing interdependence of the world economy have also shattered confidence in traditional protectionist policies. But none of these developments equate simply to obliging governments to adopt particular neo-liberal reforms in domestic economic management. Part of our purpose in this volume is precisely to emphasise that there is still considerable variety in the policies that nation-states might adopt, and that there are still a variety of credible strategies to advance the broader principles of social justice. In other words, national governments that have been forced to adapt to new pressures and demands have also retained important capacities to choose particular policies and to shape the economic environment in which they operate. The Scandinavian model of social democracy is perhaps the best evidence of this open policy space, despite the apparent supremacy of neo-liberalism and the triumph of the Anglo-American model, which has recently been threatened by global economic turbulence.

This should not be taken to imply that it is still possible to resurrect the traditional model of social market democracy 'in one country' as exemplified by the Keynesian settlement after 1945. According to Andrew Gamble, two transformations stemming from global movements have had a particular impact on social democracy, in terms of both policy frameworks and domestic political management: the new international division of labour, and the growth of migration. Historically, social democracy has used various means to protect and subsidise employment, for instance by championing national industries that could ensure sufficient levels of competitiveness and productivity. Yet the increased mobility of labour and capital as well as the dominance of global companies – who often organise their system of production transnationally – have not only created major policy dilemmas for social democratic governments, but also weakened the traditional constituency of industrial workers who are often most exposed to the pressures from global competition and restructuring. In addition, there are fears about the impact of migration on living standards, employment and the supply of housing. This has encouraged elements among the governing class of European social democratic parties to take on defensive and protectionist positions. They have sought to defend the standards and citizenship benefits that have been achieved in particular national contexts, projecting an appeal that is based on upholding traditional economic and sectional interests against the unruly forces of globalisation.

In our view this is not an adequate approach given the rise of complexity and the emergence of the new global economy. As Gamble reiterates, the transformations alluded to in this volume invalidate the defensive mind-set of traditional social democracy, and demand a quite different approach to institutional reform. The first challenge is to create a transnational system of governance which complements national authorities in delivering the services and public goods that citizens need to enjoy opportunity and security. This collection reflects on the particular role that might be fulfilled by a reformed European Union.

The challenge of governance throws up a second major issue: how to engage and involve citizens in the policy-making process given the increasing complexity of post-industrial societies, and the global scope and scale of major developments. The collapse of deference and the role of the media in fostering cynicism have made the task of governance and political leadership far harder. Politics, as Gerry Stoker suggests elsewhere, is doomed to disappoint because like any centralised collective form of decision-making, it requires trade-offs between competing interests, is prone to failures in communication, and often produces messy and muddled outcomes.[9] But the only way through the problems thrown up by globalisation and the diversity of structural pressures and demands alluded to in this volume is to construct a politics that works for citizens and communities. They will not be solved by any other means.

In summary, we argue that a conception of social justice operating within the bounded territory of the nation-state will be quite inadequate for the future. The challenges have not suddenly emerged since the late 1970s, nor are they wholly to do with economic globalisation and its impact on national policy regimes where, as we have seen, the evidence is less than conclusive. The issues are to do with governance itself and with the processes unleashed by modernity, above all advances in technology and science. And this, in turn, also has a profound impact on diverging levels of development and the widening disparity between the global rich and the global poor.

In pursuit of social justice: creating new political spaces and policy tools

This is the context that those committed to principles of social justice now need to address. Our claim is that it requires us above all else to open up new political spaces and to develop new forms of governance that transform how the state is organised and run. It is about building a different set of capabilities at the local, national and transnational level. The most obvious area for innovation beyond the nation-state is the European Union, which is gradually creating a common membership space in which all citizens are accorded fundamental rights. This is combined with the strengthening of the EU social dimension where a variety of 'hard law' and 'soft law' instruments make possible the notion of solidarity across borders. The EU has also encouraged the development of transnational schemes and collaborative partnerships designed to secure shared objectives such as improved labour and environmental standards.

The experience of European integration has opened a 'window of opportunity' for the 'un-bounding' of solidarity, as Maurizio Ferrera explains. Driven by political determination, European states have gradually pooled sovereignty for the pursuit of collective action. With the emergence of a new layer of governance and, subsequently, through a series of binding regulations and court rulings, a number of social rights have been de-coupled from national citizenship within the EU and linked merely to work and residence status. While this process has been and still is by no means free of tensions – as the rise of right-wing, anti-immigration populist movements exemplifies – it also demonstrates that finding a balance between the 'logic of closure', as a precondition for social solidarity, and the 'logic of opening', which inspires European integration, is far more credible than it once was.

Comparing different regions of the world economy, it is clear that development is increasingly characterised by a 'complex mosaic' of fast growing 'superstar regions' found in both the north and south, as Diane Perrons reiterates in her contribution.

Regional patterns of inequality coincide with interpersonal inequalities shaped by gender, ethnicity, race and social class. This poses a particular challenge for those who are concerned about the inequitable model of global capitalism, inasmuch as neo-liberal growth policies such as supporting development clusters tend to exacerbate the growing divide between different regions. Perrons argues for a new mode of regulation that would allow contemporary productivity gains to be spread more evenly. This needs to encompass both the national and the international levels in order to achieve more inclusive growth and development, while re-balancing the division of labour between women and men which, based on the extension of parental leave and childcare support, can help reduce gender inequalities.

There is not only a need to move beyond traditional policy trade-offs in tackling new governing challenges, but also a recognition that the global market alone is an inadequate instrument for ensuring an equitable and sustainable distribution of opportunities and life chances. This should not mean returning to an old-fashioned form of 'tax and spend' social democracy wholly oriented to the nation-state. That is a defensive and anachronistic means by which to secure social justice in an open world where the tendency towards inequality, as well as sentiments of insecurity and polarisation, are stronger than in any previous era of economic history. Instead, we need to develop intelligent new adjustment policies that can adequately address the pressures felt most acutely by low-skilled workers and their families.

As Anke Hassel highlights, this requires a policy mix based on four pillars of reform: investing in and protecting skills and human resources to allow workers to move between jobs more easily; addressing concerns about employability, education and economic security by maintaining sufficient levels of social protection; identifying a country's comparative strength in terms of both economic and institutional assets, using them to the advantage of social and economic cohesion; and considering the distribution of in-work benefits and wage subsidies to tackle poverty while strengthening centralised wage-setting institutions and unionisation in order to combat income inequalities. Rejecting the current orthodoxies, Hassel insists that each country must find the appropriate blend of interventions and institutional reforms.

The failure of an overly dogmatic approach is best observed in the United States where the polarising inequalities and the 'hollowing out' of the middle class have fuelled economic anxiety while undermining the country's prosperity. Overly ideological supply-side policies and the insistence on smaller government led to a situation where Americans became more sceptical of the future than ever before. While excessive redistributive policies that ignore the need for private-sector growth, upward mobility, innovation, savings and entrepreneurship do not represent a sustainable solution either, the challenge is to identify a set of policy instruments that enable 'pro-growth equity' in a globalised economy. In his contribution, Gene Sperling identifies the ingredients for 'shared prosperity', including a progressive compact on trade that should embrace higher labour standards, strengthening safety nets worldwide, and smart job creation through strategies that encourage more high-value added jobs in competitive industries, an agenda that will be taken forward by the new US president.

Towards a modern conception of social justice

Following such an approach is by no means easy. In particular, it presents a major dilemma for those who fear that politics itself may be under threat from the combination of 'hyper-globalisation' and the rise of new forms of political populism, which dispute the capacity of the state to adequately protect people from global market forces. This also relates powerfully to an earlier theme of whether there is a real possibility of conflict between social justice and global justice. According to David Miller, these trade-offs are as much to do with identity as resources: how far do people see themselves as citizens of nation-states bound together by collective historical and cultural ties, or as cosmopolitans and 'global citizens' with moral responsibilities for human beings everywhere. The issue of reciprocity and fairness regarding the access of 'foreigners' to national social protection schemes has emerged as a heavily contested feature of political debate, contributing to the decline in support for centre-left parties in western Europe since the late 1990s. The danger is that adopting more cosmopolitan identities also weakens the commitment of populations in the industrialised countries to the pursuit of social justice at home, without at the same time making them any more committed to global justice across the world.

Miller's strategy is to find ways of strengthening national citizenship while making the active pursuit of global justice integral to it: the national project should contribute in specific ways to global justice, such as devoting a proportion of GDP to meeting development goals or agreed international targets for reducing emissions of greenhouse gases. Citizens in developed countries are, of course, affected more extensively than ever before by events and processes that take place elsewhere. The traditional interpretation of the national self-interest is increasingly obsolete, as 'our' security and prosperity increasingly depend on achieving it for others through international co-operation.

Another important element of the 'social justice, global justice' agenda is to establish policies that strengthen the social rights of vulnerable low-wage workers in the industrialised north, without undermining the spread of those rights to workers in the newly industrialising southern hemisphere. That requires the pursuit of global labour standards within a framework of universal respect for human rights. This should help to reduce what Miller terms 'the justice gap', as well as addressing the need to engage citizens by opening up distinctive new spaces for political activity and debate, entrenching progressive change and helping to build enduring support for the pursuit of justice at home and abroad.

At the same time, implementing radical change domestically will only succeed if we are capable of translating our philosophical principles into practical ideas. By comparing the libertarian, social-liberal and communitarian theories of social justice, Wolfgang Merkel shows the way for a credible reassessment of social justice in the light of the new realities of the twenty-first century. His formula for social justice, drawing on John Rawls' and Amartya Sen's understanding of 'equal life chances' and 'personal capabilities', has contributed to an emerging policy framework traditionally associated with the Nordic social model. This emphasises:

- The prevention of poverty: because poverty generally prevents the development of individual dignity, integrity and autonomy.
- The necessity of education and training: because they strongly influence individual life chances.
- The goal of inclusion in the labour market: because it is here that most citizens acquire income, status and prestige.
- Upholding social security standards: because this is where social security and social assistance are organised.
- Tackling the distribution of wealth and income: this is where the unjust results of the market economy are best corrected.
- The pursuit of generational justice: since it explicitly places the opportunities and life chances of the future generation on today's agenda.
- Finally, securing greater gender equality: despite all progress in this field, particularly during the last decades of the twentieth century, there is still a gender gap which runs counter to the principle of equal life chances and the needs of a post-industrial service economy.

Social justice in the global age

The challenge as Merkel presents it is to fashion a new, more productive and socially equitable compact. A just model of globalisation implies intervening, shaping and steering at the local, national and global level. The consistent message of this volume is that national governments are not powerless in the face of global forces, but it is no longer credible to frame the case for social justice in terms of the nation-state alone. We recognise that grand theories of equality and justice may have less purchase in societies of diversity and complexity. The extent of global economic interdependence and the deregulation of markets are seen by many as an irreparable obstacle to the realisation of these principles, but that assumption is mistaken. The thorough understanding of the real impact of globalisation on existing social models and welfare-state arrangements provided by the contributors to this book is indispensable in countering such myths.

Our policy framework emphasises the importance of investing intelligently in the productive capabilities of the entire population, using governing capacities imaginatively while rebuilding trust in the democratic process itself. The objective is to develop methods and tools of governance that make possible new approaches to collective action improving human welfare and equity, in turn reinventing the governing purpose of the state itself. As this volume attests, a quite different account of social justice will be necessary for the future. Our aim in producing this book has been to stimulate and encourage a significant shift in that direction, towards the creation of a world where all citizens are able to flourish in conditions of freedom and security.

Notes

1   For an excellent discussion about why economic growth matters, see W.J. Baumol, R.E. Litan and C.J. Schramm, *Good Capitalism, Bad Capitalism, and the Economics of Growth and Prosperity* (Yale University Press, 2007), pp. 15–34.
2   See, for example, R.A. Esterlin, 'Will Raising the Incomes of All Increase the Happiness of All?', *Journal of Economic Behavior and Organisation*, 27 (June, 1995), pp. 35–48.
3   R. Inglehart, *The Silent Revolution: Changing Values and Political Styles Among Western Publics* (Princeton: Princeton University Press, 1977).
4   For a discussion about social democracy as a political ideology, see, for example, S. Berman, *Primacy of Politics: Social Democracy and the Making of Europe's Twentieth Century* (Cambridge University Press, 2006).
5   See D. Miller, *Theories of Social Justice* (Cambridge, Mass.: Harvard University Press, 1999).
6   M. Walzer, *Spheres of Justice: A Defence of Pluralism and Equality* (New York: Basic Books, 1983).

7   A good starting point for the debate about globalisation is: T. Friedman, *The Lexus and the Olive Tree: Understanding Globalization* (New York: Farrar, Straus, Giroux, 1999).

8   D. Ratha, *Leveraging Remittances for Development*, MPI Policy Brief (June 2007): http://www.migrationpolicy.org/pubs/MigDevPB_062507.pdf

9   G. Stoker, *Why Politics Matters* (Basingstoke: Palgrave Macmillan, 2005).

I

PRINCIPLES

2

Social Justice versus Global Justice?

David Miller

Few things have played a more fatal part in the history of human thought and action than great imaginative analogies from one sphere, in which a particular principle is applicable and valid, to other provinces, where its effects may be exciting and transforming, but where its consequences may be fallacious in theory and ruinous in practice.[1]

Isaiah Berlin

The idea of global justice is comparatively new: it was rarely used before the last decades of the twentieth century. The idea of social justice, by contrast, has been with us for a century or more. When a new political idea appears in the wake of a longer-established one, it is natural, perhaps almost unavoidable, to see the second as simply a development of the first. Social justice was a central idea in twentieth-century politics, in democratic societies especially. It was the banner under which the battle for equal rights, equality of opportunity, the welfare state and other such goals was fought within each separate state. Alongside the political battle, philosophers elaborated numerous theories of social justice, perhaps the most celebrated of which was that of John Rawls, as set out in his book *A Theory of Justice* and later works.[2] So when later on these philosophers and others began to think about what justice might mean on a global scale it was natural that they should start by taking familiar principles of social justice and exploring how these could be applied beyond the realm of domestic politics.[3] The implicit assumption here was that at a fundamental level social justice and global justice are one and the same, the difference between them being essentially a practical difference of scope: social justice is justice within bounded societies, while global justice is justice across humanity as a whole. In line with this, the use of the phrase 'global social justice' in popular political discourse makes this assumption evident.

It is this way of thinking that I want to challenge in this essay. Although I want to defend both the idea of social justice and the idea of global justice, I also want to argue that the relationship between the two ideas is more complex than the simple picture above suggests. To understand global justice correctly, we have to grasp how the world order as a context for justice is both similar to and different from the domestic context, the differences being sufficiently great that familiar principles of social justice – equality of opportunity, for example – cannot simply be 'stretched' and applied at a global level. We also have to explore the possibility that they might pull us in different directions – that sometimes political choices have to be made between promoting social justice at home and furthering global justice abroad. It is too neat and too comfortable to think that one fits inside the other like a Russian doll.

There are two main questions that we need to address, therefore. One is conceptual. When we talk about social justice and about global justice, is the same conception of justice being used, or are we bringing different conceptions of justice into play? In other words, is the difference between the two ideas *merely* a difference of scope, with the same principle or principles being applied in the one case to the set of persons who belong to a particular society and in the other case to all human beings, or are different principles being applied? The other question is normative. If social justice and global justice are indeed distinct ideas, are they in practical conflict with each other? Might we have to choose between promoting social justice and promoting global justice, given the practical constraints that we face – finite resources, for example? Two values can be distinct without coming into practical conflict, if what is required to promote the first also helps to promote the second, or if the demands they make are wholly independent of each other. But is this true of the two values we are considering?

I begin with the conceptual question, which like most conceptual questions is difficult. To answer it properly, we would have to tackle some fundamental questions about the nature of justice and about moral epistemology. Here I shall be less ambitious and simply suggest two possible ways in which the conceptual identity thesis – social justice and global justice are conceptually the same, and differ only in scope – could be defended.

First, it might be argued that justice is a universal value whose substance is always captured by the same principle, or set of principles, no matter where and to whom or what it is being applied. In other words, justice is not contextually variable. It is never the case that different principles of justice apply in different cases, for instance to different subject matters or among different groups of people. This is simply a matter of what justice means – it is a conceptual truth. If justice is universal in this sense, then it immediately follows that the difference between social and global justice can only be a difference of scope.

Consider, as an example of this position, the libertarian conception of justice as the non-violation of personal and property rights. These rights are held by all persons, and justice obtains insofar as they are respected. If we speak of social justice, we mean simply that the rights in question are respected among the group of people who form a society; if we speak of global justice, we mean that the same rights are respected universally. There is no conceptual difference. The same will apply to rival conceptions of justice that also claim universal status, for example egalitarian conceptions such as equality of resources. If justice can always be understood in terms of such a principle, then the difference between social and global justice can only be a difference in the principle's scope, not in its content.

Second, it might be argued that although justice may have a con-textual character, in whole or in part – it comprises distinct principles that are used in different contexts – this does not drive a wedge between social and global justice. Someone taking this view might concede, for example, that justice is not always a matter of equal dis-tribution. Whether this is so depends on what is being distributed and the social context in which the distribution is taking place. However, when we survey the various contexts that bring different principles of justice in play, we find that there are no relevant differences between bounded societies and the world as a whole. Society and globe differ only in scale, not in features that are relevant to justice.

I find neither version of the conceptual identity thesis persuasive, but the issues they raise are somewhat different. In particular the second version depends in part upon an empirical claim about the properties that societies possess and whether these are sufficiently dis-tinctive to mark them out as spheres within which special principles of justice apply. So they need to be addressed separately.

The claim that justice is a universal value whose principles are invariant across social contexts may seem patently false. After all, we often talk about legal justice, political justice, justice in families and so forth, and it is by no means obvious that when we do this we are always applying the same substantive principle or principles. However, to give the first version of the conceptual identity thesis a fair hear-ing, we should modify it so that it becomes a claim specifically about *distributive* justice, understood for present purposes as justice in the distribution of advantages and disadvantages among large groups of people. The claim, then, is that when issues of distributive justice arise, we always address them by applying the same principles, for example a principle of equality. On closer inspection, however, this seems not to be the case. What we regard as a just distribution – and by 'we' here I don't mean professional philosophers who are likely to have a particular stake in the matter, but people generally who are competent users of the concept – depends on what is being distributed, by whom and among whom. This contextual variability can be shown through experiments in which people are asked to make decisions about fair distribution having been given information which induces them to construe the context in one way or another. For example, we can construct situations in which the participants have contributed differentially to some common outcome – some have worked harder than others, for instance – and then by manipulating these situations we can explore what makes the people involved choose to reward individuals unequally according to their productive contributions, and what makes them prefer to share their resources equally.[4] Our understanding of the concept of justice ought to accommodate this evidence, which means that it cannot be spelt out in terms of universal principles that apply regardless of context. If, like Rawls, we think that a theory of justice must pass the 'reflective equilibrium' test – the requirement that an adequate theory should accommodate and explain at least most of our considered judgements of justice, those judgements that we feel confident about and that appear not to be affected by our personal emotions or interests[5] – then no context-invariant theory is going to be a plausible candidate.

Of course, there is more that could be said here. A defender of the first version might simply dismiss the appeal to ordinary usage and reflective equilibrium, or she might try to show that many of the judgements people commonly make about justice are flawed and therefore don't deserve to be counted as 'considered judgements' for the purpose of building a theory of justice. But it would take us too far afield to explore this further. My claim is that identifying social and global justice conceptually on the grounds that justice (or at any rate distributive justice) always carries the same meaning no matter in what circumstances we are applying the idea is implausible. Indeed it completely distorts the idea of social justice itself. Social justice can't be captured in terms of one or more principles that apply in all situations. It's a complex idea, and it is complex because societies and the distributive spheres they encompass are also complex. Sometimes it is about ensuring that people are treated in the same way, sometimes it is about ensuring that they are treated differently, because, for example they deserve greater or lesser rewards, or have larger or smaller needs. The principles that apply within economic enterprises are not the same as those that apply in the health or welfare services, or those that apply in specifically political settings. This complexity cannot be reduced to some underlying master-principle, or even to a fixed *set* of principles that apply whenever justice is being invoked.[6]

So let's now turn to the second version, which accepts that justice is plural and contextual, but then argues that there is nothing special about societies that distinguishes them from the world as a whole as far as distributive justice is concerned. The world is simply one big society, so social justice and global justice must conceptually be one and the same.

Obviously what we need to get clear about here is what is meant by 'a society' and which of its features are supposed to be important from the point of view of justice. The answer I think is that by 'societies' we mean 'nation-states', using 'state' here in a somewhat broad, quasi-Hegelian sense to include not only formal political institutions, but also the informal associations that make up civil society. Social justice is justice within nation-states so understood, and this is not accidental, as I have argued elsewhere.[7] But the problem now is to determine which of the several features of the nation-state matter as far as justice is concerned. There are different reasons we might have for regarding nation-states as privileged contexts of justice, and in order to settle the social justice versus global justice issue we need to know which of these counts.

There are broadly four grounds on which we might regard nation-states as special sites of justice.[8] They are first of all systems of economic co-operation whose members interact with each other to their mutual benefit to a far greater extent than they interact with outsiders. By producing and exchanging goods and services under a common set of rules, they create a surplus over and above what each might have produced by acting alone, a surplus whose allocation brings principles of distributive justice into play. Following Rawls, we can say that nation-states are 'cooperative ventures for mutual advantage'.[9] Second, they are systems of political coercion in which members agree to restrict their freedom in various ways by adhering to coercively enforced laws, restrictions that have to be justified by showing that they follow from principles that all concerned have reason to accept. Third, they are political *communities* in the real sense of that term, meaning that their members recognise a common national identity and share a common will to live their lives together, and as a result incur obligations to each other that they do not have to human beings elsewhere. Fourth, those nation-states in which the idea of social justice has taken root have also been more specifically *democratic* political communities whose members are collectively responsible for the legal and policy decisions that are taken in their name and that determine the resulting distribution of benefits and burdens amongst themselves.

With respect to each of these grounds, however, defenders of the conceptual identity thesis are able to point to features of the existing or emerging global system that suggest that nation-states are not distinctive as sites of justice. In the case of economic co-operation, for example, it is commonplace to underline the extent of economic interdependence between national economies and between individuals within those economies, and similar claims are commonly made about the coercive properties of international institutions, about multiple identities, some of them transnational, and about the growth of democratic institutions and practices at supranational level. These claims are frequently advanced in the large and expanding body of literature dedicated to the general phenomenon of 'globalisation', and I do not want to elaborate on them further. The real question is whether these various processes that are lumped together under this heading of globalisation have gone so far that there is no longer a qualitative difference between relationships that obtain between people within nation-state boundaries and relationships that cross those boundaries. This is a hard question to answer definitively. It's a bit like the old Sorites puzzle about the number of grains that have to be added before we can say that we have a heap of sand. Nonetheless the following can be said against the identity thesis and in favour of the view that *social* justice remains special.

The idea of social justice emerged in the form that it did precisely because within nation-states the features I have just itemised were combined in the same unit: they were, and to a large extent still are, at one and the same time schemes of economic co-operation, coercive legal systems legitimised by democratic institutions, and communities with shared national identities. Within units of this kind, several things happen that are necessary to give shape to the conception of social justice as it developed throughout the previous century. First, there is broad agreement on what we can call the several currencies of justice – the specific types of benefit and cost whose distribution is seen to raise questions of fairness. Thus education, health care, job opportunities, income, civil and political rights and so forth come to be seen as things to be distributed according to principles of equality, need, desert, etc., according to the case. Second, the members of national communities see themselves as forming a common reference group, so they judge the adequacy of their share of each of these types of resource by how much other members in different geographical areas, occupations, and so on, are getting. Third, the economy and its accompanying social institutions are seen as subject to coercive regulation by the state, in principle at least, so that the final distribution of costs and benefits can be brought in line (imperfectly, no doubt) with principles of justice. Against this background, a conception of social justice made up predominantly of *comparative* principles – principles specifying what share of resources relative to others individuals are entitled to – can emerge. Thus we have principles that specify equal civil and political rights, principles of equal opportunity in education and jobs, principles of need in access to health care, and so forth. Even those principles that are not directly comparative, such as those specifying entitlements to minimum levels of income, are often indirectly so, when the income poverty line is drawn in such a way as to make it relative to the national average.

There is no similar convergence of features at transnational level, even though, taking each feature separately, it is of course possible to find examples of that feature occurring at that higher level (economic co-operation across borders, etc.). And that suggests a different conception of global justice, one that acknowledges the impact of nation-states upon one another but does not presuppose that the circumstances of social justice are already present at global level. Such a conception will not be made up of comparative principles. Instead, as I have argued elsewhere, it will include the idea of a global minimum, a set of human rights that people everywhere can claim as a matter of justice.[10] I understand human rights to be rights to those freedoms, resources and bodily states that allow basic human needs to be fulfilled, and basic needs in turn are defined as the conditions that must be met if a person is to have a minimally decent life in the society to which he or she belongs. So we begin with the idea that a decent human life contains certain essential components that are reiterated across all societies, and on that basis identify generic human needs whose precise form will nonetheless vary somewhat from one society to the next (thus the need for food and shelter takes a different concrete form in tropical and in Arctic societies). Corresponding to these needs we have a set of human rights, some of which are primarily rights to non-interference (such as rights to freedom of movement and expression), but others of which are rights to positive provision (to the means of subsistence, basic health care, and so forth).

Global justice, therefore, requires first of all the protection of these basic human rights for people everywhere. Because not all states are able (or willing) to secure these rights for their own citizens, the obligation to do so may fall on outside bodies, including other states. That is why human rights protection becomes a matter of *global* and not merely *social* justice. But note that the requirements of justice here are absolute, not comparative. What is required is that everybody should be brought to the point where he or she securely enjoys rights to bodily integrity, subsistence, and so forth. So far nothing has been said about the distribution of freedoms and resources over and above the minimum necessary to reach that threshold. But there is more to be said, in light of the fact that nation-states are not isolated and self-contained units but political communities able to interact to their mutual advantage, by for example creating economic gains for each other through international trade and investment, or co-operating to solve collective action problems such as the degradation of the global environment. When these interactions take place they raise questions of fairness.

How are the benefits to be shared among the various parties? What rules should be applied to set the terms of trade, given that alternative sets of rules will benefit to varying degrees producers and consumers in different countries? Or in cases where political communities have to incur costs in order to solve global problems – cutting down on their use of natural resources or reducing their carbon emissions, say – what is a fair allocation of the costs in question? These questions are often now resolved in practice by self-interested bargaining among the various parties, a practice that tends to produce results that favour richer and more powerful states. What justice requires, by contrast, is a more complex matter, which may involve taking account not only of what would be a fair assignment of costs and benefits going forward but also of the historical background to the present situation. I shall not try to give a full account of what we might call *transactional* global justice, except to say that one leading principle is the equal sharing of costs and benefits between the parties. Notice, however, that equality here applies only to the fruits of the interaction – for example to the economic surplus that is created by trade. If we say that each party to the transaction should receive a roughly equal share of this surplus, we are not attempting to equalise their overall position. Global justice does not require that all countries should be equally rich, for example, or that their members should enjoy equal opportunities relative to all their global counterparts.

My argument, then, is that we should reject the conceptual identity claim, whether in the first or the second version. Social justice and global justice are different concepts, and in order to understand global justice correctly, we need to focus attention on the nature of relationships between people across the globe who at the same time belong to different national communities. But in saying this, I am not rejecting the idea of global justice outright. On the contrary, wealthier states especially may be subject to quite demanding obligations of global justice, either to intervene to protect human rights outside of their borders, or to forgo some part of their bargaining advantage in international negotiations in the name of transactional fairness. So my position is not that of writers such as Thomas Nagel who argue that, because the conditions for social justice are not met at global level (Nagel focuses on the political coercion condition, the absence of a world state), the idea of global justice makes no sense.[11] For Nagel, our obligations to people beyond the borders of the state are essentially humanitarian in nature, not matters of justice. In my view the interactions between nation-states and individual people at global level are sufficiently intense to bring principles of justice into play, but not comparative principles of the kind that belong to the concept of social justice. Thus the capacity of states to intervene in various ways beyond their own borders to protect the human rights of non-citizens is what makes such protection a matter of global justice.

This concludes my discussion of the conceptual question about social and global justice. But what now of the normative question? Are they conflicting values, and if so which is the more urgent? This will of course depend on how we understand each value. In line with my discussion up to now, I will assume that global justice should be understood as demanding the universal protection of human rights and fair terms of interaction between nation-states. Others may want to advance more demanding conceptions, for example some form of global equality. In the case of social justice, I assume that it embraces comparative principles such as equality of opportunity and equal access to medical care for those with similar needs. Interpreted in this way, it seems clear to me that these two values often do place conflicting demands upon us. At the most elementary level, if we assume that the global protection of human rights sometimes requires rich countries to make resource transfers to poor countries, then we as democratic citizens may have to choose between, say, increasing the foreign aid budget to promote global justice and increasing the budget for pre-school education to promote equality of opportunity at home. It is a debated question whether social justice is a satiable goal, in the sense that we might reach a point where there is nothing more that we can do by way of reallocating rights and resources between people that might make their shares of resources more distributively just. There is reason to think that it is not satiable, when we consider, for example, expenditure on health care, on disability, and indeed on measures to try to correct inherited inequality of opportunity. That is, there will always be more interventions that we might make that will have the effect of meeting medical needs more adequately, giving people with disabilities opportunities that are nearly the same as those enjoyed by the able-bodied, and correcting for the effects of inherited social position by, for example, intensive pre-school education for children from disadvantaged families. In each of these areas, and others, we could decide to put more resources into pursuing social justice, and there would always be at least marginal gains from doing so. Since GDP at any time is finite, however, these resources would have to come from somewhere: either other forms of public expenditure would have to be retrenched, or rates of taxation raised (but eventually, we should assume, the tax yield will fall if the rate rises beyond a certain point). If that is the case, then practical trade-offs between social and global justice are going to be with us indefinitely.

There is also a more subtle reason why we might think that social justice and global justice are conflicting values. This involves looking not at the resources needed to meet the demands of the two ideals, but at the conditions under which people are willing to support each of them respectively. Here I am assuming that there is some practical connection between identity and justice: people's willingness to support and comply with principles of justice, particularly principles that are likely to work to their disadvantage, depends on how far they identify with the constituency within which justice is going to be practised. If that is true, and if we want democratic support for policies designed to promote social justice and global justice respectively, then we may have to choose between fostering a national and a cosmopolitan sense of identity: between encouraging people to see themselves primarily as members of a particular political community, and as responsible for the welfare of people belonging to that community, and encouraging people to see themselves as citizens of the world, with responsibilities owed equally to the needy and vulnerable, no matter where they live. So for example if, as many countries now do, we include citizenship education as part of the school curriculum, then a choice has to be made about how far the content of this education should be such as to encourage future citizens to think of their identity as primarily national in character and how far as cosmopolitan. Should they learn mainly about the history, institutions and political traditions of their own country, or mainly about global problems and how to tackle them? Of course these two options do not exclude one another completely. One can learn to be a citizen of one's country, but also recognise responsibilities and obligations to people elsewhere, perhaps responsibilities stemming from the historical record of that same country. Nevertheless a decision has to be made about where to place the emphasis. It is not the case that national and cosmopolitan identities can simply be juxtaposed, since a national identity carries with it the idea that its bearer has special responsibilities to his or her compatriots that are not owed to people at large. It is sometimes suggested that there is no real conflict here, because one may have a cosmopolitan identity but at the same time recognise that, because one is physically a member of a particular society, one's first task is to promote justice at home. By doing so, one at the same time contributes to cosmopolitan goals. But this assumes that there are no real choices to be made of the kind described in the last paragraph, where resource constraints mean that one cannot meet both the needs of compatriots and the needs of outsiders in full. Faced with such a choice, a person has to ask herself where her strongest commitments really lie – whether it is her fellow-citizens or human beings as such that matter most to her when the chips are down.

If conflicts between social and global justice are unavoidable, we should next ask whether there are priority rules that might resolve them. Should we give priority to global justice, and say that social justice may only be pursued subject to that constraint, as Kok-Chor Tan, for example, has argued?[12] In defence of this position, it could be said that global justice, particularly if interpreted in the way I have suggested, represents a more urgent set of ethical demands. Assume that our political community has achieved at least a modicum of social justice within its own borders, a reasonable assumption if we are thinking about one of the economically advanced liberal democracies. It may then seem more important to secure the basic human rights of people abroad than to take further steps to promote equality or fairness within our own political community. It matters more that people living in sub-Saharan Africa should have adequate nutrition and clean water than that inequalities in access to medical care in a country like Britain should be ironed out – since even comparatively badly off people in Britain are still far better off than most of those living in sub-Saharan Africa.

If one takes what Nagel has called 'the view from nowhere', this conclusion follows easily.[13] But what if we ask the same question from the point of view of the citizens of a particular political community having to decide on their policy priorities? Suppose the choice is this: we could save money on health expenditure by closing down a few outlying hospitals and requiring the people affected to travel long distances to the big city units, which will mean some inequality of access to health care (people will be deterred from making the trip, and some may suffer medically from having to take long rides in the ambulance). The money saved will be used to fund life-saving drugs in developing countries. Is it now so clear what our choice should be? There are two questions that we have to consider. One has to do with the division of responsibility. It is not disputed that the human rights of people living in sub-Saharan Africa include the right to receive essential medical supplies, given that these supplies are available – the drugs exist and it is feasible to deliver them to the people who need them. But whose responsibility is it to fulfil this right? How much, if anything, must we in this community do, given what we and others have done in the past, and given what others are now capable of doing? The second question has to do with our treatment of those who will be disadvantaged if we decide in favour of global justice by funding the drugs programme. Is it consistent with the underlying principle of equal citizenship – the principle of equal concern and respect, as it is often labelled – to choose to widen inequality of access to health care, albeit for good reasons? It is tempting to sweep this second question under the carpet by supposing that the pursuit of global justice only requires uniform sacrifices on the part of fellow-citizens – each of us must give up a few pence a day to help raise the position of the global poor – or at least to suppose that if the sacrifice is unevenly distributed this can be compensated for by other policies. But this may not always be so. You can't in fact compensate the person who dies in the ambulance making the longer journey to hospital; the same applies to the soldier or aid worker who is killed in the course of a humanitarian intervention to protect human rights.

So once we abandon the view from nowhere and consider the matter from the point of view of the citizen in a democracy deliberating with his fellow-citizens about policy choices, we are going to have to accept that there will be practical conflicts between social and global justice in which global justice will have to yield, even on the fairly restrictive conception of global justice that I have proposed. There is no reason to think that these conflicts will be all-pervasive: clearly anti-poverty programmes directed at people within your political community will contribute to both social and global justice. But given the demanding nature of social justice, we can't rule out cases in which pursuing it would mean retrenching on policies and programmes designed to protect human rights abroad, and we can't say that in these cases global justice must always take priority. This means that there may be what I shall call a justice gap: people in poor countries may have claims of justice against the citizens of rich countries – claims for resources to be sent in their direction, or for protection against various forms of local oppression – which those citizens can justifiably refuse to meet in the name of social justice. This is not, I should stress, simply a claim about motivation. The point is not just that citizens may be unwilling to send resources abroad because their altruism is limited. It is a point about justice, and what we should do when different claims based on justice collide. It relies, therefore, on my earlier argument that justice is contextual, not universal, and on my claim that there is something special about social justice.

I have not, however, tried to provide an independent argument for giving priority to social justice in cases such as those described. Instead I have appealed to what I hope may be shared understandings on the part of readers of what is owed to fellow-citizens. I am not sure what to say to someone who is already committed to a strong form of cosmopolitanism which would rule out any such special consideration for compatriots. At the same time, I do not want to suggest that the claims of social justice must always take precedence over claims of global justice. It is easy to think of cases where the priority should be reversed – for example, few of us would believe that making available a supply of very cheap clothes to poor people in our own society justifies allowing our corporations to source their goods from third-world sweatshops employing child labour. For a justice gap to exist, it isn't necessary that social justice should trump global justice whenever they collide; it's only necessary that social justice should win sometimes.

The argument of this essay can be summed up in three main claims. The first is that if we are to develop an intelligible conception of global justice, we must begin by taking a close look at the human relationships to which our conception will be applied. The world, now and for the foreseeable future, is made up of independent, though interacting, political communities, within each of which there are different shared understandings of the central values of human life and of what, therefore, the goals of the state should be. Even though most nation-states are multicultural internally, there is no real equivalent to this political diversity inside them. So we cannot form our conception of global justice simply by drawing from ideas of social justice that have evolved within nation-states. We cannot assume that principles that make sense in these domestic contexts will continue to apply once we move to the international arena. Our theory of global justice must stand independently of existing theories of social justice.

The second claim concerns the agency that we hold primarily responsible for carrying out the task of promoting distributive justice. In the case of social justice, that agency is the state. Of course the state mainly furthers social justice indirectly, through legislation, public policy and fostering norms that citizens are encouraged to follow – so social justice relies on widespread co-operation on the part of the public who have, for example, to pay their taxes and claim their benefits honestly, to follow appropriate, non-discriminatory rules when making decisions about who to employ, who to buy from and sell to, and so forth. Nevertheless part of the state's job is to say authoritatively what each person must do in the name of social justice and often to follow up with sanctions if a person fails to comply. There is no equivalent to this in the case of global justice, no single agent who can be held responsible for protecting human rights or for ensuring that the international trading system is fair. We might imagine states agreeing with each other to co-ordinate their activities so that these goals are achieved, but even if such agreements can be reached – and as recent negotiations over humanitarian intervention, trade rules and measures to combat climate change show, this can itself be very difficult to achieve – they cannot be effectively policed. There is no authority with the power to enforce what has been agreed against a recalcitrant state. This is the background to what I have called the justice gap: no state can be obliged, as a matter of justice, to take up the slack that others have left. This makes the achievement of global justice precarious in a way that the achievement of social justice is not.

The third claim is about the real possibility of conflict between pursuing global justice and pursuing social justice, a possibility that seems often to be denied by progressives who see the former as simply a logical extension of the latter. I have noted that there may not only be resource conflicts but also identity conflicts: there may be a trade-off between seeing ourselves as citizens of nation-states bound by historical and cultural ties to other citizens, and seeing ourselves as cosmopolitans whose ties to any particular place are only sentimental but not ethical or political. Although the institutions and practices of social justice are now well entrenched in most liberal democracies, it is also true that public attitudes in these societies have shifted somewhat over the last quarter-century or so, broadly towards liberal individualism and away from liberal egalitarianism. That is, there is a stronger sense that people should be free to choose how they want to live their own lives, and be willing to take responsibility for those choices, and a weaker sense that it should be part of the state's job to protect people from the effects of their choices by measures to promote equality of outcome. (Symptomatic here may be the recent debate, in Britain, about inheritance tax, where it has proved hard to convince people that there is something unfair about the hugely unequal effects of the inheritance of wealth in the absence of such a tax). In other words, social justice has been on the back foot in recent decades as far as popular attitudes are concerned.[14] Under these circumstances, we should be concerned to strengthen communal identifications, national identities especially, that might help to reverse this trend.

Contrariwise, encouraging people to adopt a more cosmopolitan identity may weaken their commitment to social justice still further without at the same time making them any more committed to global justice. In other words, rather than strong principles of distributive justice for the world, we get weak principles of justice for those at home – perhaps a social safety net and not much else. A better strategy, it seems to me, is to strengthen national citizenship, but then make it a part of citizenship so understood to be active in pursuit of global justice. In other words, alongside established national goals such as domestic security, economic growth and environmental protection, it should become part of the national project to contribute in specific ways to global justice. It might become a matter of national pride to have set aside a certain percentage of GDP for developmental goals – perhaps for projects in one particular country or group of countries – or to have met agreed international targets for reducing emissions of greenhouse gases. This does of course require citizens to be willing to look beyond national interest in the conventional sense when deciding which policies they are prepared to support. But with a relatively modest conception of global justice along the lines I have sketched, the demands that are made on them should not in general be excessive. Since co-ordination between independent political communities cannot be guaranteed, the justice gap will still exist: there will be cases where people in poor countries have claims of justice that no rich community feels obliged to meet. But if we can enlarge our understanding of citizenship so that it comes to include the discharge of responsibilities of global justice, it will at least have been narrowed significantly.

Notes

1 I. Berlin, 'European Unity and Its Vicissitudes', in Isaiah Berlin, *The Crooked Timber of Humanity*, ed. H. Hardy (London: Fontana, 1991), p. 197.
2 J. Rawls, *A Theory of Justice* (Cambridge, Mass.: Harvard University Press, 1971).
3 Rawls himself, however, did not take this path. When, near the end of his life, he wrote at length about international justice for the first time in *The Law of Peoples* (Cambridge, Mass.: Harvard University Press, 1999), he was explicit that the principles he had defended in his theory of social justice did not apply beyond the nation-state. For discussion see the essays collected in R. Martin and D. Reidy (eds), *Rawls's Law of Peoples: A Realistic Utopia?* (Oxford: Blackwell, 2006).
4 See my overview of the evidence in *Principles of Social Justice* (Cambridge, Mass.: Harvard University Press, 1999), ch. 4.
5 See Rawls, *Theory of Justice*, section 9.
6 For an extended argument to this effect see Miller, *Principles of Social Justice*, esp. ch. 2.
7 Ibid., ch. 1.
8 This fourfold distinction follows P. van Parijs, 'Global Distributive Justice', in R. Goodin, P. Pettit and T. Pogge (eds), *A Companion to Contemporary Political Philosophy*, 2nd edn (Oxford: Blackwell, 2007). Van Parijs, however, in each case dismisses the alleged reason for limiting the scope of distributive justice. I consider the first three grounds at greater length, and more favourably, in 'Justice and Boundaries' (forthcoming), on which the present paragraph draws.
9 Rawls, *Theory of Justice*, p. 4.
10 See D. Miller, *National Responsibility and Global Justice* (Oxford: Oxford University Press, 2007), ch. 7.
11 T. Nagel, 'The Problem of Global Justice', *Philosophy and Public Affairs* 33 (2005), pp. 113–47.
12 K.-C. Chan, *Justice without Borders: Cosmopolitanism, Nationalism and Patriotism* (Cambridge: Cambridge University Press, 2004).
13 T. Nagel, *The View from Nowhere* (New York: Oxford University Press, 1986).
14 This point should not be overstated. People will still declare themselves in favour of equality of opportunity, the social minimum and government's responsibility to narrow the gap between rich and poor. But as the inheritance tax example shows, they may not always be willing to support the policies that would be necessary to achieve these aims. For some recent evidence, see R. Jolley, 'The British Do Support Equality', *Fabian Review* 119: 3 (Autumn 2007), pp. 4–7.

3

Towards a Renewed Concept of Social Justice

Wolfgang Merkel

Justice is a term that has animated political philosophy since Aristotle. The term is as old as the controversy over its concept. Even one of the most outstanding works of political philosophy in the twentieth century, John Rawls' *A Theory of Justice* (1971), could not develop a paradigm of justice that achieved unanimous agreement. While it has not been able to achieve such consent, however, it has undoubtedly inspired a highly productive theoretical debate in recent decades. Yet practical policies have been slow to follow this renaissance in the theory of justice.

The wave of neo-liberalism initiated by Margaret Thatcher and Ronald Reagan had first to ebb before the discourse of justice could secure a sound and prominent place in political discussion. Since the mid 1990s, however, politicians – at least in Europe – have had to confront the crunch question: Do you believe in social justice? There are various reasons for this. For one, the gap between rich and the poor has widened continuously during the last two decades, even in western industrialised nations. Another reason concerns the pressure and impact on the welfare state in continental Europe. In the future, the forces of globalisation and individualisation will continue to take their toll, while the demographics of European societies will undergo significant restructuring.

Such an overhaul of policies and of the welfare state as a whole demands new regulative ideas of social justice if government action is not to be dictated solely by arguments of economic efficiency or by the path dependency of the traditional welfare state. Since Rawls' *A Theory of Justice*, the field of political philosophy has been developing an ever-growing number of ideas, principles and norms of social justice. Are these philosophical theories and principles of social justice, such as emerged in the last third of the twentieth century, still valid in the era of globalisation? Can they guide progressive politics through the beginning of the twenty-first century? What kind of adjustments might be needed in order to make them applicable as regulative ideas for socially just policies in the global age? In order to answer these overarching questions, I will structure my analysis in four steps:

- What is social justice?
- How should progressives define social justice?
- How should progressives translate the philosophical principles into regulative ideas?
- Social justice in the globalised age of the twenty-first century.

What is social justice?

It appears trivial to point out – although the issue is often confused in everyday semantics – that inequality of distribution is by no means unjust per se, any more than equality of distribution is just per se. Indeed, the opposite may be true: equal distribution may be unjust, and unequal distribution may be just. Aristotle's *Iustitia Distributiva*, then, has a problem with finding criteria on which to base concrete policy decisions. This is the subject matter of theories of justice, and of progressive politics as well. Theories of justice approach the problem by starting from a different articulation of our moral preconceptions and by using specific justificatory strategies, in order to arrive at different principles and validity claims. Since it is impossible even to outline all these numerous theoretical enterprises here, I will simply examine three very influential theories of the last three decades, using the following two criteria to justify my selection.

The first criterion refers to a basic intuition concerning the relationship of individual and communitarian theories of justice. Both can be located on a continuum ranging from the absolute individual to the absolute community, that is, from individualism to collectivism. The second criterion refers to the distributive implications of the competing theories of justice and ranges from a position opposed to redistributive measures to one embracing them. These two criteria establish the axiomatic positions available to any theory of justice. Contrary to popular assumption, the second axis – concerning the desirability of (re-)distributive measures – is logically separate from the individual–community axis. Considerations of distributive justice, for example, may take the individual as their point of departure but nonetheless still lead to (re-) distributive consequences further-reaching than alternative theories that justify their positions by recourse to the community. A crossing of these two axes produces four quadrants within which to locate different political philosophies of justice (see figure 1).

The first quadrant comprises all theories that, starting from a strictly individualistic axiom, conclude with a clear aversion to political (re-)

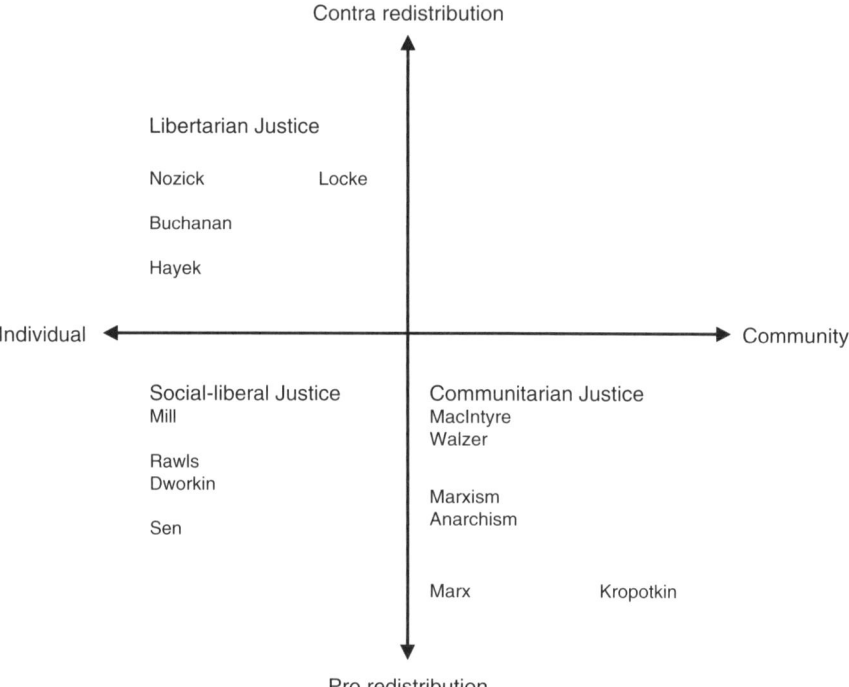

Figure 1 Axes of Social Justice

Source: Author's own compilation.

distribution. This group includes theorists such as John Locke, liberalism's modern forebear, as well as Robert Nozick, James Buchanan and Friedrich August von Hayek among our contemporaries. I choose Hayek as the best exponent of this position since he – of all the theorists mentioned for this field – had the largest political impact until the end of the twentieth century. The second quadrant is occupied by theories that also take the individual as their point of departure, but arrive at principles rather more inclined towards redistribution. Such a position was held by John Stuart Mill in the nineteenth century, and today most prominently – and expanding greatly upon Mill – by Rawls, Ronald Dworkin and Amartya Sen.[1]

I have initially chosen Rawls as representative of this position both because of his undisputed dominance in the philosophical debate about justice in the last quarter of the twentieth century and, of course, because of the power and complexity of his theory. However, he will later be complemented by Sen. In the third quadrant, enclosed by the axes 'community' and 'contra redistribution', there are no positions of consequence. A theory that is at the same time community-oriented and yet opposed to redistribution would be far too inherently contradictory to satisfy any criteria of theoretical consistency. In the fourth and last quadrant, describing positions that are both community-oriented and open to redistributive measures, we find a large number of political philosophies of justice. An extreme version can be found in Peter Kropotkin's work, more moderate ones with Jean-Jacques Rousseau and Michael Walzer. As a moderate and contemporary of ours, Walzer will represent this quadrant in my philosophical inquiry into theories of justice.

The libertarian position: Friedrich August von Hayek

For Hayek, as for all liberal and libertarian philosophers who concern themselves with questions of justice, individual autonomy takes precedence normatively over the public sphere of political decision-making. Therefore, any limitation of this autonomy, such as interference by a welfare state, would have to be subject to a particularly stringent test of its legitimacy. According to Hayek, the institutionalised redistribution of the welfare state designed to correct market outcomes does not pass this test for three major reasons:

- *Logical argument.* The societal outcomes of market exchanges are the unintended consequences of individual actions. If, however, intentionality and thus responsibility for their results are not given, these actions cannot be evaluated according to any theory of justice. The statement that 'markets are unjust' is therefore absurd. The popular demand for 'more social justice' is nothing but a 'semantic mirage' of socialist quacks or populist politicians.
- *Cognitive argument.* The market, that is, the voluntary and legally bound co-operation of individuals, creates a 'spontaneous order in society'. From this voluntary co-operation grow cumulative traditions and institutions that form their own 'evolutionary morals'. 'These moral rules exceed the abilities of reason',[2] and should therefore be altered neither by political majorities, nor according to abstract principles of rationality.
- *Efficiency argument.* In addition, the market is the sphere of unequalled efficiency. It is cumulative and evolutionary and not created by rationalist design. 'Whether progress continues might well depend on man consciously choosing not to exercise the domination that is today within his power.'[3]

All in all, these three arguments lead Hayek to clearly reject the correction of market-induced property, income and welfare relations by the state. The state should only guarantee a basic economic minimum to all those 'who cannot support themselves'.[4] As a result, Hayek recommends a society based on equality before the law, plus maximum security of contract (in the market) seconded by a transfer-supported minimum social protection. Any further restrictions to the (economic) freedom of contract would have illiberal results and thus cannot be justified. Hayek's emphasis on the market and individual meritocracy would fit a Darwinian neo-liberal project for the global age.

Besides the unpleasant consequences of his theory, it becomes very clear after some deliberation that Hayek's claims are not as well founded as they might seem at first glance. Hayek himself, talking about evolutionary morals, must be asked why the 'real' morals are too hard for human reason to grasp. Efficiency is certainly very laudable. Nevertheless, one should not forget that when talk of efficiency ends, only then may talk about justice begin. For the existence or non-existence of efficiency refers only to the Pareto optimality of an actual state; it tells us nothing about its ethical dimension: whether this state is *good* or not.[5]

The social-liberal position: John Rawls

Rawls and Hayek share an uncompromising point of departure: to think any philosophy of a just society strictly from the individual. Rawls, however, develops a different method in order to justify his principles of justice and, not least for that reason, arrives at diametrically opposite rules of distribution. Rawls, unlike Hayek, does not treat justice as an individual virtue but rather views a society's institutional structure as the prime addressee of any demands for justice since it co-determines people's life chances. While the market does possess the attribute of unsurpassed efficiency of allocation, the creation of just social conditions is not one of its features. The principal reason for this ethical blindness lies in the unequal and unjust conditions of access to the market. Rawls' idea is to provide all individuals with an equal set of basic goods that correct the 'scandalous lottery of nature' and the inequality of life chances. Intelligent or stupid, beautiful or ugly, from a sheltered or neglected family background, with rich or poor parents – such factors should not decide an individual's life plan and his or her chance to implement it. Therefore, institutions need to be inscribed into the political, economic and social constitution of a society which fairly distributes those basic goods necessary for the creation of equal life chances. Most important among these basic goods are rights and liberties, powers and opportunities, an adequate income and wealth, as well as the social conditions for self-respect.[6]

To that end, Rawls develops two principles of justice. The first, lexically superior principle demands an absolutely equal distribution of basic liberties and political rights. This is not controversial and has long been guaranteed in democracies based on the rule of law. The second rule outlines a principle of socio-economic justice, according to which socio-economic inequalities are permissible only if they 'are to everybody's advantage and are tied to positions and offices that are open to everyone'.[7] The application of Rawls' second principle would doubtlessly require considerable redistribution of wealth and of life chances in most OECD countries. However, the question arises whether it can cope with globalised markets, open societies and the necessity of certain standards of social cohesion. I will return to this question.

The communitarian position: Michael Walzer

Rawls attempted to force the complex, pluralistic and fragmented societies of the late twentieth century under the stewardship of two universalistic principles of justice. Walzer avoids this. In his book *Spheres of Justice* (1983),[8] he postulates the existence of separate spheres of justice, both descriptively and normatively. Walzer argues that there cannot and must not be a single overarching logic of distribution for such diverse spheres as citizenship, social security and welfare, money and commodities, office, free time, upbringing, kinship and love, mercy, recognition and political power. The conclusion is: every sphere of goods and every sphere of life has its own rules of distribution. The imperative is: no sphere-specific rule of distribution shall 'infringe' on another sphere. That is especially the case with the sphere of money. For reasons of social justice there have to be goods whose distribution does not depend on money – among others, health care or education, whose distribution should not be determined by the market, but rather by the equality principle and by need.[9]

At first glance, this appears similar to the familiar demands of traditional social democracy. Walzer, however, does not want it to be codified according to the standards of social rights as in T.H. Marshall, or those of continental European welfare states.[10] This would only create bureaucracy and dry out society's participatory resources. Walzer's communitarian suggestion, then, is to link a state-guaranteed social minimum to diverse additional local contributions. Participation by the recipients should be encouraged and decisions about distributive transfers should be left to local communities. Equality through the standardised distribution of social transfers and services is thus sacrificed to participation-oriented methods of distribution. Forms of distribution and transfers are made contingent – at least partially – on the particular consent of shifting democratic majorities in communities.

Yet at least some part of social transfers would thereby acquire a charitable character that is hard to calculate with any degree of accuracy.

Furthermore, it seems problematic that Walzer assumes a possible consensus on questions of distribution. That might be conceivable in his own idyllic upper-class community of Princeton, but it would hardly work in the Bronx or Harlem, which are barely an hour away. Like all communitarians, Walzer underestimates the justice-enhancing functions of efficient bureaucracies and overestimates the capacity of civil society for self-organisation. Paradoxically, the 'communitarian' Walzer emerges in the distributive consequences of his theories as a more cautious 'liberal' than the liberal Rawls, who depends on state regulation and an efficient distributive bureaucracy.

How should progressives define social justice?

If the usefulness of Walzer's theory for justifying a state-organised system of redistribution and legally guaranteed social security in complex heterogeneous societies is limited, Hayek can be excluded altogether from considerations of progressive justice that are open to redistributive measures. His assumption that the meritocratic principle[11] develops best in unregulated markets may be either naive or ideological, but is certainly characterised by a substantial lack of realism. It underestimates tendencies towards concentration, cartelisation and monopolisation, which necessarily impede the unfolding of the meritocratic principle. It neglects differences in starting positions resulting from an individual's social background, and their impact on future life chances and possibilities of development. It largely ignores the production of collective goods in health, education, research, the environment and infrastructure, subordinating them to the efficiency of the market and the free choice of citizens. It thus conflicts with the meritocratic principle that Hayek himself propagates.

Paradoxically, the liberal Rawls is best suited to be used for considerations of justice by a modern redistribution-friendly welfare state. However, his emphasis on just institutions should be complemented by Sen's insistence on the intrinsic and instrumental value of personal 'capabilities'.[12] Sen goes beyond Rawls in criticising the latter's confusion of means of freedom and real freedom itself. There is a logical difference between the endowment of certain primary goods and the real choices a person has in everyday life. What is missing in Rawls' theory 'is some notion of "basic capabilities": a person being able to do certain things'.[13] Sen's notion of capability is defined as a set of functionings among which a person is able to choose. A person's capability is an 'alternative combination of various "doings and beings", with quality of life to be assessed in terms of the capability to achieve valuable functionings'.[14] The answer to Sen's own question 'Equality of what?' is clear: equal chance to acquire equal capabilities. The society and its state have to provide these opportunities. Such a state can be neither neo-liberal nor paternalistic, but has to be an 'ensuring state'.[15] Both access to individual empowerment and its enabling by an active state can provide the opportunity structure for a just distribution of 'life chances'.[16] The main arguments for this conclusion are as follows:

1. By using the concept of the individual as their point of departure, Rawls' and Sen's principles of justice take into account not only the precept of the freedom of the individual but also the individualisation of values and lifestyles in the post-industrial societies of the twenty-first century.
2. Rawls' and Sen's concepts of justice grant the individual freedom and political rights to the greatest possible extent and protect him or her against authoritarian or paternalistic impositions by the state or by society. They heighten his or her degree of freedom and broaden opportunities for a self-determined individual choice.
3. Despite this priority of individual freedom, Rawls' second principle of justice[17] and Sen's focus on capabilities call for considerable redistribution, as long as it promotes equal and fair life chances for the least privileged.
4. Sen emphasises the promotion of individual *'capabilities'*. At the centre of this concept stands the capability of the individual as the agent of his own interests. Equal, broad and early access to education and employment strengthens the individual's autonomy, self-esteem, integration into society and capacity to adapt to the ever-changing economic challenges.

As far as basic capabilities are concerned, Sen is a strong utilitarian. But inequalities can be just if they fulfil two requirements: first (and similar to Rawls), if they lead to efficiency gains which are to the benefit of everybody; second, if they are a consequence of conscious individual decisions. Therefore, collective efficiency and individual choice can justify the inequality of income and wealth.[18]

How should progressives translate the philosophical principles into regulative ideas?

Drawing on Rawls' and Sen's principles of justice, at least five concrete priorities can be derived, capable of guiding progressive politics and policies in the twenty-first century. They will be supplemented by two additional guiding ideas of particular relevance for the future:

- Prevention of poverty: because poverty generally prevents the development of individual dignity, integrity and autonomy.
- Education and training: because they strongly influence individual life chances.
- Inclusion in the labour market: because it is here that most citizens acquire income, status and prestige.
- Maintaining social security standards: because this is where social security and social assistance are organised and redistribution attempted.
- Distribution of wealth and income: this is where the unjust results of the market economy should be corrected.
- Generational justice: since it explicitly places the opportunities and life chances of the future generation on today's agenda. This was already taken into account in Rawls' *A Theory of Justice*, albeit in a very abstract way.
- Gender justice: despite all progress in this field, particularly during the last decades of the twenty-first century, there is still a gender gap which runs counter to the principle of equal life chances and the needs of a post-industrial service economy.

Prevention of poverty

All other goals of distributive justice must be subordinated to the prevention of poverty. A life above the poverty line is thus considered the fundamental basic right of justice-oriented politics. Individual autonomy and the best possible utilisation of life chances are only feasible above the poverty line. Only then can real inclusion into the developed affluent societies of western democracies be achieved. Only then can the equally irreplaceable basic right to 'negative freedom' develop the complementary content of 'positive freedom'.[19] Poverty not only entails inequality of income, wealth and resources, it also creates the real danger that the poor no longer have access to all civic and political rights. The Latin American political scientist Guillermo O'Donnell once referred to this as 'low intensity citizenship'. The right to not have to live in poverty in affluent societies thus acquires the status of an inalienable basic right to social justice. However, a life above the poverty line is by no means sufficient, but is merely a necessary condition for genuine integration into society. A passive strategy of fighting poverty via unconditional social assistance or a work-free basic income, even if this is a guaranteed right in a welfare state, might relieve material need, but in the work-centred societies of developed countries it does not bring about social inclusion.

Education and training

Intensive investment in education and training is the least contro-versial of all goals in philosophical as well as in political discussion. It is certainly less controversial than the question of how to finance education as a public good. Hayek would rely on private funding for both secondary schools and higher education. Walzer and Rawls argue that there is a public responsibility to finance high-quality secondary schools.[20] While this applies to elementary schools as well, it does not necessarily include universities. Rather, an inversion of the structure of privilege looms here. Privately paid tuition fees are not only justi-fied but are also socially just, contrary to universities that are financed from 'general' tax revenues which reward graduates with improved 'individual' income and life chances.

A general argument for the primacy of education – supported by all, from Hayek to Walzer – is the overriding importance of knowledge for the present and future wealth of developed societies. However, it can also be derived from the important role education plays in empower-ing individuals to pursue a self-determined life.[21] Knowledge is the fuel for economic prosperity and the precondition for a free choice of individual life plans. Therefore education should be one of the core policies for progressives in the twenty-first century.

Inclusion in the labour market

One weakness of both Walzer's and Rawls' conceptions of justice is a certain blindness towards issues that concern the labour market. Unemployment, however, is not primarily an economic problem that can be solved simply through extensive transfer payments. It is first and foremost an ethical challenge,[22] because unemployment, and long-term unemployment in particular, damages individual auton-omy, undermines self-respect, and usually also leads to an irreversible disadvantage in the materialisation of future life chances. So long as not only income but also status, self-respect and social standing in developed societies are primarily distributed via paid employment, inclusion in the labour market must have high political priority. Sen argues convincingly that even very generous social transfers cannot nearly compensate for, let alone prevent, the negative consequences of unemployment. Sen statistically proves that unemployment leads to:

- social exclusion and a dramatic loss of freedom of choice;
- long-term damage through the loss of abilities, cognitive skills and motivation;

- psychological suffering through social discrimination;
- higher illness and mortality rates;
- the loss of human relationships and familial cohesion;
- an exacerbation of ethnic and gender inequality since women and ethnic minorities are often over-represented among the unemployed;
- a loss of social values and responsibility.[23]

A welfare state that provides incentives for people to abstain from gainful employment or even discourages them to do so by way of unconditional basic incomes, generous social assistance and loosely defined 'welfare-to-work' criteria, while simultaneously fencing off the labour market to outsiders through high (supposedly social) regulations is, from this perspective, socially unjust.[24] Standards of social security must therefore be adapted to the dynamics of the labour market when they weaken the dynamism of labour markets and block access to gainful employment, thereby creating long-term unemployment and social exclusion. This is true not only for reasons of economic efficiency, but above all for reasons of social justice. On the one hand, this would reduce rational free-riding in the welfare state and, on the other, would prevent the exclusion of a substantial part of the population from civil society. However, this must and should not lead to the logic of the 'marginal' welfare state, but rather to public policies that activate, enable and ensure access to the labour market and ensure social security.

An unconditional basic income, which would encourage a temporary withdrawal from gainful employment and the partial realisation of Marx's utopia of 'to each according to their needs', carries substantial risks. These would probably chiefly affect young people for whom the basic income might be sufficient to satisfy consumption desires in a particular phase of their lives. If, however, they wanted to re-enter the labour market after a while, they would have to pay for the socially financed leave with a substantial loss of career opportunities. The basic income would then become a 'hedonism trap' so long as the basic institutional structure of the economy and society could not guarantee non-prejudicial possibilities of resuming gainful employment after a long period of absence from the labour market. Guaranteeing such possibilities may in fact be utopian, and would mean overestimating the reach of politics in capitalist democracies.

Social security and the activation of the welfare state

If one sees social inclusion and the prevention of poverty through education and integration into the labour market as a primary justice-related objective, one has to demand a thorough overhaul of the welfare state. The passive elements of ex-post compensation have to be discarded and the activating components must be strengthened. The welfare state has to be structured so as to prevent, a priori, socio-political 'damage', particularly in the labour market. This requires shifting resources towards education, reducing the tax-burden on the production of labour, and tougher conditions for receiving redundancy payments that enforce a swift resumption of gainful employment.

The model for this restructuring, however, cannot be the 'marginal welfare state'[25] of the United States, as suggested by neo-liberals. First of all, it has no strong activating elements; second, it is insensitive vis-à-vis those who cannot be blamed for their inability or weakness in the labour market. Denmark, with its combination of high investment in education, active labour-market policy, generous social transfers coupled with comprehensive duties on the side of beneficiaries to avoid social and fiscal free-riding, provides an example of real social inclusion for the lower and upper end of society that is worth emulating. The goal of inclusion in the labour market requires that the tax system be as employment-friendly as possible.[26] However, it is also necessary to (re-)establish the symmetry of tax collection, which has been coming apart at the seams. The voluntary 'self-exclusion' of the rich from their civic tax-paying duty at the upper end of society is, from the perspective of social justice, just as scandalous as the 'involuntary exclusion' of the poor and unemployed from economic and cultural participation at the lower end.[27]

Reduction of income and wealth gaps

Relative to the four goals of social justice presented above, the reduction of income and wealth gaps is secondary. This statement, however, is valid only if the first four preferences have been realised. If the prevention of poverty, the creation of equal opportunities and life chances through education and training, inclusion in the labour market and an activation of the welfare state are achieved, the call for the equalisation of wealth and incomes loses much of its justice-oriented justification. This applies especially where an income gap leads to increased productivity, economic output and substantial profits for the most disadvantaged of society. In that case Rawls' rule of admission for socio-economic inequality would partially concur with the findings of neo-classical economic theory. Inequality becomes problematic, however, where a necessary degree of social cohesion cannot be sustained.

Generational justice

Generational justice has become a disputed topic in continental politics. The most recent trends indicate that the older generation lives at the cost of the young or of future generations. One strand of argument refers to the ecological burden the present generation will leave to following generations; the other strand puts its emphasis on the public debts which encumber or 'tax' our children and grandchildren. Whereas the ecological argument can hardly be contested, the indebtedness argument has to be treated with caution. Not every kind of indebtedness has to be a burden on future generations. We have to distinguish between debts caused by public consumption and debts caused by public investment. Investment in education, research and development can be considered as temporary indebtedness which will yield high returns in the future, and is therefore to the benefit of the coming generations.

In any case, it must be emphasised that the inter-temporal dimension of justice is crucial. Each theory has to include a saving principle. Punctual justice would be easy to achieve since the state could finance a high and equal income for everybody simply by running massively into debt over one limited period of time; but facing the future, there is clearly a trade-off between the inter-temporal sustainability of the welfare state and present social ambitions.

Operationalising these seven dimensions of social justice by empirically accessible indicators, a picture of social justice in the OECD world emerges (see table 1).

The four Scandinavian countries are at the top. They represent the best practices of a strong enabling state which provides the most equal capabilities throughout social classes, gender and age. The more market-oriented Switzerland ranks before the Bismarckian insurance states of the European continent such as Austria, France and Germany. Belgium ranks even behind New Zealand, Australia, the UK and the United States which represent the Anglo-Saxon type of 'uncoordinated capitalism'.[28] The Catholic, Orthodox, or Muslim democratic and capitalist latecomers are at the bottom of the OECD ranking. With their heavy and early spending on education, childcare, training, retraining and inclusion in the labour market, the Scandinavian welfare states come closest to Sen's imperative of social justice enhancing the capabilities of each citizen.

Reducing the gender-justice gap

Despite some progress in translating legal and constitutional equality into the effective equal distribution of life and career chances between men and women during recent decades, there is still a considerable inequality of opportunities. This becomes obvious if one takes into account the unequal employment rates as well as the unequal distribution of top positions in the economy, in politics, and in society

Table 1. Index of Social Justice in OECD Countries (1990–2006)										
Countries	Index (w)	Index (uw)	Rank (w)	Rank (uw)	(1) Poverty	(2) Education	(3) Labour	(4) Social exp.	(5) Income	(6) Generations	(7) Gender
Sweden	22.86	7.26	1	1	1.33	1.25	0.71	0.85	0.98	1.04	1.09
Denmark	21.41	6.73	2	2	1.43	1.47	0.72	1.23	0.94	0.13	0.80
Norway	19.65	6.48	3	3	0.68	1.56	1.09	0.98	0.87	0.45	0.85
Finland	16.22	5.35	4	4	1.05	0.91	−0.19	0.57	1.14	0.83	1.04
Switzerland	13.99	4.08	5	5	0.56	1.01	1.06	0.50	−0.05	0.61	0.39
Iceland	10.25	3.43	6	6	na	0.44	1.12	0.47	na	0.48	0.92
Austria	9.53	3.00	7	7	0.40	0.85	0.63	0.45	0.34	−0.02	0.35
France	8.16	2.54	8	9	0.66	0.52	−0.57	1.03	0.13	0.39	0.37
Luxembourg	6.37	2.60	9	8	1.08	−1.09	0.41	1.06	0.72	1.01	−0.61
Czech Republic	6.04	1.85	10	11	1.38	−0.77	0.10	−0.50	1.00	0.29	0.34
Canada	6.00	1.72	11	12	0.02	0.82	0.48	0.11	−0.03	−0.37	0.69
New Zealand	4.71	1.45	12	13	0.22	0.13	0.50	0.20	na	−0.06	0.46
Netherlands	4.66	1.41	13	14	0.93	−0.26	0.18	−0.06	0.60	−0.07	0.09
Germany	4.49	2.09	14	10	0.14	−0.16	−0.28	1.12	0.39	0.57	0.32
Australia	2.46	0.54	15	15	−0.06	0.07	0.18	−0.15	−0.37	0.50	0.36
United Kingdom	1.19	0.12	16	18	−0.28	−0.21	0.31	0.14	−0.87	0.46	0.57
United States	1.02	0.30	17	17	−1.65	1.05	1.01	−0.06	−1.17	0.51	0.60
Belgium	1.02	0.51	18	16	0.54	0.43	−0.86	0.78	0.63	−0.93	−0.07
Korea	−1.66	−1.00	19	19	na	−0.78	0.88	−2.13	na	1.30	−0.27
Hungary	−3.48	−1.62	20	22	0.53	−0.59	−0.71	−0.59	−0.17	−0.51	0.41
Portugal	−6.28	−1.65	22	23	−0.99	0.14	0.07	−0.51	na	−0.68	0.31
Japan	−6.57	−1.43	23	20	−1.07	−0.59	0.78	−0.44	na	−0.02	−0.09
Poland	−6.94	−2.53	21	21	0.04	−0.46	−1.26	−0.89	−0.08	−0.35	0.47
Slovak Republic	−8.45	−1.76	24	24	na	−1.21	−1.47	−0.63	1.31	−0.24	0.49
Ireland	−11.44	−3.79	25	25	−0.77	−0.33	−0.87	−0–46	−0.67	−0.34	−0.35
Spain	−13.35	−4.34	26	26	−0.37	−0.45	−1.50	0.56	−0.71	−0.51	−1.35
Italy	−15.41	−4.95	27	27	−0.85	0.15	−1.30	0.34	−0.67	−1.48	−1.15
Greece	−22.45	−7.15	28	28	−0.88	−1.35	−1.00	−0.30	−0.91	−1.44	−1.27
Turkey	−33.01	−9.99	29	29	−1.44	−1.93	−0.69	−1.77	na	−0.72	−3.44
Mexico	−33.16	−11.79	30	30	−2.63	−1.15	0.43	−1.91	−3.36	−0.83	−2.34

Notes: 1. Poverty = poverty rate as 50% of median income; 2. Education = public expenditure on education % GDP; public expenditure on education per capita; 3. Labour = employment rate, unemployment rate, long-term unemployment rate; 4. Social expenditures = social expenditures as % GDP; public expenditures on health per capita; 5. Income inequality = Gini index; 6. Intergenerational justice = government debt; investment into research and development % GDP; 7. Gender justice = INT [1 − employment rate (men) / employment rate (women)] → INT = absolute value of the difference. na = not available; w = weighted; uw = unweighted.

Sources: OECD database; OECD Factbook (2005, 2006); Education at a Glance (1992–2005); Luxembourg Income Study (2000).

in general. Just societies cannot tolerate this offence against the just distribution of effective opportunities. There can be no doubt that the most serious discrimination against equal opportunity is not in politics, but in the economy. The representative inequality of men and women in the higher management of the finance, banking and corporate sectors is much greater than in parliaments and governments. As important as the gender-fair distribution of top political positions is, the idea that an automatic spill-over from politics into the headquarters of the capitalist economy will occur appears to be an illusion. Gender mainstreaming alone will not reduce the gender equality gap effectively. Moreover, gender mainstreaming itself is not unproblematic in terms of justice, and may violate some rules of equal opportunity between individuals, i.e., it may discriminate against individual men. However, just as all policies ought to be screened on whether they improve the position of the least advantaged, they ought also to be screened on whether they contribute to gender justice.

Social justice in the globalised age of the twenty-first century

The globalised age of the early twenty-first century will be driven by intense economic restructuring, dynamic social change, and political interdependency in the OECD. These economies and societies will be more open than ever and will demand from people, whether as producers, consumers or merely as citizens, a high capability and willingness to adapt to a rapidly changing environment and to shape their individual fate and well-being autonomously. The individual's personal capabilities will define their range of choices and life chances. Just societies and just policies will be measured by the opportunities they provide for citizens to develop their potential.

The passive welfare states of continental Europe, tailored to compensate citizens ex post after they have failed to integrate into demanding labour markets, will prove to be outdated, costly and unjust. They cure the symptoms, but do not address the sources of unequal life chances and of injustice. Those welfare states and policies which empower individuals will be considered up to date and just because they enable people to choose their own life plans. This was already true in the last decades of the twentieth century, but it will be even more so in the twenty-first century, when the demand and reward for low-skilled work will decline. Education will be the key to individual empowerment and life chances, which are not only the sources of personal autonomy but also the main drivers of collective welfare.

However, to create the institutional framework for a just society along Sen's premises, the social contract of most OECD countries needs to be rewritten, as Gøsta Esping-Andersen has proposed.[29] The new social compact should focus on empowering people and should open equal life chances for all citizens. It should entail at least three specific partial contracts in the form of new child, gender and employment contracts.

The *new child contract* must focus primarily on investment in children. This includes generous but child-conditional income guarantees for families (to avoid child poverty), quality-based support for children in childcare or all-day schools, and maximising female employment, since double-income households provide the best protection against child poverty. Poverty traps limit the life chances of children fundamentally and marginalise their families in society. To reduce such inherited deprivation has to be of utmost priority. Therefore, generous income guarantees for families should be conditional on the parents' preparedness to work. The state and society should provide training schemes and facilitate the access of parents to the labour market. Working parents can impart to their children useful work ethics that are necessary in order to recognise life chances, to develop capabilities and to have choices. There is a substantial risk, if not a high probability, that unemployed parents will impart the opposite. Thus, an unconditional basic income for every citizen may induce low-skilled parents to abstain from the labour market thereby trapping their children in a world of low education, a low work ethic, unemployment, and substantially reduced life chances.

If a just state ought to uphold 'equal concern'[30] for each citizen, it must offer children high-quality pre-schooling, in particular those children who come from lower-class and immigrant families. The positive incentives and negative sanctions have to be strong enough so that these families send their children to public pre-schools. Even affirmative action for the least privileged children can be justified in order to translate Dworkin's 'equal concern' for all children into a reality.

The *new gender contract* must be more efficient than the common, bureaucratic policies of gender mainstreaming. In previous years, women's level of education has exceeded that of men in many areas. Additionally, today's service-oriented societies have supplied women with chances they never enjoyed in the industrial economies of the previous century. However, employment for women has to be made a viable non-discriminatory option on a much larger scale by making it compatible with familial responsibilities. This does not mean that men should not be held accountable any more in this respect – on the contrary. But neither women nor society can afford to wait until the perception and attitudes of men have changed fundamentally. An increase in economic independence for women would not only represent progress in gender justice but also an improvement in collective social productivity.

Economically, it does not make any sense to invest in women's education only to later prevent them from joining the workforce by failing to offer institutionalised opportunities and incentives that make career and family compatible. Discrimination against women no longer takes place in education, at least in most OECD countries. Women are discriminated against in the labour market above all by the tax system (e.g. household taxation), the (continental) welfare state (e.g. contribution-based lower pensions), and the lack of day-care facilities for children. To dismantle this source of discrimination is not at all utopian since it would lead to a knowledge-based economy with a high-skilled labour force, thereby enhancing productivity as well as contributing to closing the justice gap between men and women.

The *new employment contract* must reduce unemployment first and foremost through increasing employment, and not through work-time reduction or the redistribution of stagnating employment rates. Non-wage labour costs must be slashed and the retirement age increased. The cautious deregulation of the labour market must be accompanied by activist programmes to secure social justice, through vocational, re- and further training.

However, realistically, 10 to 20 per cent of the employable population, even in highly qualified service-oriented economies, will only be able to find employment in a less qualified sector with low wages. To avoid the neo-liberal disease of the working poor, therefore, these jobs need to be subsidised, or a minimum wage certainly well above the US level needs to be introduced. Programmes for education, qualification and geographical mobility should be developed further to avoid the pauperisation of families and their entrapment at the bottom of society. Hereditary poverty over generations, which is establishing itself in Germany and on the European continent generally, must be fought against. Education, activation and integration into the labour market are a better solution than solidifying poverty through welfare payments, no matter how generous.

Conclusion

There is a fear among many that global economic interdependence and the deregulation of markets leave no room for a socially inclusive economic policy, since low-wage competition and the international race for scarce financial capital compel nation-states to act according to a neo-liberal agenda. Given that this debate has now reached epic proportions, it would take a lengthy discussion to deal with it in detail. I will therefore confine myself to a few brief comments. First, both advocates and opponents far overestimate the phenomenon of economic globalisation in terms of its size and impact. The intensity of international trade, the integration of capital markets and the transnational diffusion of production are simply not deep enough to enforce a total rejection of social standards in the OECD countries in the near future.

Second, discussion and critique of globalisation most often disregards the most fundamental economic laws of international trade, such as Ricardo's theorem of comparative cost advantages or the Heckscher-Ohlin model. These tell us that trade liberalisation in general will be to the benefit of all countries involved, because it fosters an efficient division of labour and the use of economies of scale. Nevertheless, globalisation has and will probably have two major negative consequences. On the one hand, it is expected that some groups – for example, unqualified workers in the OECD countries – will be among the losers since the status of their manpower has changed from relative scarcity to relative abundance in the globalised economy. However, it is possible in principle to compensate these groups for their losses. On the other hand, it can be observed that certain political instruments such as fiscal redistribution have lost their effectiveness due to economic globalisation.

It might be – and indeed is – argued that the state, precisely because of this development, will fail to carry out the necessary redistribution. True, we cannot expect the state to regain its power with regard to, e.g., an effective taxation of interest revenues and capital gains. However, the share of corporate taxes and taxes on interest revenues in total tax revenues is relatively small, so why should it not be possible to balance out these losses by other means?

Third, the exact shape of globalisation suggests that the wealth of one country depends mostly on *local* factors, above all on local productivity – that is, on the technology and the human capital its labour force disposes of. This leads to the conclusion that the best way to increase a country's economic performance and individual wealth is by *local* investment in education as well as research and development, as well as by a local active labour-market policy and labour-market deregulation to facilitate the unemployed re-entering the labour market.

Here the cycle of constraints posed by globalisation and individualisation on the one hand, and social justice on the other, closes. Libertarian concepts of social justice relying exclusively on the structure of the market cannot solve the problem of equal access to the market and its opportunities. Markets alone do not produce collective goods such as education, but tend to privatise them. The result is an unmeritocratic privileged access to education and life chances. It is not merit but the 'lottery of nature' (Rawls) that largely determines an individual's life chances.

Communitarian theories of justice display an analogous problem of unjustified inequality, but at the community level. Well-off communities can provide better education, better services and more capabilities than poor communities. Only the equal treatment of all communities, enforced and enabled by the central government, could overcome this problem of unjustified inequality. However, such a standardisation of social services and educational opportunities would contradict the essential paradigm that single communities and their respective civil societies determine the mode and quality of public goods and services themselves. Communitarian theories have no explicit proposals for how to empower (especially young) people with those capabilities needed to cope successfully with a rapidly changing globalised knowledge economy.

If a globalised knowledge economy and society distributes life chances essentially according to the human capital accumulated by an individual, then equal access to a good education turns out to become crucial for a just society. The window of opportunity for such an equal and just education opens and closes in the early phases of the life cycle. Children learn fast and easily in their early childhood and, most importantly, they acquire learning skills important for the rest of their lives. Just societies have to be keen to open this window in particular to children of lower-class and immigrant families. Missed chances in these formative years can rarely be made up for. Education is not every-thing, but without education everything is nothing. However, the new compact for children and education must be complemented by a new compact for employment and gender equality in order to help the seeds of an equal, fair, and good education yield fruits throughout the life cycle of an individual. There can be no doubt that Sen's focus on the equal provision of capabilities can solidly underpin Esping-Andersen's proposal for a new social compact in order to achieve a productive economy and a just society, even in the age of globalisation.

Economic efficiency and social justice demand higher investment in children. However, an ageing society cannot allow a simple shift of financial resources from the old to the young. Health care and elderly care have to be offered through high-quality public services. The serv-ices have to be of high quality, otherwise the middle classes will not accept collective provision. Part of the increased costs could be covered by higher female employment and the extension of the working age. The other part has to be financed by taxes on income, property and consumption.

Progressives must restore the legitimacy of the tax state. It is an illusion that low taxes and excellent public services can be provided simultaneously. The tax policy of New Labour and the Red-Green Government in Germany (1998–2005) to some extent encouraged this illusion. This trend has to be stopped soon, if not reversed. However, to reduce the retirement age, to prevent the extension of weekly working hours, to regulate the labour market, to increase corporate taxes, to pay generous unconditioned unemployment compensation and social assistance as the trade unions in France, Germany and Italy and other traditional leftists demagogically propose, would be a retreat to the past. It would lead to a disastrous loss in international competitiveness. This does not mean a return to the old-fashioned tax-and-spend state or the tax levels of the 1970s. Investment in children will pay off already in the medium term, and a longer working age and higher employment quota will help to cover the higher costs for the elderly.

The market alone will not bring about the necessary changes. The state has a crucial role to play in allowing people to choose by investing in them, their capabilities and life chances. The primary focus has to be on children, women and families. A new, more productive and socially more just compact, better education, female employment, social security for families, and a longer and more flexible working life are unavoidable. The social democratic social contract must be rewritten. Anglo-Saxon capitalism and continental European welfare states would be well advised to inform their policies by Rawls' and Sen's principle of justice and by best practice in the Scandinavian countries.

Notes

I would like to thank Dennis Badenhop for his critical comments, suggestions, and co-operation.
  1 This strand of 'social', 'developed' or 'modern' liberalism calls upon the state to guarantee its citizens not just formal, but actual equality of resources and opportunities. See, e.g., J. Rawls, *A Theory of Justice* (Cambridge, Mass.: Harvard University Press, 1975 [1971]) and *Political Liberalism* (New York: Columbia University Press, 1993); R. Dworkin, 'What is Equality? Part I: Equality of Welfare', *Philosophy and Public Affairs* 3 (1981), pp. 185–246, 'What is Equality? Part II: Equality of Resources', *Philosophy and Public Affairs* 4 (1981), pp. 283–345, 'What is Equality? Part III: The Place of Liberty', *Iowa Law Review* 73 (1987), pp. 1–54, and 'What is Equality? Part IV: Political Equality', *University of San Francisco Law Review* 22 (1988), pp. 1–30; A. Sen, 'Equality of What?' The Tanner Lecture on Human Values, delivered at Stanford University, 22 May 1979: http://www.tannerlectures.utah.edu/lectures/documents/sen80.pdf; *Choice, Welfare and Measurement* (Cambridge, Mass.: Harvard University Press, 1982), 'Well-Being, Agency and Freedom. The Dewey Lectures 1984', *Journal of Philosophy* 4 (1984), pp. 169–221, *Inequality Reexamined* (Cambridge, Mass.: Harvard University Press, 1992), and *Development as Freedom* (New York: Alfred A. Knopf, 1999).
  2 F.A. von Hayek, *Die Anmaßung von Wissen* (Tübingen: Mohr, 1996), p. 6.
  3 F.A. von Hayek, *Die Verfassung der Freiheit* (Tübingen: Mohr, 1971), p. 48.
  4 Ibid., p. 382.
  5 Robert Nozick, in contrast to von Hayek, allows for a certain redistribution of goods if their current possession results from unfair transfers or acts of appropriation in the past. While Nozick's theory is in this respect certainly more adequate than von Hayek's strictly non-redistributive conception, it is as a whole not better founded; its core, the 'historical principle of justice', is entirely unpractical; and where Nozick tries to reformulate it as an applicable

guideline for policy-makers, he ends only by saying that Rawls' difference principle would be a good approximation. See R. Nozick, *Anarchy, State and Utopia* (New York: Basic Books, 1974), p. 231.

6   Rawls, *A Theory of Justice*, p. 62.

7   Ibid., p. 60.

8   Quotations are from the German version: *Sphären der Gerechtigkeit* (Frankfurt: VS Verlag, 1992).

9   M. Walzer, *Die Vergesellschaftung des Wohlfahrtsstaates* (Frankfurt: Campus, 1988), p. 161.

10 T.H. Marshall, *Citizenship and Social Class* (Cambridge: Cambridge University Press, 1950).

11 The term 'meritocratic principle' is often somewhat imprecisely translated as 'achievement principle'. 'Meritocracy' refers to merit, that is, something one has legitimately earned as a result of one's efforts and achievements.

12 See, for example, A. Sen, *Ökonomie für den Menschen. Wege zu Gerechtigkeit und Solidarität in der Marktwirtschaft* (Munich: dtv, 2000).

13 Sen, 'Equality of What?', p. 218.

14 Sen, 'Capability and Well-Being', in A. Sen and M. Nussbaum (eds), *The Quality of Life* (Cambridge, Mass.: Harvard University Press, 1993), p. 31.

15 A. Giddens (ed.), *The Progressive Manifesto* (Cambridge: Polity, 2003), pp. 13ff.

16 See R. Dahrendorf, *Lebenschancen. Anläufe zur sozialen und politischen Theorie* (Frankfurt: Suhrkamp, 1979).

17 The final version of the second principle of justice ('principle of difference') reads: 'Social and economic inequalities are to be arranged so that they are both: (a) to the greatest benefit of the least advantaged, consistent with the just savings principle, and (b) attached to offices and positions open to all under the conditions of fair equality of opportunity' (Rawls, *A Theory of Justice*, p. 302).

18 Sen, *Inequality Reexamined*, p. 138.

19 I. Berlin, *Four Essays on Liberty* (Oxford: Oxford University Press, 1969).

20 This argument is supported even more strongly by the pronounced resource-egalitarianism of Dworkin. See R. Dworkin, *Foundations of Liberal Equality. 1989 Tanner Foundation Lectures* (Salt Lake City: University of Utah Press, 1990).

21 Rawls, *A Theory of Justice*; A. Giddens, *The Third Way: The Renewal of Social Democracy* (Cambridge: Polity Press, 1998); Sen, *Development as Freedom*.

22 A. Sen, 'Soziale Gerechtigkeit und Ökonomische Effizienz', in Julian Nida-Rümelin and Wolfgang Thierse (eds), *Philosophie und Politik II* (Essen: Klartext-Verlag, 1998), pp. 14–26.

23 Ibid., pp. 19–20.

24 Such structures are to be found especially in the continental welfare states (e.g., Germany, France, Belgium).

25 G. Esping-Andersen, *The Three Worlds of Welfare Capitalism* (Cambridge: Polity Press 1990), and *Social Foundations of Postindustrial Economies* (Oxford: Oxford University Press, 1999).

26 F.W. Scharpf, 'Sozialstaaten in der Globalisierungsfalle', lecture to the annual general meeting of the Max Planck Society, Munich, June 2000: http://www.mpi-fg-koeln.mpg.de.

27 Giddens, *The Third Way*, p. 103.

28 P. Hall and D. Soskice, *Varieties of Capitalism: The Institutional Foundations of Comparative Advantage* (Oxford: Oxford University Press, 2001).

29 Esping-Andersen, *Social Foundations of Postindustrial Economies*.

30 R. Dworkin, *Sovereign Virtue: The Theory and Practice of Equality* (Cambridge, Mass.: Harvard University Press, 2000).

II
ANALYSIS

4

Winners and Losers of Economic Globalisation

Lionel Fontagné

Globalisation and social justice are generally seen as at odds with civil society – a perception persistently confirmed in political debates and discourse. Against this background, the relatively balanced conclusions reached by many economists are often caricatured as neglecting the social aspect of the globalisation 'story'. In contrast to popular perceptions of such economic analysis, it can be suggested that globalisation offers dramatic opportunities to unleash growth and alleviate poverty in those regions of the world with sound civil institutions and an educated population. Yet even such a prudent assessment must be qualified, given that many regions of the developing world do not possess such structures. Economic globalisation has therefore been linked to the contemporary global disparities and extraordinary levels of inequality.

First, we need to understand 'inequality' in a global perspective. We could, for instance, look at the inequalities of personal wealth within countries (inequalities between individuals); or, alternatively, we could consider the inequalities arising from international differences in the average income per capita (inequalities between nations); or, finally, we could examine population-weighted international differences in average income per capita (inequalities between populations).

If we treat the weight of every country equally, regardless of the size of its population, inequalities between nations have increased as a result of globalisation.[1] In contrast, income inequalities between populations (considered on the basis of their average income in relation to the size of the population) have declined, thanks mainly to the emergence of China.[2] Finally, there is some evidence of increasing inequalities between individuals within countries in most regions of the world – and there is evidence for this in a large number of developing countries too.[3] In accordance with the Luxembourg Income Study dataset for industrialised economies, the International Monetary Fund has pointed to systematic increases in interpersonal income inequalities, with the exception of low-income countries, over the last two decades.[4] This increase in inequalities is particularly marked in China. Indeed, China contributes to the reduction in inequalities between populations as its average income per capita increases, while simultaneously contributing to the deepening of interpersonal inequalities as increases in average income per capita are not evenly distributed among the Chinese population. As a result, 60 per cent of overall global inequalities at the level of individuals are attributable to inter-country inequalities.[5]

Second, we need to define 'social justice' in the context of this chapter. Viewed from a global perspective, we could defend the idea that social justice should prioritise the elevation of income per capita of the poorest countries in the world. Alternatively, we could focus on the alleviation of poverty in developing countries – including those partially developed national economies where large fractions of the population still lie beneath the poverty threshold. However, the crucial question is to deal not only with the 'average' country, but to establish whether globalisation has been associated with the impoverishment of certain countries. Using the latter approach, Bourguignon et al. have identified two dozen countries where this has been the case.[6] Hence, depending on how the data is weighted, we can conclude that inequalities have increased or worsened among countries over the last two decades.

Yet, if we shift the focus of analysis to the inequalities within our own (developed) societies coping with globalisation, conclusions are far from clear-cut. The process of understanding the overall impact of globalisation on inequality and social justice is far from being achieved. And some of the qualifications made with regard to social justice at the global level have to be kept in mind even when we are considering our industrialised economies. Using a relatively restrictive criterion of social justice, we should ask whether globalisation has particularly affected those with the lowest incomes, or, moving beyond generalisations, whether individuals have been negatively affected by globalisation.

This chapter aims to evaluate general trends in the distribution of the benefits and burdens of globalisation within industrialised societies, based on the (indirect) evidence associated with a detailed analysis of trade flows. Such an approach is challengeable: trade in goods is only one part of the story. Foreign direct investment (FDI), the activity of foreign affiliates, financial flows and migrations, should be considered too (e.g. Anderson, on the role of migrations on inequalities during the first wave of globalisation in the nineteenth century).[7] The 2007 IMF report contrasts the respective impacts of trade and FDI, and finds that FDI has increased interpersonal inequalities by more than trade has decreased these inequalities, leading to an overall increase in the dispersion of individual incomes in most countries.[8]

Of course, we could challenge this conclusion on the basis of the definition of trade considered, as well as on the basis of the joint determination of trade and FDI. The two variables are all but independent. We could also stress that not all categories of exchanges have the same impact: in particular, trade in cultural goods is indirectly impacting the rest of trade flows, via the transmission of culture, preferences and representations. However, the trade in goods is extremely well documented and provides us with a useful level of detail to match our empirical research with recent research developments in the field of international economics.

Thus, a number of questions are addressed here. Who are the main economic beneficiaries and losers in this era of increased global economic integration and competition? How does economic theory explain this puzzle? What are the main characteristics of the competition between industrialised and emerging economies? What is the division of labour put in place by globalisation and what are its consequences? In particular, can we infer from this characterisation of the international division of labour what the impact of international trade with low-wage economies on labour compensation within industrialised nations is?

As such, this study is organised as follows. The theoretical mechanisms linking trade and inequalities are surveyed in the first part. The second part looks at the labour content of trade and the related competitive pressure, in particular on blue-collar workers. The third part addresses the issue of off-shoring, often perceived as the main vector of inequalities in the developed economies. The fourth part puts forward the key argument developed here: international specialisation is now taking place at a level of detail going much beyond what has generally been considered in studies addressing the impact of trade on inequalities.

Understanding the link between trade and inequalities

The economic analysis of the mechanisms linking trade to inequalities is anything but clear-cut. Much of the policy debate implicitly relies on the workhorse of the standard trade theory, the so-called Heckscher–Ohlin–Samuelson model. Under this framework, trade arises as a result of international differences in relative autarkic prices of goods. Accordingly, trade is leading to a convergence of relative prices: the relative price of the good which a country is advantaged in will increase, while the relative price of the good it is disadvantaged in will decrease.

Since goods are differing in their relative content in skilled versus unskilled labour, changes in relative prices of the goods will translate into changes in the relative prices of production factors. For a skill-abundant country, advantaged in the production of skill-intensive goods, specialisation will have the following consequences. The skill-intensive sector will expand while the unskilled sector will contract. As production of the importable good decreases, unskilled as well as skilled workers are displaced. But the predominantly unskilled sector is actually freeing more unskilled labour than the skill-intensive sector can employ efficiently at the current relative wage; and recipro-cally, the exportable sector is seeking more skilled labour than that displaced by the importable sector at the current relative wage. These imbalances will translate into an excess supply of unskilled labour and an excess demand for skilled labour at the autarkic wage.

Therefore, in the skill-abundant country trade will reduce the wage of unskilled workers and increase the wage of skilled workers. Alternatively, when the labour market is ailing, this ultimately leads to unemployment for the unskilled workers. From a policy perspective, this point of view opposes continental Europe, where the adjustment mainly takes place in terms of quantities, to the United States, where larger adjustments of production factor prices can be observed.

In order to better understand what is at stake in the policy debate, we need to consider the following caveat: if factors are substitutable, the relative employment of unskilled labour will increase in both sectors as a result of changes in factor prices. Both sectors become less intensive in skilled workers. Incidentally, this factor substitu-tion smoothes the magnitude of the changes in factor returns. In an economy advantaged in the unskilled sector the change in the relative prices of goods will be opposite to the one considered here, while the change in relative factor prices will also be symmetrical. It is precisely this hypothesis, known as the Stolper–Samuelson theorem, which nurtures the widespread fears associated with open-ness to globalisation: the real return to the abundant production factor will decrease as the real return to the scarce production factor will increase.

The limits of standard trade theory

Following the theory described above, the wage gap between skilled and unskilled labour should increase in industrialised countries and decrease in developing countries. There are, however, a number of further qualifications to be made before relying on such an approach. In our case, we have used the simplest framework, namely two countries in order to have international exchange, two homogeneous goods in order to have inter-industry specialisation, and two factors in order to tackle distributive impacts. Yet, in a more general framework one would have to impose very restricted criteria in order to reach these predicted outcomes. Ultimately, only empirical assessment could validate this claim.

First, we have to consider the kind of relationship between products and factors. Ethier introduced the useful notion of the 'natural friend' of a production factor.[9] A 'natural enemy' is defined in the same way: when the price of a good increases the return to the factor decreases. In the 'even case', where the number of goods and factors is equal, every factor has a good which is its natural friend and a good which is its 'natural enemy'.[10] More precisely, for the increase in the price of every good, holding the prices of the other goods fixed by assumption, there must be at least one factor that loses and one factor that gains. According to economic textbooks, sticking to the two factor–two countries case, the reason why every factor has one enemy and one friend is straightforward. However, in a general framework this one-to-one relationship is weakened. Problems worsen when the number of goods and the number of factors differ.

A second concern refers to the so-called condition of diversification: for a given set of goods, similar countries will produce the same subset of goods and, hence, produce these goods with the same production techniques and the same factor prices. In contrast, countries exhibiting large dissimilarities in their factor endowments will produce a different subset of goods with different factor prices.

When imports do not compete with domestic production, cheaper imports boost the purchasing power of households. Accordingly, countries at very different levels of development and having very different factor endowments should not produce the same bundle of goods, and factor price equalisation should not hold. As Leamer has argued, there are 'paths of development' that countries will rather deterministically follow.[11] In a nutshell, developing economies will integrate into the world economy by exporting, for example, clothing, shoes, or toys, and thereafter progressively upgrade their bundle of exported goods as they accumulate physical and human capital. Helpman and Krugman show that the net factor content of trade will be larger between rather dissimilar countries, but that very dissimilar countries will not equalise their factor prices.[12]

To summarise, the standard view is based on a factor proportion framework, where certain factors of production gain and other factors lose in real terms with trade openness. These gains and losses increase in magnitude with the net factor content of trade. But when countries largely differ in their factor endowments, complete specialisation arises and factor price equalisation no longer holds.

Moving beyond the standard approach

There are additional dimensions of inequality which are not addressed within the standard approach and that are key policy issues. For instance, whenever the employment of production factors is highly specific, inequalities among sectors will be recorded. Hence, if workers in the clothing sector are hardly employable in the pharmaceutical sector as a result of the highly specialised nature of the tasks they perform in their sector of origin, then any adverse shock on the textile sector will harm these workers.

Another issue concerns gender. If different sectors employ female workers in very different proportions, and if female and male workers are not perfectly substitutable on the labour market, any adverse shock on the sector employing a large amount of female workers (e.g. clothing) will translate into an adverse shock on this segment of the market.[13] One way of thinking about this is to consider that there is some sector specificity of the skills in the short run, and that a transitional cost will be faced by individuals employed in sectors facing a surge in competitive imports.

Lastly, the relevance of the Stolper–Samuelson effect for economic policy is questionable when there are various sources of individual or household income. Inequality between individuals or between households can be the result of the distribution of different sources of primary income. In particular, returns to assets have to be taken into account. The magnitude of real changes in income also depends, of course, on consumption patterns. Income can be tackled before or after redistribution. For rural households, self-consumption has to be added.

As a result, every individual, or every category of household, will be affected differently given the vectors of changes in goods prices and in factor returns.

All of these issues make it difficult to compare the distribution of income across countries. And they raise equally serious questions when one addresses the response of income inequality to a given shock. Typically, income equality substantially differs with or without returns to assets, and pre- or post-income redistribution. Finally, using household data, it may be the case that shocks are smoothed by the different evolutions in the different sources of income in the household.

What does the empirical evidence tell us?

Despite the numerous limitations of the standard theoretical approach, the policy debate on trade and inequalities has been driven by its underlying rationale. While extensive empirical work attempts to assess the validity of its alarming conclusions, three major obstacles have thus far impeded any clear-cut measurement. First, the magnitude of the trade-related changes in factor prices appears to be very limited.[14] But given the limited share of industrialised economies' trade with developing countries, this does not come as a surprise. The labour content approaches, referred to below, reach the same conclusions.

Second, what is observed on the labour market is an increase in demand for skilled labour, despite the increase in the compensation of skilled workers. Hence, we do not detect the expected factor substitution when the wage gap is widening between skilled and unskilled workers. A shock must have exogenously increased the demand for skilled labour and many believe that this is due to a skill-biased technological progress. In line with this, trade is not responsible for the rising wage inequalities observed in many OECD countries.[15]

Finally, we can also observe increases in inequalities in emerging markets (e.g. in Mexico), contrasting with the expected reduction in the gap between the compensation of skilled and unskilled labour in the global south. The question then is how did such skill-biased technical progress identically affect countries at very different development levels? This is where recent academic interest matches the concerns of civil society: off-shoring is the new suspect. But before addressing the specific responsibility of off-shoring, we will try to quantify the overall contribution of trade with low-wage countries to the displacement of workers in the manufacturing sector in industrialised countries.

If theory fails to provide policy-makers with an appropriate tool to analyse the impact of globalisation on inequalities, it comes as no surprise that the debate has been largely nurtured by a-theoretical estimates of the impact of trade on the labour market. These approaches are generally referred to as the 'labour content of trade'.

The labour content of trade

For policy-makers, the key issue is how many jobs in the manufacturing sector have been displaced respectively by domestic forces and by trade, in particular trade with developing economies. In principle, the standard economic theory referred to above challenges such an approach: jobs are neither created nor destroyed in the full employment general equilibrium. The labour force is simply re-allocated to more efficient uses, or re-employed in the industry facing foreign competition thanks to a factor substitution driven by changes in relative factor prices. However, addressing the number of jobs displaced by foreign competition more directly attempts to reply to widespread policy concerns, asking in particular for the short-term adjustment costs.

The labour content of trade can be tentatively measured, either by using an 'Input–Output' approach or by relying on an econometric estimation. In both cases, the number of workers displaced by trade in general, and by trade with developing economies in particular, remains rather small, pointing to the paramount importance of domestic factors.

Input–Output tables

The first method commonly used is based on the labour content of exports and imports as measured using an 'Input–Output' table. Such a table provides all inter-industry relations, upward and downward, for a given economy decomposed in a certain number of industries. Combined with the information on the labour content of one dollar's worth of production in every industry, one can infer the total content in labour of one dollar of additional demand (e.g. exports) to a given industry. Similarly one can get information on the labour content of one dollar of imports (actually of one dollar of domestic substitutes for these imports). Combining this information on production techniques with information on employment in industries, one obtains the total labour contained in exports (imports) to (from) the world or a given region (e.g. low-wage countries). The same calculation can be done by skill levels of workers in order to get an insight into inequalities.

Typically, the magnitude of the associated job displacements is very limited, pointing to the conclusion that domestic factors explain a much larger share of observed variations in employment, or of impacts differentiated by skill levels. Two studies are exemplary for this. In the early 1990s, the French administration carried out an assessment of the labour content of French trade in manufactures with developing economies. Overall estimates pointed to a 'loss' of 319,000 jobs due to imports, and a 'gain' of 446,000 jobs due to exports. The observed positive net impact was the result of a French trade surplus. A second calculation by Bonnaz et al. took into account the problem of non-competing imports.[16] The plants producing goods competing with low-wage countries have been closed and are no longer part of the statistics. Thus, in order not to underestimate the labour content of imports, the technique to be considered should not be the one present in the actual data of the input–output table.

The authors propose an upper bound of the losses, which corresponds to a substitution in physical terms rather than in value terms (one domestic pair of shoes for one imported pair of shoes, instead of one dollar for one dollar). Given the average ratio of unit values (values divided by quantities) for French (exported) products and French imports from developing economies for the same categories of products, equal to 2:1, the value of the domestic production displaced by imports has to be increased accordingly. As a result, the net loss of jobs after this correction was 330,000. This upper bound represented roughly one-tenth of the observed unemployment at that time.

Gallais and Gauthier have refined this calculation for France: they disentangle labour by skill categories and take into account not only manufactures but trade in goods and services (except tourism).[17] As opposed to Bonnaz et al., they include all trade relationships, with developed as well as developing countries. On the one hand, not focusing on low-wage countries should dilute the observed effects on employment. On the other hand, considering trade as a whole should lead to a larger impact on employment in absolute terms. Lastly, they compute the actual balance in employment, after correcting for the trade imbalance. The net loss of blue-collar jobs is 58,000 and the net gain of white-collar jobs is 33,000. These amounts are tiny and point to the negligible overall impact of trade on inequalities.

A similar approach has been followed by Baily and Lawrence, who investigated the role of trade in US manufacturing job losses after 2000.[18] They estimate separately the impact of imports and exports on the observed decline in manufacturing employment between 2000 and 2003. They observe that manufacturing employment fell by 2.85 million over this period and that 89 per cent of the fall was due to weak domestic demand combined with a strong productivity growth. The rest was due to trade, but the induced loss of jobs was the result of an export weakness, itself due to an overvalued dollar.

Econometric approaches

Net labour contents of trade can alternatively be estimated econometrically. Two recent examples are worth highlighting, since they identify separately the estimated role of trade with low-wage countries. Boulhol and Fontagné[19] replicate and extend to 2002 (instead of 1994) the estimations made by Rowthorn and Ramaswamy,[20] and ask what is the contribution of trade with emerging economies to the observed deindustrialisation in sixteen OECD countries. Using a simple framework comprising two sectors (industry and services), and linking relative prices to productivity, they point to a 'natural'

decreasing share of industry in the labour force because of rapid productivity gains. The fall in industry prices will not lead to a continuous
rise in relative industry output. In total, and in real terms, one should
observe an increase in the relative value added of industry until a certain threshold of income per capita, before the evolution reverses.

Using trade and production data for 1970 to 2002, Boulhol and
Fontagné show that an increase in the net imports from low-wage
countries of 1 point of GDP reduces the manufacturing employment
share by 4 per cent in the long term.[21] In contrast, an increase in the net
imports from OECD countries of 1 point of GDP reduces the manufacturing employment share by 1 per cent only. The order of magnitude
for the labour content of imports from developing economies relative
to that from developed economies is 3.5.

Based on these estimates, the total contribution of trade with low-
wage countries to the changes in the manufacturing employment share
can be computed. The contribution of trade with low-wage economies
would explain on average one fifth of the observed decline in the manufacturing employment share. Stated differently, trade with low-wage
countries is associated with an average decrease of around two points
in the manufacturing employment share. As a last piece of evidence,
Boulhol and Fontagné calculate what manufacturing employment in
2002 would have been had the countries involved maintained their
trade ratios with low-wage countries at 1970 levels.[22]

Looking for example at the US, the displacement of jobs in the
manufacturing sector amounts to approximately 3.3 million. For
Japan and France, it amounts to respectively 1.4 million and 350,000
manufacturing jobs. Such contributions can be calculated for two sub-
periods, before and after 1986, in order to check what the impact of
the recent deepening of globalisation has been. Doing so, Boulhol and
Fontagné observe that the phenomenon is twice as large in the second
sub-period, but that this is due to the increase in trade flows only, and
not to the increase in the labour content differential of one dollar's
worth of net trade.[23] Finally, the differences between countries in the
magnitude of job displacement are sizeable: the largest contribution
is observed for Italy, with a contribution of trade with low-wage countries peaking at up to 36 per cent; the weakest is observed for Sweden,
with a contribution of 7 per cent only.

Off-shoring and inequalities

Nowadays, off-shoring has taken a prominent place in the debate
about inequalities. In fact, its surge to prominence had been prepared
by a long series of works on the new organisation of the international division of labour. Specific methods have been used to tackle

the contribution of this phenomenon to the increasing gap between skilled and unskilled wages.[24]

In a nutshell, firms reorganise themselves on a global level to take advantage of international cost differentials. They accordingly specialise their overseas subsidiaries in different segments of the production process, or engage in subcontracting production segments to foreign firms. The associated fragmentation of production processes is leading to a growing recourse to imported parts and components from low-wage countries.[25] Imports, in turn, become a complement of, rather than a substitute for, domestic inputs.[26]

It has been recognised for a long time that trade in intermediate goods is leading to additional gains, as compared to trade in final goods.[27] Ranking production segments along a continuum of production stages has been proposed by Sanyal: since productivity evolved at a different pace across countries along the continuum (from upstream to downstream of the activity), the latter was split at some point, leading to trade in intermediate goods, or, in today's semantics, to outsourcing.[28] Models of the same spirit have been proposed by Sanyal and Jones[29] and Dixit and Grossman.[30]

Modelling the impact of outsourcing on inequalities

What is new in the literature of the late 1990s is that the implications for the factor markets are tackled as the core issue. Instead of explaining trade patterns, interest has shifted to their impact on inequalities. In models used by Feenstra and Hanson, activities are ranked along the continuum in sequential order. Hence, one goes from the less skill-intensive to the more skill-intensive. Each country specialises according to its comparative advantage and trade in intermediate products takes place.

Let us assume that the skill-intensive country is also the one well-endowed in capital, and that the economy is the domestic one. If returns to capital are higher in the foreign country, there will be foreign investment in production plants. This will affect the specialisation of the two countries. The domestic economy shifts its specialisation towards the most skill-intensive stages, while the foreign country adds the off-shored segments to its former bundle of produced intermediate goods. Every segment that is outsourced is more skill-intensive than the most intensive one previously produced in the country hosting the off-shored activities. Accordingly, the average skill content of the bundle of goods produced by this country increases. The demand for skilled labour increases in both countries, and consequently the skill premium increases in both countries.

This is one potential trade-related explanation of the shift in the labour demand curve, explaining why wage inequalities between skilled and unskilled are increasing in all countries, regardless of their skill intensity.[31] Ignoring in this context the Stolper–Samuelson reasoning is helpful, but needs to be validated empirically. What is the actual contribution of outsourcing to the observed increase in the share of skilled labour in the value added? The simplest method for evaluating the impact of outsourcing on inequalities is to statistically explain the observed change in the shares of factor incomes in the value added (factor cost shares) by a series of variables including outsourcing and the other suspect: technical progress.

This approach has been extensively used in the existing literature and is in line with the hypothesis that outsourcing has shifted the demand for skilled labour, exactly as has a skill-biased technical progress. However, relying on data from individual firms and tackling their trade in intermediate products is not an easy task. This is why most studies rely instead on the share of imports in intermediate consumption, categorised by industry. This can be done by considering either all the intermediate consumption of an industry (e.g. steel, rubber, glass, for the car industry) or intra-consumption only (the intermediate consumption of the products of the car industry by the car industry).

The other common explanation refers to technical progress, in particular in line with information technologies (e.g. investment in computers). Available studies conclude that the contribution of outsourcing to the increase in the share of skilled labour in costs is in the range of 15 per cent to 30 per cent in the US, in the UK and in France.[32]

Specialisation in varieties within products

In contrast to the previously mentioned standard trade theory, in a multi-product setting, the bundle of imported and exported goods is indeterminate. However, the alternative approach based on net factor contents received very weak empirical support, leading in turn to the introduction of new considerations, such as differences in technology.[33] One of the explanations for such discouraging evidence was the use of trade data at the sector level. Indeed, there is growing unease with approaches in terms of sectors or products. On the contrary, it turns out that countries specialise in varieties within products, rather than on any one product overall. Hence, studies focusing on sectors or products may miss their target and, in the end, it may be the case that industrialised and developing economies are not direct competitors, but rather complement each other.

Even if factor abundance (the story about skill-abundant and skill-poor sectors) is likely to be used to explain the specialisation of countries, intra-sectoral or intra-product variation of production techniques is very large. In this context, Schott looks more precisely at the role of technology, concluding that countries either do not produce the same bundle of goods with the same technique (this is Trefler's interpretation)[34] or else they do not produce the same bundle of goods at all (this is Schott's hypothesis).[35]

Fontagné, Gaulier and Zignago rely on a newly developed database covering all countries and all products in the world, over a decade.[36] Using such exhaustive data makes it possible to disaggregate trade flows across many countries according to unit values (values divided by quantities, at the most detailed level). Products belonging to the same item of classification and exported by two different countries may have largely different prices: the authors consider in this case that these are different varieties of the same products. They reconstruct world trade in three ranges of prices for each product and analyse what the market positioning of exporters is for their different products and on their different destination markets.

Based on this assumption, they conclude that a new form of international specialisation is taking place, in terms of quality within industries and within product categories. This form of specialisation plays an important role in the dynamics of north–south competition. North and south are very similar in terms of exported products, at least if we consider emerging economies competing with the north, but this similarity vanishes when it comes to varieties within products exported. Such specialisation of countries at different levels of development within products and across varieties has important implications.

First, it is mirrored in the recent shifts in world market shares of the main world competitors: these shifts are very different across quality segments. Emerging economies are not gaining market share in high-value portions of trade patterns, but instead are making progress in the bottom segment of the market. Second, if north and south are not competing head-on, fears of large redistributive impacts of north–south competition may be misplaced. However, the authors conclude that differentiating products is the result of different production functions. The factor bundle used to produce low-range and top-range products is very different. As with technical progress, the shift of firms towards high-priced goods necessitates a reliance on more R&D, more skills and more technology; and this may indirectly impact on the demand for unskilled labour.

Conclusion

The consequences of the new assessment for specialisation are of paramount importance in terms of economic policy. If low-wage and high-wage countries completely specialise in differentiated varieties of the same bundle of goods, instead of partially specialising on the same products, the relationship between product prices and factor prices is fundamentally weakened. A further fall in import prices translates into purchasing power (benefiting low-income households if it concerns consumption goods), while not putting pressure on blue-collar workers' income. On top of this, if the production process is actually fragmented and if countries do completely specialise in different segments, this will translate into competitive gains.

Depending on the importing country, we can observe a variable proportion of the two mechanisms. Using median unit values of products imported from emerging economies and domestic substitutes, and reclassifying products according to their use (intermediate, consumption, etc.), we can compute the respective contribution of imports of the different types to the overall potential gain. For instance, in the case of the US, we observe for 2005 that 60 per cent of the total accrues to producers and their productivity efforts (intermediate imports and investment goods imports). This is to be compared with 55 per cent for Japan, 40 per cent for Germany, 35 per cent for the UK and 18 per cent for France.

Finally, in many cases the bulk of globalisation gains accrue to consumers, not to producers, as is well illustrated by the French case. In order to evaluate this gain, we can use product-by-product information on value added instead of relying on medians. By doing so, we observe that the gain per French household has been rather stable over the period 1999 to 2005 if we keep the consumption basket constant: roughly 1,000 euros per French household per year. These are only potential gains since the distributor's mark-up can vary over time as globalisation goes on. But if we take into account the change in the consumption basket, this potential gain triples, thanks to the rapid diversification of the export bundle of developing economies.

Notes

1   See R.J. Barro and X. Sala-i-Martin, 'Convergence', *Journal of Political Economy* 100:2 (1992), pp. 223–51, and D.T. Quah, 'Empirics for Growth and Distribution: Polarisation, Stratification, and Convergence Clubs', *Journal of Economic Growth* 2:1 (1997), pp. 27–59.

2   See CEPII, *L'économie mondiale 2005* (Paris: Editions Repères, 2004).

3   S. Chen, and M. Ravallion, 'Absolute Poverty Measures for the Developing World, 1981–2004', World Bank Policy Research Working Paper 4211 (2007).

4　International Monetary Fund, *World Economic Outlook* (October 2007), ch. 4: Globalisation and Inequality.

5　F. Bourguignon and C. Morrisson, 'Inequality Among World Citizens: 1890–1992', *American Economic Review* 92:4 (2002), pp. 727–44.

6　F. Bourguignon, V. Levin and D. Rosenblatt, 'Declining International Inequality and Economic Divergence: Reviewing the Evidence through Different Lenses', *Économie Internationale* 100 (2004), pp. 13–25.

7　E. Anderson, 'Globalisation and Wage Inequalities, 1870–1970', *European Review of Economic History* 5:01 (2001), pp. 91–118.

8　International Monetary Fund, *World Economic Outlook* (October 2007).

9　W. Ethier, 'Some of the Theorems of International Trade with Many Goods and Factors', *Journal of International Economics* 4 (1974), pp. 199–206.

10　R. Jones and J.A. Scheinkman, 'The Relevance of the Two-Sector Production Model in Trade Theory', *Journal of Political Economy* 85:5 (1977), pp. 909–35.

11　E.E. Leamer, 'Paths of Development in the 3-Factor, N-Good General Equilibrium Model', *Journal of Political Economy* 95 (1987), pp. 961–99.

12　E. Helpman and P. Krugman, *Market Structure and Foreign Trade* (Cambridge, Mass.: MIT Press, 1985).

13　See E. Anderson, 'Trade-induced Changes in Labour Market Inequalities: Current Findings and Methodological Issues', ABCDE Tokyo conference paper, 29–30 May 2006: http://siteresources.worldbank.org/INTDECABCTOK2006/Resources/EAnderson_paper_.pdf

14　See for instance M.J. Slaughter and P. Swagel, 'The Effect of Globalization on Wages in the Advanced Economies', IMF Working Paper 97/43 (1997).

15　R.Z. Lawrence and M. Slaughter, 'International Trade and American Wages in the 1980s: Giant Sucking Sound or Small Hiccup?', *Brookings Papers on Economic Activity: Microeconomics* 1993:2 (1993), pp. 161–226, and P. Krugman and R. Lawrence, 'Trade, Jobs, and Wages', NBER Working Paper 4478 (1993).

16　H. Bonnaz, N. Courtot and D. Nivat, 'Le contenu en emplois des échanges industriels de la France avec les pays en développement', *Économie et Statistique* 279 (1994), pp. 13–34.

17　A. Gallais and B. Gauthier, 'Structure des qualifications et échanges extérieurs français', *Économie et Statistique* 9/10 (1994), pp. 4–10.

18　M.N. Baily and R.Z. Lawrence, 'What Happened to the Great US Job Machine? The Role of Trade and Electronic Offshoring', *Brookings Papers on Economic Activity* 2 (2004), pp. 211–84.

19　H. Boulhol and L. Fontagné, 'Deindustrialisation and the Fear of Relocations in the Industry', CEPII Working Paper 2006-07.

20　R.E. Rowthorn and R. Ramaswamy, 'Growth, Trade and Deindustrialization', IMF Working Paper, 98/60 (1998).

21　Boulhol and Fontagné, 'Deindustrialisation and the Fear of Relocations in the Industry'.

22　Ibid.

23　Ibid.

24　See R.C. Feenstra and G.H. Hanson, 'Global Production Sharing and Rising Inequality: A Survey of Trade and Wages', in K. Choi and J. Harrigan (eds), *Handbook of International Trade* (Oxford: Blackwell, 2003).

25　See L. Fontagné, M. Freudenberg and D. Ünal-Kezenci, 'Statistical Analysis of EC Trade in Intermediate Products', *Eurostat* Série 6D (March 1996), and D. Hummels, J. Ishii and K.M. Yi, 'The Nature and Growth of Vertical Specialization in World Trade', *Journal of International Economics* 54:1 (2004), pp. 75–96.

26 B.Y. Aw and M.J. Roberts, 'The Role of Imports from the Newly Industrializing Countries in US Production', *Review of Economics and Statistics* 67:1 (MIT Press, 1985), pp. 108–17.

27 R.N. Batra and F.R. Casas, 'Intermediate Products and the Pure Theory of International Trade: A Neo-Heckscher–Ohlin Framework', *American Economic Review* 63:3 (1973), pp. 297–311.

28 K.K. Sanyal, 'Vertical Specialization in a Ricardian Model with a Continuum of Stages of Production', *Economica* 50:197 (1983), pp. 71–8.

29 K.K. Sanyal and R.W. Jones, 'The Theory of Trade in Middle Products', *American Economic Review* 72:1 (1982), pp. 16–31.

30 A.K. Dixit and G.M. Grossman, 'Trade and Protection with Multistage Production', *Review of Economic Studies* 49:4 (1982), pp. 583–94.

31 R.C. Feenstra and G.H. Hanson, 'The Impact of Outsourcing and High-Technology Capital on Wages: Estimates for the U.S., 1979–1990', *Quarterly Journal of Economics* 114:3 (1999), pp. 907–40.

32 For the US see R.C. Feenstra and G.H. Hanson, 'The Impact of Outsourcing and High-Technology Capital on Wages: Estimates for the U.S., 1979–1990', *Quarterly Journal of Economics* 114:3 (1999), pp. 907–40. For the UK see R. Anderton and R.P. Brenton, 'Outsourcing and Low Skilled Workers in the UK', *Bulletin of Economic Research* 51 (1999), pp. 267–86; A. Hijzen, 'Fragmentation, Productivity and Relative Wages in the UK: A Mandated Wage Approach', GEP Research Paper, 03/17, University of Nottingham (2003); and A. Hijzen, H. Görg and R.C. Hine, 'International Fragmentation and Relative Wages in the UK', IZA Discussion Paper, 717 (2003). And for France see V. Strauss-Kahn, 'The Role of Globalisation in the Within-Industry Shift Away from Unskilled Workers in France', NBER Working Papers, 9716 (2003).

33 See D. Trefler, 'The Case for Missing Trade and Other Mysteries', *American Economic Review* 85: 5 (1995), pp. 1029–46.

34 Ibid.

35 P. Schott, 'One Size Fits All? Heckscher–Ohlin Specialization in Global Production', *American Economic Review* 93:3 (1999), pp. 686–708.

36 L. Fontagné, G. Gaulier and S. Zignago, 'North–South Competition in Quality', *Economic Policy* 23:53 (2008), pp. 51–92.

5

Globalisation and Demographic Imbalances

Germano Dottori

The US Declaration of Independence, which is more than two centuries old, states that men are created equal and share a common right to the pursuit of happiness.[1] A call for equality is also made in several other relevant declarations adopted by the United Nations and ratified by many individual states.[2] However, at the beginning of the twenty-first century we are still confronted with cleavages and levels of global inequality that obstruct the pursuit of happiness for a huge proportion of the world's population. A large part of contemporary mass migration may stem from these cleavages, yet such a phenomenon is a complex geopolitical reality, explained by a combination of demographics, economics and politics. This chapter will therefore attempt a multidimensional and multifaceted analysis, taking into account these different factors and seeking a more comprehensive approach to policy solutions.

The supremacy of the demographic factor

While many polemicists around the planet tend to blame globalisation for mass migration – and often a lack of social justice and global equality at large – the role of demography deserves more serious consideration if we are to fully understand the roots of this phenomenon.[3] This focus may seem a rather disturbing assumption to some, given that demographic trends are largely unamenable to political will, be it short-term or long-term, international or national, and instead depend more heavily on a wide range of local social and economic factors, cultural attitudes, and inherited collective behaviours. Nonetheless, however troubling it may be to the political realm, a demography-based explanation of today's large, international migration flows fits the set of available data better than any of the alternatives.

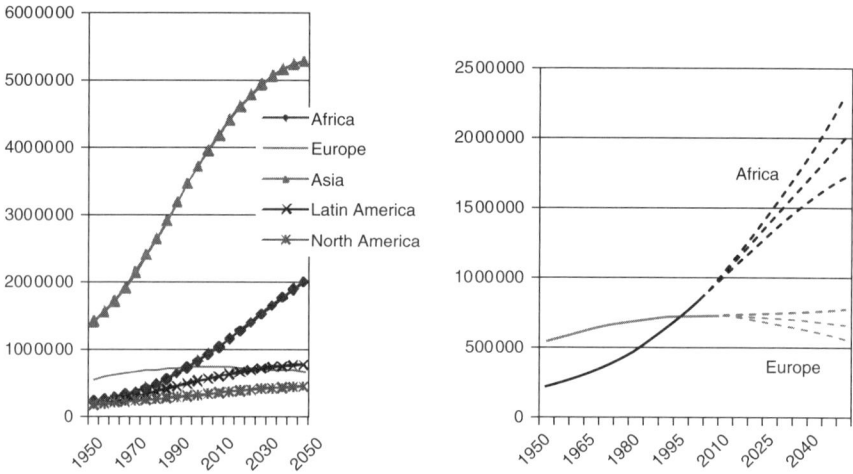

Graph 1   Demographic Trends: Major Areas Populations 1950–2050

Source: UN (2006) as quoted by the Italy Ministry of Foreign Affairs, 'Rapporto 2020' UN baseline scenario forecasts.

Most simply, migration is best understood by the fact that fast-growing populations export manpower. People in such circumstances will often seek better job opportunities elsewhere, experiencing a deficit of opportunities in their own countries thanks to the surplus population. In some instances, it is even possible that, faced with rapidly expanding populations, some states will encourage emigration in the hope of improving their citizens' overall standards of living. For example, in the first half of the last century, two international conferences on migration were convened in Rome by the then Kingdom of Italy, with the express aim of better asserting the right for Italian citizens to move abroad.[4] State support for emigration has in fact always been such a relevant political issue in Italy that a committee for 'Foreign Affairs and Emigration' still exists in the Italian senate.[5] A similar attitude can be seen today in many African countries, whose governments openly oppose any EU policy suspected of seeking to prevent immigration.

The opposite is also true: most states experiencing demographic decline, stagnation, or ageing populations, are inclined to import manpower. It was unsurprising, for example, that many European states recruited labour from around the world to fill shortages left by the Second World War. The Federal Republic of Germany achieved its post-war economic miracle largely thanks to millions of *Gastarbeiter* ('guest workers'), who were mainly recruited from Turkey. Even the German Democratic Republic, Federal Germany's 'twin' communist state, managed – and needed – to fuel development by attracting large

Table 1. **Demographic Distribution According to Age and Median Age in Selected Countries**				
	Median Age (y.o.)	**0–14 y.o. (%)**	**15–64 y.o. (%)**	**More than 65 y.o. (%)**
Japan	42.64	14.3%	66.2%	19.5%
Germany	42.16	14.4%	66.7%	18.9%
Italy	41.77	13.9%	66.7%	19.4%
Russian Federation	38.15	14.6%	71.3%	14.2%
USA	36.27	20.6%	67%	12.4%
People's Rep. China	32.26	21.4%	71%	7.6%
Turkey	27.7	26%	67.3%	6.7%
India	24.66	31.2%	63.9%	4,9%
Iran	24.23	27.1%	68%	4.9%
Nigeria	18.63	42.3%	54.6%	3.1%

Source: CIA World Factbook (2006).

numbers of foreign workers, despite the tight Soviet-imposed regulations on cross-border mobility.[6] In addition, similar policies to recruit much-needed foreign labour were adopted by France, Belgium and Britain.

Today, we are still living in times of serious demographic imbalances, driven by a number of rapid changes that have occurred in recent decades. Europe and post-Soviet Asia plunged into structural demographic decline after the 'baby-boom' years of the 1950s and 1960s, while Africa and Southern Asia have experienced unprecedented population growth. Something similar also happened in the western hemisphere, giving rise to a clear global demographic fault line that ranges from Casablanca to Vladivostok, and is mirrored across the Atlantic at the Rio Grande. North of that geographical border, the demographic landscape is characterised by stagnant or declining populations, while to the south the pressure of demographic growth is powerful.

Furthermore, as can be seen from table 1 above, the structure of the prevailing demographic pyramid in the global 'north' is different from that in the global 'south'. The median age in Japan, Germany and Italy, for instance, is well over forty years, while in India and Iran the average age is barely twenty-four, and in Nigeria it is even under nineteen. The older generation represents a mere 3 per cent of the Nigerian population, but constitutes nearly one fifth in Japan, Italy and Germany.

Economic, social and political consequences of demographic imbalances

These demographic realities produce far-reaching economic, social and political consequences both in the OECD area and outside. As Henry Kissinger remarked several years ago, in almost all European countries birth-rates are no longer able to sustain the

> present population, which is already inadequate to meet the needs for labour in a globalised economy. With improvements in medicine, the percentage of those having to be supported by a shrinking labour force will rise dramatically; the overall population of most European States will drop precipitously – and this in the face of mounting demographic pressure from the poor countries at the fringes of Europe to the East and the South.[7]

First of all, especially in the EU, demographic stagnation is putting pressure on the costly welfare systems established in western Europe after the Second World War. An ageing population means greater health expenditures and increasing percentages of GDP devoted to those in retirement. This, by consequence, places a relatively heavier burden on younger, working generations. In Italy, for example, the ratio between working and retired people is changing dramatically, heading rapidly towards the critical 2:1 threshold. Faced with such a possibility, the European Commission has resorted to closely monitoring Italy's social policies, beseeching Rome to implement sustainable structural reforms to its welfare system. Demographic pressures on the welfare state not only represent one of the most serious challenges currently facing many European governments, but also mean that one of the strongest arguments in favour of permissive immigration policies is made by the fact that immigrant labour can help to ease such burdens.

In political terms, ageing populations may also potentially lead to a decreased propensity to invest in the future of younger generations, in fixed assets, in social infrastructures and, indeed, in the pursuit of power politics. It is plausible that when ruling classes hail predominantly from older generations, they will be less inclined to actively build up and project their forces of power and less inclined to seek the exportation of their own ideologies and cultural norms to the rest of the world. Political conservatism and concern for domestic stability will tend to prevail over innovation and the pursuit of idealistic political programmes – notably those aiming to foster a certain degree of social justice in the international arena. As a result, countries experiencing demographic ageing are likely to also experience a net loss of economic competitiveness and a decline of political power over time. However, among the more positive effects of predominantly older

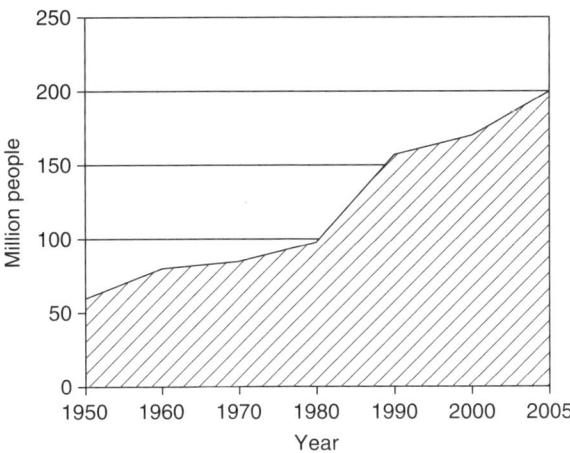

Graph 2   Million people living abroad

Source: William A.V. Clark (2007).

populations will be greater stability and predictability within the international arena.

The opposite of course applies to countries with comparatively younger populations. These reveal a greater propensity to invest in the future and are less risk-averse. By the same token, younger populations may be more ready to accept sacrifices in the name of national and political ideals – even possibly the ultimate sacrifices demanded by war – and by consequence may be more inclined to support aggressive 'revisionist' foreign policies.

Such socio-political implications can be noted in the different political environments that prevail in the so-called global 'north' and 'south'. While north of the Casablanca–Vladivostok fault line we find the relatively stable advance of globalisation, high per capita incomes and ageing populations, the regions south of this symbolic border are often characterised by instability, war, poverty, low personal incomes and young populations. Richard Cincotta, Robert Engelman and Daniele Anastasion even coined the phrase 'security demographic' in order to portray these political and military effects of underlying demographic imbalances. According to them, 'security demographic' should be defined as 'a distinctive range of population structures and dynamics that make civil conflict less likely'.[8] Given the current global climate, which sustains such geopolitical inequalities, it is understandable that demographic and political pressures have prompted the large flow of emigrants from the 'south' to the more affluent and stable societies of the 'north'.

Furthermore, such migration patterns are entirely consistent with the demographic arguments outlined above: abundant manpower

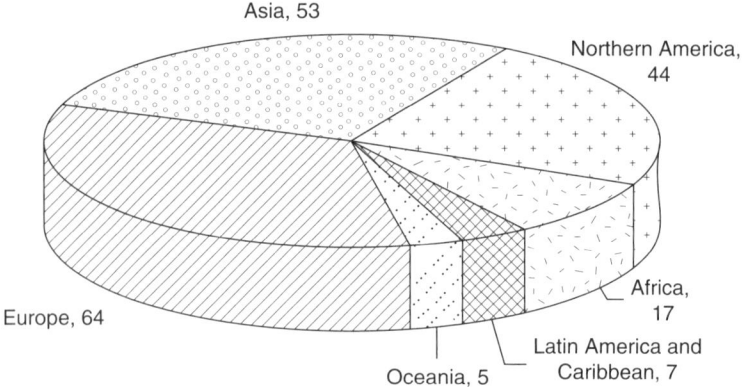

Graph 3   Geographical distribution of international migrants. Millions of settlers according to their final settlement

Source: United Nations Economic and Social Affairs (2005).

goes where it is scarce. Whilst conflict and economic hardship may be factors in the scale and direction of current migration flows, no such sustained migration flows could exist without a structural excess of labour on the source side and a comparative lack on the destination side. As a matter of fact, according to William Clark, of an estimated 200 million people settled in a country other than that of their birth, approximately 30 to 40 million are Chinese. India, he remarks, contributes at least 20 million to the total number of international migrants, and the Philippines account for a further 7.7 million.[9] It is illustrative, therefore, that both the People's Republic of China and the Indian Union are currently the most populated states of the planet. As far as the Philippines are concerned, their position among the leading exporters of manpower is apparently explained by the active role played by the Catholic Church in organising Filipino emigrants, which, as we have seen, is a role very familiar from past experiences in Italy.[10] Europe, by contrast, is not only experiencing demographic decline, but also, according to UN estimates, is the world's largest recipient of foreign settlers, hosting around 65 million migrants. Demographics clearly matter when it comes to migratory flows, and they matter more than economics.

The role of economics and politics in fuelling mass migration

None of this is to deny the relevance of the powerful forces of the international economy. Economics certainly matter, not only because high per capita incomes attract those from poorer countries, but also because there is currently an approximately ten point income gap – perhaps even higher – between people in the northern hemisphere and those in the south. However, the view this chapter supports is that economic inequalities alone cannot be the primary cause of large, long-term flows of migrants, and that such flows would not be sustained without underlying demographic imbalances.

Economic inequalities can certainly fuel short-term influxes from poorer to richer countries, or some forms of limited 'brain drain', involving only rather tiny numbers of high-skill migrants. For example, since the fall of the Berlin Wall, and to a certain extent even before, Britain, Germany, France, Austria, Spain and Italy have experienced a significant wave of immigration from a number of the former communist countries. This particular phenomenon cannot have been explained purely by demographics. States like the Baltic Republics, Poland, Romania, Ukraine and most of the Balkan states (excepting Albania), were all source countries for large flows of (often illegal) immigrants to western Europe in the 1990s.

However, all these countries have in fact been suffering the same demographic trends that have affected Germany, Spain or Italy. They all have similarly ageing populations and, as far as Ukraine is concerned, may even show sharply declining populations. [11] According to the favoured demographic explanation put forward by this chapter, such population patterns should have made them more eligible to be recipients than generators of substantial migratory flows.[12] Therefore, in context-specific circumstances such as this, where regional fluxes of migrants occur between states with relatively similar demographic features, economic, or even political, factors clearly provide a more suitable explanation.

Yet, even wide economic gaps cannot sustain long-term steady flows of migrants without simultaneously strong demographic pressures. This is because shortages of manpower will eventually emerge in the source countries, making emigration a less attractive choice. In fact, economic logic would imply that as labour shortages in the source states increase, wages will be driven upwards, thereby actually weakening or even erasing any incentive to emigrate. Conversely, excesses of manpower in the destination countries will make the task of finding a job more difficult, exerting a negative pressure on wages and indeed ultimately serving to reduce the overall economic gap.

There is already some evidence in the European Union that such a dynamic is at play: fluxes of migrants from eastern European states of the former Soviet bloc to the old 'fifteen' are beginning to slow. This migratory pattern is particularly visible in Italy, where although immigration to the Peninsula can still be described as twofold, the relative numbers coming from different sending regions are changing.

Previously large, the numbers of migrants from eastern Europe are now falling – with some people from Poland and Romania even returning home or choosing alternative destinations – giving way instead to a bulk of immigrants arriving from the African continent and the Asian subcontinent.[13] These new arrivals are certainly more motivated by the inabilities of their home countries to generate enough jobs for ever-increasing populations, rather than by calculated evaluations of pure economic opportunity.

It should also be recognised that politics itself can play a significant, if subordinate, role in provoking international migration. According to some UN reports, about one fifth of the increase observed in the number of international migrants during the 1990s was the result of the break-up of the Soviet Union, Czechoslovakia and, of course, the Yugoslavian Federation. These political ruptures affected global estimates of migratory flows, transforming internal into international migrants, and explaining the discontinuity observed in the data available after 1991. The record numbers of refugees and displaced people emerging from these post-Soviet crises, however, have not continued to bolster numbers of international migrants. According to more recent UN figures, refugees accounted for just 7 per cent of the total world stock of migrants in the year 2005, thus also disputing claims that political conflicts are the primary cause of recent large-scale migration flows.[14]

Such data thereby strengthens the assumption that demographic imbalances are the key determinants of migration patterns. Without the backing of simultaneous demographic pressures pushing and pulling the movement of people, neither huge economic inequalities nor short-lived political upheavals can sustain steady migratory fluxes over extended periods of time. Sooner or later, these sources will dry up.

Governing migration: the difficulties of both restrictive and permissive approaches

First of all, and in light of the argument outlined above, it must be recognised that even the most restrictive immigration rules adopted in recent years by some western countries – in particular the US, France and Italy – have failed to subordinate the migratory pressures created by such global demographic realities. In fact, as the recent large-scale demonstrations in favour of regularisation and citizenship rights, held by illegal immigrants in the US and elsewhere, have shown, restrictive policies more often serve to force migrants to enter through irregular channels and to turn to the black economy, leaving such people to an existence on the fringes of society. It is apparent, and understandable,

Table 2. Registered Foreigners in Italy, 31 December 2002–31 December 2006					
	2002	**2003**	**2004**	**2005**	**2006**
Registered Foreigners	1,549,373	1,990,159	2,402,157	2,670,514	2,938,922
% out of Total Population	2.7	3.4	4.1	4.5	5

Source: ISTAT (2008).

that these communities eventually seek to regularise their status and gain access to rights, if not of citizenship, then at least of protection under the law.

Italy's own experience testifies to this reality: despite the draconian measures brought in under the so-called 'Bossi–Fini law', the total number of registered foreigners living in Italy doubled to nearly 3 million in the period from 2002 to 2006. Such large and rapid increases were in fact the result of a number of regularisation programmes similar to those carried out in the US following changes to the law in 1986. They are therefore evidence of the massive numbers of workers who had succeeded in living and working clandestinely in Italy despite the restrictive regulations. As table 2 shows, and in keeping with the steady ageing of Italy's native population, the presence of so many new arrivals had a profound effect on Italy's demographic landscape. The foreign-born population, which had previously constituted only 2.7 per cent of the overall population, rose to 5 per cent in just four years.

In the United States, too, even the most ambitious attempts made to stop or at least slow immigration from Mexico and Central America have expressly failed, as the growing percentages of Hispanics living in US today clearly show. According to an estimate made in March 2006 by the authoritative Pew Hispanic Center, and shared by the US General Accounting Office, the so-called 'undocumented' population living in the States ranges from 11.5 to 12 million individuals, mostly hailing from Mexico and Central America.[15] Hispanics also account for not less than 1.3 million of the 2.8 million increase in the American population between mid 2004 and mid 2005. Neither physical fences built on the borders nor tighter regulations introduced at the state level have so far been able to turn these trends around, making immigration one of the most sensitive issues in American politics.

Immigration is therefore undoubtedly a complex challenge for any government. It is, however, all the more so for progressive ones. This is because, as immigrant numbers inevitably grow, social tensions can often become more acute, and accommodating various competing needs can present greater challenges to the goal of social justice. Newly arrived immigrants, for instance, commonly find themselves facing extremely poor standards of living, a reality which already raises questions about the extent of social justice achieved even in the most advanced and presumed 'civilised' nations of the world. Furthermore, contrasts in living standards are even greater with regard to irregular migrants, who, very often the victims of unscrupulous people-traffickers, can find themselves hostage to transnational or local criminal gangs. Such realities may be particularly prevalent in southern Mediterranean countries such as Italy or Spain, where large-scale immigration is a fairly recent, and therefore often uncontrolled, phenomenon. They are, however, also present in states with long histories of inward migration and more sophisticated immigration systems, such as Britain and France.

For these reasons, there are strong arguments to be made in favour of more permissive immigration regulations. More restrictive regimes may not only be more ineffective, but actively provoke greater recourse to irregular migration. This in turn gives rise to large communities existing on the margins of western societies, and thus both frustrates attempts to ensure social justice in such countries, and exacerbates the tensions surrounding immigration. More permissive regimes, it is argued, would help to relieve these tensions by allowing for dramatic improvements in the social and economic conditions of foreign settlers.

However, before embarking on an uncritical call for open borders, there are also potential drawbacks to such an approach that must be considered. Despite the relevant, and evident, problems created by over-restrictive policies, there are some aspects of conservative arguments that deserve closer examination. It is claimed that in the light of widespread concerns among western populations, a large and uncontrolled influx of immigrants may not only provoke identity-fuelled and xenophobic reactions, but also cause social conflicts among different classes of have-nots competing for the benefits of the welfare state. Indeed, human labour is unlike other capitalist commodities that can be traded and exchanged liberally across the global economy. Migrants bring, together with their intellectual and physical assets, their own cultures, habits and expectations. They have needs, at both the economic and the socio-cultural levels, which demand recognition from their host countries.

Accommodating the needs of newcomers and balancing them with the demands and concerns of 'native' populations is not an easy feat. However, whilst there are many who accuse European governments of failing to fully appreciate the far-reaching social and political ramifications of rapid, large-scale immigration, legal and illegal migration has already had a profound effect on the ethnic, cultural and also political landscape of several European states. In fact, Italy provides a very good case study of the rapid social and demographic transformations that recent experiences of immigration have created, and of the difficulties that have been posed.

The Peninsula, a relatively mono-racial and mono-cultural society since the age of the Roman Empire, has suddenly found itself among the most ethnically diverse countries in Europe. As we have seen, the impact of immigration on Italy's demographic make-up has been intensified by the natural decline of the 'native' Italian population. In recent years, the percentage of foreign-born inhabitants has grown to exceed 7 per cent in some regions. More than 14 per cent of newborn babies in northern Italy are not ethnically Italian, and more than 20 per cent of newborn babies in the country at large have at least one foreign-born parent.

Furthermore, the unexpectedness of this dramatic change can be better understood if we remember that Italy's very recent history was one of mass *emigration*. As the poet Giovanni Pascoli described, Italy was the 'great proletarian' (*la Grande Proletaria*), with more than 27 million Italians emigrating to the US and South America, or towards the richest states of continental Europe such as Germany, France and Belgium. Italy's first experience of inward migration came in the 1980s, when relatively small numbers of asylum seekers arrived from Poland following the 1981 coup in Warsaw. Whilst these newcomers were accepted and assimilated fairly easily, thanks in no small part to their common Catholic religion and Italians' identification with their plight, today's phenomenon is a far more complex challenge for Italian society and its political system as a whole.

It is proving much more difficult for Italy to adapt what is a largely traditional society to the cultural habits and norms of people coming from very different parts of the world. For example, concerns and questions have arisen about how to deal legally and morally with Islamic traditions of polygamy, and even the unacceptable practice of 'infibulation' found among groups hailing from certain parts of Africa. Such tensions were exemplified by a case in Tuscany a few years ago when, in an attempt to reduce the risks of this operation being carried out illegally, a proposal was made to introduce surgically assisted 'infibulation' performed under controlled environments in state hospitals. The massive public outcry that followed reveals the immense difficulties progressive governments face when trying to balance minority group rights, equality rights and the individual human rights that have come to be accepted in our societies.

Such polemics are not unique to Italy. Across Europe, and particularly since the events of 9/11, certain voices have been actively propagating divisive fears about the perceived threat posed by Europe's large – and relatively recent – Muslim population and the spread of radical Islamism. In addition, riots, demonstrations and hostilities in France,

Denmark and the UK, have brought to the fore and heightened the possible link between immigration, increasing ethnic diversity and growing political support for right-wing populism.

For example, the geographical distribution of support for the French Front National, a xenophobic party led by the inflammatory Jean-Marie Le Pen, is particularly concentrated where large communities of immigrant origin are found, such as the region of Alsace and the city of Marseille. In Italy, too, such trends are observable. In the region of Lombardy, the cities of Veneto, Brescia, Treviso and Vicenza all have relatively large foreign-born populations, over 8 per cent, and well over the national average. These cities also happen to be strongholds of the Northern League, a party that has capitalised greatly on anti-immigrant fears.

Such fears are not only focused on cultural difference and new encounters with previously unknown practices. They also revolve around more general concerns about crime, security and legality. In Italy, for instance, citizens have tended to equate immigration with rises in crime. This has been thanks to the large number of undocumented workers, and therefore the potential for them to be drawn into the black economy or be involved in other criminal activities. As a result, drug and human trafficking, as well as exploitation and prostitution, are now commonly perceived as crimes that immigrants are solely responsible for, despite evidence to the contrary and the long and well-known dominance of the Italian mafia in these realms.

There is limited room for progressive governments to manoeuvre, therefore, when faced with these pressures and with intense public opinion on the matter of immigration. In fact, the polarising nature of the immigration debate can be seen by the splits over the issue that have arisen even amongst the left in many European countries. In May 2007, the Italian daily, *La Repubblica*, ran a first-page piece by a self-declared leftist reader. In the article the author, Claudio Poverini, proclaimed:

> Why am I suddenly compared to Eichmann if I ask for the immediate expulsion of violent illegal immigrants? . . . I don't want to give the right the monopoly of legality and so I don't understand why we should give immigrants the right to a local vote after having been five years in our country, when no other state of Western Europe does the same.[16]

In line with the argumentation above, it is not prudent for progressive governments to pursue blindly permissive policies in the hope of counteracting these negative effects. As we have argued, extremely rapid, uncontrolled, or mismanaged inward migration can pose equally as many problems for liberal societies. Instead, a more moderate approach appears the most advisable, balancing the economic and demographic inevitability of migration with the concerns of both host societies and newly arrived communities.

Concluding remarks: options for the future

Indiscriminate restrictive policies have proven an ineffective means to check immigration flows, serving instead to bolster illegal channels of entry for desperate migrants all across the Mediterranean basin. For example, despite the European Union's refusal to be a 'safe haven' for immigrants,[17] and their numerous efforts to thwart illegal flows – including the establishment of a new international border enforcement unit, Frontex[18] – immigration continues, both legal and illegal, to be a reality in European societies. Equally, however, permissive, more 'integrationist' approaches, especially if adopted without careful planning, have the potential to impose heavy social burdens on societies already under stress.

This chapter therefore suggests that since demographic pressures will continue to sustain migration patterns from the 'south' to the 'north', common (international) policies, for example agreed at the EU level, could be more helpful and effective, sharing risks and burdens relating to the integration of immigrants among a large number of states. If EU member states were to co-operate on these policies at a regional level, they would also provide a more compelling and coherent front when seeking to better manage migration through means of institutional north–south co-operation. Even the recent proposal for a Mediterranean Union made by the French President Nicolas Sarkozy and endorsed by the European Council on 14 March 2008, however limited, deserves to be considered as one option to explore. Critically, Euro–African dialogue must also be developed and strengthened.

However, as this chapter has also argued, there is no room for illusion. Behind the mass migratory flows currently underway are strong demographic pressures that no policy can hope to effectively tackle in the short term, either at the nation-state level, or at the regional or global levels. Without doubt, Europe and the United States will not be able to close their gates to mass migration in the near future. No new Hadrian's Wall will work, however technologically advanced it may be. This is a matter of fact: an undeniable geopolitical reality, depending on both long-term demographic and short-term economic inequalities, and their political consequences, at least for the time being.

Yet political processes are not totally powerless. Instead we should accustom ourselves to the idea of adapting our societies to just such realities. Instead of trying to insulate ourselves from the phenomenon of migration, we should focus our policy approach on the long-term horizon, simultaneously attempting to mitigate, as far as possible, the most negative effects of mass migration. In this regard, even a modest reduction in the intensity of current migratory influxes could potentially help OECD and EU member states implement successful domestic social justice policies.

Progressives should also be aware that unless immigration proceeds in a controlled and steady manner, there are questions of social stability, welfare and domestic peace at stake. The incredible rate of recent immigration – both legal and illegal – has created a 0.5 per cent year-on-year increase in the population in some western European societies, putting immense strain on what have traditionally been mono-ethnic nations. While the mono-ethnic history of Europe may be largely absent from the consciousness of today's citizens, the current stability enjoyed in the continent was hard-won through centuries of bloody wars. More recently, the horror of the Holocaust and the tragedies of ethnic cleansing in the Balkans should serve to highlight the fragility of social cohesion, even when it appears an unquestionable feature of our affluent and peaceful societies.

Therefore, in order to ease the process of integration and mitigate the social tensions that can arise, the pace and speed of immigration must be taken into account. This is particularly true when the host economy is sluggish, or slow to generate many new job opportunities for newcomers, as is unfortunately the case in much of continental Europe today. It is the responsibility of policy-makers to ensure that mass migration is managed effectively so as to insure against any possible return to the dark days of ethnicity-, identity- and religion-driven conflicts.

Once again, the link between demography and development cannot be overstated, and is a point equally important for our own societies as it is for those nations seeking to join the ranks of the developed world. Whilst the so-called 'west' cannot sustain its own levels of economic growth with severely depleting populations, population explosions also pose threats to the fragile social, economic and political systems of the developing world. As Lester Thurow bluntly, but correctly, wrote more than a decade ago in his *The Future of Capitalism*, no country has ever achieved advanced economic success without having simultaneously managed to maintain a long and stable period of moderate demographic growth. Ultimately, per capita incomes are unable to significantly increase if a given population grows faster than real GDP.[19]

The 'One Child Policy' adopted by the People's Republic of China two decades ago was widely criticized, but it actually obviated an estimated 400 million net increase of its population, thus also restraining to some extent the number of Chinese migrants. Some promising developments are also occurring on the southern shores of the Mediterranean Sea, since significant slowdowns in the birth-rates of Morocco and Syria were recently recorded.

Indeed, controlled levels of population are necessary to avoid further serious environmental degradation and the forced migration of many millions more people as a result of climate change. Migration and demography are therefore intimately linked, and impact directly on the way in which globalisation will proceed for the developed and developing worlds alike. Such facts must not be ignored in immigration policy-making processes of the future.

What seems both feasible and commendable is a long-term strategy aimed at addressing underlying demographic and economic imbalances. Such a strategy should include measures both to bolster development in the so-called 'third world', and to revive demographic growth in the post-industrialised world. Foreign direct investment, trade and public development aid programmes must all be considered tools to generate more job opportunities abroad. Debilitating trade barriers should also be disbanded in order to avoid entrenching further long-term damage in developing economies.

In short, what is most desperately needed is a responsible globalisation: a system in which the more advanced economies of the world accept the competitive challenge presented by newly emerging economies, investing in these global markets and refusing to give scope to a backlash of protectionism. Managing migration needs to be brought into the equation – both 'at home' and in the international arena. Political leadership in this respect will, no doubt, be of paramount importance.

Notes

1 The Preamble of the US Declaration of Independence, approved on 4 July 1776, states: 'We hold these truths to be self-evident, that all men are created equal, that they are endowed by their Creator with certain unalienable Rights, that among these are Life, Liberty and the pursuit of Happiness.'
2 Article 4 of the Universal Declaration of Human Rights, adopted and proclaimed by the UN General Assembly on 10 December 1948, holds that 'All human beings are born free and equal in dignity and rights. They are endowed with reason and conscience and should act towards one another in a spirit of brotherhood.' Furthermore, article 23, 2, of the same Declaration dictates that 'everyone, without any discrimination, has the right to equal pay for equal work'. The French Declaration about Man and Citizen Rights, adopted by the French revolutionary National Assembly on 26 August 1789, similarly states that 'Men are born and remain free and equal in Rights. Social distinctions cannot be founded on anything but the general good (article 1). All political associations aim at preserving the natural and imprescriptible Rights of Man. These Rights are Liberty, Property, Security and Resistance to oppression (article 2).'
3 United Nations Organisation, Population Division, *Replacement Migrations: Is it a Solution to Declining and Ageing Population?* (New York, 2000).

4 The first symposium was held in 1921, with the participation of Albania, Austria, Bulgaria, Czechoslovakia, Hungary, Italy, Yugoslavia, Poland, Portugal, Romania and Spain. The convention founded a Permanent Secretariat of Emigration Countries. In 1924, the second International Conference received delegations from a larger number of states, fifty-nine, both exporting and importing manpower. But no agreement was reached regarding the most sensitive issue of cross-border workers' mobility. See P. Bevilacqua, A. De Clementi, and E. Franzina (eds), *Storia dell'emigrazione italiana* (Rome: Donzelli Editore, 2001–2), p. 448.

5 Furthermore, the more 'modern' Camera dei Deputati also maintains the comparable Foreign Affairs and International Trade Committee.

6 On 11 April 1980, the German Democratic Republic Government signed a treaty with the Socialist Republic of Vietnam stipulating the 'temporary employment and training of Vietnamese workers in companies of the German Democratic Republic'. See *German History in Documents and Images*, Volume 9, *Two Germanies, 1961–1989*: http://germanhistorydocs.ghi-dc.org/pdf/eng/Chapter4Doc9Intro.pdf. According to some estimates, no less than 7,000 Vietnamese workers settled in the GDR. Other immigrants were 'imported' from Poland, Mozambique, Angola and Cuba.

7 H. Kissinger, *Does America Need a Foreign Policy? Toward a Diplomacy for the Twenty-first Century* (New York, London, Toronto, Sydney, Singapore: Simon and Schuster, 2001), p. 53.

8 R. Cincotta, R. Engelman and D. Anastasion, *The Security Demographic: Population and Civil Conflict After the Cold War* (Washington, DC: Population Action International, 2003), p. 14. According to the authors, evidence collected from more than 180 countries, about half of which experienced civil conflict at some time from 1970 through 2000, show that the decline in the annual birth-rate of five births per thousand people corresponds to a decline of about 5 per cent in the likelihood of civil conflict during the following decade.

9 See W.A.V. Clark, 'Human Mobility in a Globalized World: Urban Development Trends and Policy Implications', in H.S. Geyer (ed.), *International Handbook of Urban Policy: Contentious Issues* (Cheltenham: Edward Elgar, 2007), quoted in L. Muscarà, 'Il mondo in diaspora' [World in Diaspora], *Limes* 4 (2007), pp. 63–74.

10 However, the Philippines also show a typical manpower exporter demographic profile. Their population is well above 90 million and its annual growth rate is 1.7%. The local median age is 22.7 years and the fertility rate is 3 children born/woman.

11 Ukraine lost some five million people in the fifteen years following the break-up of the Soviet Union and is experiencing an annual 0.6% decrease of its population. The local total fertility rate is 1.24 children born/woman and the median age is 39 years. Similar demographic profiles emerge in Romania and Poland.

12 It is not surprising that some of these countries are already importing manpower, in order to satisfy a steady demand for labour, which is particularly strong in their building industry: while still a source of migratory fluxes, Romania especially has become a destination for Chinese and Indian immigrants. See P. Sartori, 'Passano per i Balcani le vie della disperazione' [The Routes of Despair Cross the Balkans], *Limes* 4 (2007), p. 191.

13 African and Asian people, for instance, represent most of the illegal immigrants reaching the Mediterranean outpost of Lampedusa, in the Channel of Sicily, as well as the Sardinian shores, after a dangerous trip at sea. The majority of migrants arriving in Italy through Greece are also Asian.

14 United Nations Organisation, *Trends in Total Migrant Stock: the 2005 Revision* (New York, 2006).

15 See Pew Hispanic Center Factsheet, published on the www.pewhispanic.org website and www.gao.gov/new.items/d06775.pdf

16 Claudio Poverini, 'Aiuto, sono di sinistra ma sto diventando razzista', *La Repubblica*, 7 May 2007.

17 See C. Mercuri, 'Frattini: La polizia italiana pattuglierà il deserto libico' [Frattini: The Italian Police will Patrol the Libyan Desert], *Il Messaggero*, 12 March 2007.

18 See the EU website, according to which Frontex was created as a specialised and independent body tasked to co-ordinate the operational co-operation between member states in the field of border security. The activities of Frontex, which is based in Warsaw, are intelligence-driven. Frontex complements and provides particular added value to the national border management systems of the member states.

19 See L.C. Thurow, *The Future of Capitalism: How Today's Economic Forces Shape Tomorrow's World* (New York: William Morrow, 1996), Chapter V. According to Thurow, the critical threshold is a demographic increase of 1 per cent per year. Economic development should be attainable only by keeping population below that rate.

6

Globalisation and the New Social Realities in Europe

Roger Liddle

To what extent has globalisation shaped the social reality of today's Europe? Does globalisation constrain Europeans' potential to address social injustice? Drawing on work undertaken for the European Commission's 'social stocktake' in 2006–8, this chapter summarises the evidence on current social trends in Europe. It then considers how far globalisation is a factor in shaping them. The analysis concludes that much social change is internally driven – a product of occupational shifts, demographics and changing values. However, 'globalisation' accentuates the trend by which greater opportunities for many are matched by an increased risk of polarisation.

Globalisation is often treated as an issue concerning the consequences of global market integration and trade for skills and inequalities, in particular how the 'globalisation' of labour impacts on the position of the low-skilled and those with skills that are potentially 'outsourceable' in developed countries. These questions are of central importance, but there are others.

Migration has grown as globalisation has deepened. In the last five years the EU has absorbed more legal migrants than the United States. But migration encounters popular resistance. Citizens still tend to think of migration as something that the nation-state has powers to control, powers that it should more firmly exercise. Politicians respond in kind, even though in reality their capacity to act is limited. The inevitability of migration into the EU, at least to an extent – and indeed its necessity, given the underlying demographic realities – is rarely argued. In addition the diversity which migration brings, for all the objective benefits to migrants and host countries alike, makes a solidaristic response to new social risks more problematic.

Other facets of globalisation are climate change and rising commodity prices – for energy and food in particular. We are still at the early stages of judging the potential impact of these phenomena on European societies. On climate change there is widespread genuine public concern, but this is not yet an election-deciding issue, and to date the much-talked-of policies to promote mitigation have hardly begun to bite. As for commodity prices, their rise (in 2008) is a relatively new shock: earlier globalisation was characterised by falling prices for consumer goods such as clothing, shoes and electronic equipment. Rapid increases in food and oil prices are creating bewilderment and uncertainty. No one is absolutely sure whether the processes under-way represent cyclical movements, speculative bubbles or long-term structural shifts. Given Asia's rising demands for natural resources, a significant element must be structural and long term. The distributive implications for Europe are at present ill thought through.

There is also an unresolved debate about how far globalisation can be held responsible for what many see as a disturbing ongoing transfor-mation towards a harsher, less consensual and far more inegalitarian capitalism – and whether Europe is powerless in face of this profound change. On all these issues, the precise balance sheet is unclear. What we do know from economic and social history, however, is that struc-tural shifts result in large-scale winners and losers. If the 'winners' from globalisation want to go on winning (and there is plenty of evi-dence that the potential winners in our societies are much broader than a tiny elite), public policy needs to focus much more intently on improving the life chances of the potential 'losers' on grounds of both social equity and prudent pragmatism.

Globalisation as the shaping factor of political discourse

In the mid 1990s, globalisation was a concept coming into fashion among sociologists; now it is part of popular vocabulary. Globalisation is widely seen as the most powerful shaping factor of modern times. It clearly is changing the contours of politics. As the British Prime Minister Gordon Brown said in his first Lord Mayor's Banquet Speech,[1] the differences between 'over here' and 'over there' are eroding fast. Questions of migration, climate change and security are now at the centre of our domestic politics. And the economic consequences of globalisation are clearly dramatic, not least the rise of China and India. This ongoing shift in global economic power is perceived as driving ever-faster economic change in our societies, accentuating the disappearance of 'traditional working-class jobs' in mass manu-facturing industries, and increasing polarisation between Europeans with skills appropriate to the modern world and those without them. Globalisation is seen to offer opportunity for some, perhaps a major-ity, yet increased insecurity for others and greater inequality all round.

In the United States debate raged around these questions during the 2008 presidential campaign. If the distribution of income in the US had remained as it was in 1979, then 80 per cent of American families would today on average be around $7,000 a year better off.[2] Of the productivity gains achieved in the US in the past generation, 50 per cent have been appropriated by the top 10 per cent of wage earners. The rise in US inequality is equivalent to 1 per cent of US GDP being transferred to the top income groups every three years.[3] This profound shift to a more unequal society has taken place over three decades since the 'Great Compression' of the post-Second World War Keynesian 'golden age' was followed in the 1980s by the 'Great Widening', with those on low incomes falling behind. In the past decade America has witnessed a 'Great Polarizing' as the top leaves the middle far behind.[4]

Does US experience mean that in the global age Europeans are condemned to live in a steadily more unequal society? Will this be another case of delayed transatlantic catch-up with devastating consequences for the 'European Social Model'? If the causes of rising inequality in the US can mainly be attributed to globalisation, then truly Europeans have something to fear, because in terms of trade and the relative openness of the economy the European Union is more exposed to new sources of competition than the United States.

Fears certainly exist. Polling of public attitudes in the EU reveals a disturbing contrast between contentment in the present and widespread unease about the future. A recent Eurobarometer poll[5] suggested that 64 per cent of the European public believe life will not be as good for their children as it has been for them, with only 17 per cent thinking it will be better. This goes alongside widespread feelings that welfare states and pensions will not prove sustainable. Life satisfaction in the present is highest in Europe's most developed welfare states – the Nordic and Benelux countries. Europe's optimists are concentrated in countries like the Baltic States, Finland, Greece, Ireland, Poland, Portugal and Spain that have either succeeded in 'catch-up' or are making rapid progress towards it. By contrast, Britain, France and Germany all share above-average social pessimism about the future, despite the fact that political stances towards globalisation varied between obsessive defamation (France) and over-enthusiastic embrace (UK).

Indeed, Europe sits uneasily between two contrasting attitudes. On the one hand, placing excessive blame on globalisation for the ills of our societies runs the risk of exaggerating its causal impact, fuelling protectionism and obscuring the need for alternative policies that might correct present social ills. On the other, refusing to recognise adequately the problem of the 'losers' from globalisation in our societies carries the opposite risk of ignoring social trends that could in time undermine a progressive consensus behind openness.

The importance of internally driven change

For all Europe's diversity, analysis reveals many common social challenges: not least the challenge of recognising how fundamentally our societies have changed in the last generation. The social models of the past were built on the solidaristic foundations of a mass manufacturing industrial society and a relatively homogeneous, 'male breadwinner' welfare state. The social challenges of our societies today are quite different. We now live in a world of a knowledge and service economy that is becoming rapidly post-industrial (two-thirds of jobs are in services), with change accelerated by European economic integration, but in origin the result of technological developments and the new demands of consumers whose preferences change with increasing affluence. In this knowledge and service economy of multi-diversity, citizens define themselves more as consumers than producers, and values are becoming more individualist and post-materialist.

Family life has changed out of recognition in a generation, partly as a result of falling birth-rates, greater gender equality and the weakening bonds of the extended family. As a result, welfare states with an ageing population have problems of sustainability, maintaining equity between the generations, and difficulties in adjusting to new social risks. Low birth-rates at present levels threaten the sustainability of our societies. Some member states face a real prospect of sharp population shrinkage. There are big issues of generational equity between young and old. Childcare and work–life balance issues around support for what is now the norm of the 'dual-earner' family are crucial.

At the same time, Europe needs more migrants, but most member states have great difficulty in integrating them successfully, in both their school systems and labour markets. Ethnic minorities, with some notable exceptions, perform badly in schools, even in the second generation, and the most comprehensive analysis of ethnic minority experience concludes that in the job market in many countries they face barriers of discrimination in accessing better paid, more secure jobs.[6] Ethnic diversity in Europe is not a recent product of globalisation: initially it resulted from strong demand for unskilled labour during Europe's post-war recovery, which was met by migration from former Empire colonies and guest-worker programmes. Unlike in countries such as Canada, this has left a legacy of embedded generational disadvantage which has yet to be overcome.

There are other new risks of social polarisation. New social risks have emerged with a widespread rise in depression, mental illness, obesity and alcohol misuse. The incidence of child poverty appears to be rising in many member states. Social mobility may well be in decline – as measured for instance by the percentage gap between the proportion of young people going to university from homes where their parents went to university and from homes where their parents did not. Inequality in pre-tax incomes is rising – with pay at the top racing ahead in a number of member states and the 90/10 gap widening in most. Many younger people, either out of work or in insecure or temporary jobs, are at the sharp end of disadvantage. The share of wages in national income has fallen particularly fast in continental Europe, less so in the UK and US. However, inequalities – after tax and social benefits are taken into account – have not risen as fast in many member states as they have for example in the US in the last quarter-century. This suggests that national political choices can still make significant differences to distributional outcomes, even in the global age.

Increased insecurities are in part to do with economics, but their drivers are more complex. Later well-being in life owes a lot to the relative advantages of the home into which one is born; but it then depends on succeeding at school and college, finding the right life partner, successfully combining two jobs with family, the luck of a stable relationship, how well one's children do at school and keeping them out of trouble with drugs or the police, accessing good-quality public services, caring for aged parents, living in communities that are far more fluid than were those of one's parents or grandparents, and coping well with the multiple stresses of modern life.

Life is complex in the modern world. Individuals can reach for the stars but the costs of personal failure are more keenly felt. Most people think everybody has a chance to succeed, even if objectively the chances are pretty weighted one way or the other by birth and circumstance. When people feel disadvantage it is as likely to be directed at scapegoats such as the unfair access to public services that most people think migrants enjoy. The unfairnesses that people perceive relate not so much to the old structures of class but to the way 'they' – ill-defined groups perceived to be in authority – behave. Governments are expected to sort things out, but in their attempts to address popular unease politicians are bad at explaining what they can and can't do, which reinforces mistrust of politics itself, and not least of politics at its most remote from the citizen, as practised at the level of the European Union.

Existing welfare states are not on the whole well attuned to new social risks that lessen access to life chances. Old 'social models' that were designed for the age of male-breadwinner households in a mass manufacturing society have not fully adjusted to present social realities. Without positive action to create fresh opportunities, the weak and disadvantaged are at risk of falling through the extensive gaps in existing social provision. Pessimism, however, should not be overdone. There are many grounds for optimism:

- Life satisfaction and happiness is higher in Europe than in any other part of the world.
- Life expectancy has increased and could increase a lot further, as could the possibilities of leading healthier as well as longer lives if citizens take more responsibility for their own good health.
- The jobs people do in the knowledge economy have more potential to be more fulfilling.
- Educational opportunity is expanding.
- Women are more independent and in control of their own lives.
- Diversity has the potential to be a great source of creative strength.
- Successfully managed migration can help meet Europe's economic and social needs.

Yet there are clearly serious risks of new forms of polarisation in our societies just as many thought the old social divisions had been overcome. The big success of the European welfare state has been in the reduction of poverty in old age. Although one in six older people, mainly elderly women, still live in poverty, and huge challenges of social care are emerging for an ageing population, Europe has made great strides in overcoming the problem of pensioner poverty that so afflicted the post-war generation. For the majority, pensions are adequate; it is the burden of financing them that is the greater problem and that in 'pay-as-you-go' systems inevitably falls on the younger generation. On the other hand, it is striking how many of the most pressing social problems in the Union at present concern younger people:

- A disproportionately high youth unemployment.
- One in six 16 year olds still leaving school with few skills.
- The prevalence of job insecurity and short-term employment contracts among younger people.
- Rising wage inequalities that primarily affect the young.
- Declining social mobility as the opportunity gap widens between families (including a new generation of active fathers) who are able to invest huge amounts of time and money in their children's future and those from disadvantaged backgrounds, often combining emotional as well as economic deprivation.
- Risks of dropping out due to drug and alcohol abuse, mental health problems, and involvement in crime.
- The particular problems of poor educational performance and failed labour-market integration among many ethnic minority groups, including second and third generations.
- Increasing pressure on young people in setting up households of their own and postponing the birth-rate of the first child as a result

of rising housing costs and inadequate social support for the 'dual-income' couple.

The social consequences of occupational and gender shifts

The most striking features of the modern labour market in Europe are rising demand for skills, the growth of low-skilled service jobs in both the public and private sectors, and the rapid erosion of 'good working-class jobs' principally for men. The skills that the modern labour market demands are not necessarily 'traditional skills'. A quarter of jobs are now thought to demand IT skills in some shape or form. Also 'personal' skills are often as important as technical competences in the growing number of service jobs that require direct contact with the client or customer. This has encouraged the fashion for education and training to focus on generic as opposed to more specifically vocational skills. While the widespread demand for the 'Polish plumber', in the labour migration that took place in the immediate aftermath of the EU's 2004 enlargement, demonstrated the continued importance of traditional skills in our economies, the new 'softer' skills in great demand are more suited to the articulate, particularly women, and less to working-class men.

The factors driving this occupational reshaping of the labour market have little to do with globalisation. The demand for skill is primarily driven by technology; the demand for services by changing consumer preferences as our societies get richer and more affluent consumers steadily climb up Maslow's hierarchy of needs. In the early phases of post-Second World War affluence, rising prosperity manifested itself in strong demand for cars, television sets, washing machines and other manufactured goods. But as productivity in manufacturing has risen, primarily due to technological advance – consistently faster than in the economy as a whole – the numbers employed in producing them have tended to fall as have their prices to the consumer. At the same time, with growing affluence consumer preferences have shifted to services such as meals out, sport, recreation and tourism. Among the faster-growing occupations in our societies today are relationship counsellors and gym instructors – service responses to the stresses of modern living.

On balance these occupational shifts should be positive for well-being. As Europe becomes more of a knowledge economy, and as the workforce becomes more highly educated and skilled, for the majority jobs should become more satisfying, more autonomous and less routine, with more focus on teamwork and less on hierarchy. This should result in greater intrinsic as well as instrumental satisfaction from work. Whether or not their job is intrinsically satisfying, most people are happy with it, even when they are short of money. Eighty-four per cent declare themselves very satisfied or fairly satisfied with their working conditions. At the same time safety at work has been continuously improving, a feature of the decline of heavy manual and industrial work. Between 1994 and 2004 the incidence rate of fatal work-related accidents fell by 38 per cent and that of accidents leading to more than three days' absence from work by 29 per cent. And Europeans enjoy more leisure time. Europeans famously work shorter hours than Americans. Annual hours worked per employee were an average of 1,552 in 2004, by contrast with the US figure of 1,817: six weeks a year less on the basis of a 36-hour week. In 1960 the position was reversed with Europeans working 2,082 hours per year and Americans 2,033.[7] There is a whole academic literature on whether this represents a preference for leisure or the malfunctioning of European labour markets. Recent years have seen some lengthening of hours as a result of competitive pressures, particularly in German manufacturing. Nevertheless the overall picture and the huge differences in working hours that persist between Europe and America are hardly suggestive of globalisation forcing people to work harder and longer.

However, labour markets may be generating new stresses and new risks of polarisation despite shorter hours, better safety and the decline of manual work. Structural economic change is giving rise to the need for a more competent labour force with higher skills; it may be forcing changes in work organisation, content and pace as well as requiring continuous restructuring of firms. Twenty-eight per cent of the European workforce feel their health is at risk because of work or declare that they are suffering from non-accidental health problems caused by work or made worse by their current or past employment.[8] Work intensity may be rising,[9] with more complaints of backache and muscular pain as well as stress. As a result, high rates of sickness absence are a problem in many member states. This may in part reflect increased competitive pressures, which may owe something to globalisation – but the phenomena apply across the board in public and private sectors, in those sheltered from foreign competition and those not.

One likely explanation of the universality of rising stress is that pressures of work–life balance are growing in Europe. The gender employment gap continues to narrow fast. This has been one of the strongest sources of recent employment growth particularly in southern Europe and Germany. This fundamentally represents value shifts in our societies, not the economic pressures of globalisation. The modern family follows the 'dual-earner' model. Yet in the UK, for instance, much of the debate about the modern family has been sidetracked into a discussion about the status and benefits of marriage, when in fact the debate should be focusing on the inadequacies of support for the 'dual-earner couple' regardless of their marital status. Levels of support for the 'dual-earner couple' vary enormously across Europe in terms of the availability of childcare, family-friendly employment policies, as well as relationship support and counselling.

The disappearance of 'good working-class jobs' and the rise of permanent social exclusion

'Good' industrial working-class jobs, often in unionised large firms, are disappearing and tending to be replaced by 'Big Mac' service jobs – in low-skilled service occupations such as supermarkets, garages, hotels and restaurants, in specialist retail in the private sector, and in health and social care in the public sector. These jobs are often perceived as offering little status or prospects. Many working-class young men resent the fact that these are the type of jobs the modern labour market offers them. Because of conflict with their gender stereotypes, big issues of 'respect' and self-respect arise. Migrants are often needed to do jobs that 'British workers' are reluctant to do.

The best new jobs in the knowledge economy often require IT and personal skills. But 30 per cent of the EU labour force has no skill qualifications at all. Young people especially are at risk, too many of whom – one in six – are still leaving school early and even more lack the basic skills for economic survival in the knowledge economy. When one examines the performance of European educational systems, there is still massive room for improvement. In several member states educational performance appears to be in decline. Education is increasingly seen as the gateway to a decent job, but this message can come across as extremely threatening to those groups in society whose families have traditionally failed in the education system. Far from promoting a culture of aspiration in schools, it can smother it.

Has globalisation made the disappearance of 'good working-class jobs' faster than it would otherwise have been? The switch from manufacturing to services began in the 1970s. The trends were long in existence before the word globalisation took off in the 1990s. Nonetheless globalisation is reinforcing these trends. Witness the squeeze on the key clothing and footwear sectors of the Italian economy as a result of new competition from emerging economies: the best firms prosper by retaining their design and marketing skills in Italy, but outsourcing production elsewhere. Consider the possibility that Chinese and Indian companies may soon challenge European car makers in their mass market ranges. Also, if Europe is serious in its commitment to take a global lead in mitigating climate change, then it must be prepared to face up to the consequences for its energy-intensive industries before the rest of the world has to, and face the inevitable restructuring required.

Economists will blithely say that an increased rate of job changing is perfectly manageable so long as the right adjustment policies are in place. But polarisation and inequality in our societies have been greatly increased by past failures of labour-market adjustment, with the rise of employment inactivity and the increased risks of permanent social exclusion as a consequence. A striking feature of Europe's deindustrialisation has been the concentration of unemployment and long-term labour-market inactivity among particular regions and groups:

- Workers with few skills are three times more likely be unemployed than graduates.
- Even in the EU15, never mind the 'transition' economies of the new member states, over a tenth of the workforce live in regions with more than 15 per cent unemployment.[10]
- Unemployment is concentrated at either end of the age range: for prime age (25–55) males, employment activity rates in Europe are around the same as they are in the United States.
- Unemployment among under-25s has been around double the unemployment rate across the EU overall: in 2005 over a fifth didn't have a job in France, Italy, Poland and Spain.
- The last three decades of the twentieth century saw a massive fall in labour-market participation among 55–64 year olds: over 40 per cent of men had by the turn of the century dropped out of the labour market.[11]

This concentration of high unemployment and low activity in particular regions and among particular groups has undoubtedly had serious social consequences. Nearly 20 per cent, or 18 million, of the EU's under-18s are at risk of poverty on the standard relative measure. The last three decades have seen a pervasive increase in child poverty rates which in all member states are higher than poverty rates among the population as a whole. Children with the highest risk of poverty live in *single parent families*. These account for only 4.4 per cent of all households, but a third of them are at risk of poverty. Child poverty is also prevalent in *jobless households*. Across the EU, 10 per cent of all children live in jobless households, 60 per cent of whom are at risk of poverty. The child poverty rate in *large families* is also high where mothers are full-time carers and the male breadwinner is low-paid: around 6 per cent of all employees are at risk of poverty.

Poor children experience a disproportionate share of deprivation, disadvantage, bad health and bad school outcomes. When they grow up, they are more likely to become unemployed, to get low-paid jobs, to live in social housing, to get in trouble with the police, and are at a greater risk of alcohol and drug abuse as young adults. Moreover, in most countries, they are likely to transfer their poverty of opportunities to their own children.

A structural rise in food and energy prices would be a serious issue, embedding such poverty trends. A larger share of poorer people's budgets goes on these essential items, reducing disposable incomes for other purposes. Yet if price rises are needed to signal a permanent shift in Europeans' pattern of consumption, it cannot make long-term economic sense to intervene artificially in an attempt to shield the poor from the consequences. One obvious response would be to let prices find their new market levels, but channel extra help to poor and vulnerable families, for example through winter heating allowances, child benefits or higher school-meal subsidies. Another is to increase taxes on those resources which society needs to economise on in the long run, but hypothecate the proceeds for investment in energy conservation and less wasteful patterns of food production and distribution.

Increased risks of insecurity?

Old jobs are being lost and new ones created at an ever-faster pace. Young people are more likely to have changed jobs for whatever reason. A Eurobarometer survey showed that while 23 per cent of retired workers and 21 pent of the over 55s had *never* changed employer, this figure is only 16 per cent for all younger age groups.[12] But job changing in itself is not necessarily a bad thing. Denmark has one of the highest rates of job changing in Europe, but because of its social investment in 'flexicurity' Danish workers fear job losses the least of all citizens in the EU.

Labour-market insecurity has risen because of the growth of non-permanent labour contracts in many member states. Fixed-term contracts now account for a fifth of jobs in Portugal, a third in Spain, and have grown rapidly in some new member states – in Poland to over a quarter of all jobs. In Germany there has also been a growth of part-time, non-standard jobs outside the normal rules of the social insurance system. Over half of fixed-contract workers would prefer a permanent job if they could get it.

The social consequences of these developments are difficult to estimate. In Europe over the last five years employment has risen very fast. Many people who have these new jobs are on short-term employment contracts. In the last decade the consensus among labour-market reformers and policy-makers at European level has very much become that 'a job is the foundation of economic opportunity and the best answer to poverty'. Critics object to what they see as 'poor quality' jobs and fear the creation of massed ranks of working poor. But this can be avoided by developing in-work benefits for the working poor such as tax credit schemes or negative income tax. Such policies have their drawbacks, particularly in terms of incentives, but is this worse than tolerating an increase in working poverty or opting for enforced idleness as a more 'social' outcome?

Many people undoubtedly face insecurity and marginalisation in the contemporary labour market. However, the main culprit may be insider–outsider divisions between 'insiders' who enjoy high levels of legal protection against dismissal and 'outsiders' on temporary contracts who have minimal security and no incentive to learn or be taught new skills. French evidence suggests that this has led to growing generational inequalities: the gap between the average earnings of people at 30 and at 55 has increased from insignificant levels to 20 per cent in the past quarter-century.[13] Even 'flexible labour markets' like the UK have seen a growth in insecure 'agency work', where the answer is better employment protection. But such legislative protection has to strike a balance. Too high a level of security for some means greater insecurity for others.

What seems clear is that the labour-market position of the low-skilled is worsening: without opportunities to learn and relearn skills, and manage labour-market transitions better, too many run the risk of finding themselves stuck on a carousel of bad jobs and unemployment. This affects not just the economically inactive over-50s who have lost 'good working-class jobs' in successive rounds of industrial restructuring, but also young people, especially the low-skilled, trying to establish a foothold in the labour market. However, if the Danes can address these problems more or less successfully through 'flexicurity', without damage to their economic performance, can it really be argued that globalisation is preventing the rest of Europe from following suit?

In the United States some economists have in part attributed the decline of low-skilled wages to migration. There is no clear evidence of this in Europe, though many migrants do perform badly in our education systems and labour markets. This reflects deep problems of integration evidenced by 'white flight' from schools in racially diverse areas leading to de facto educational segregation and discrimination in access to apprenticeships and training opportunities. Migrant families are often perceived unfairly as 'abusing' public services because they appear more dependent on them, but these stresses often occur in disadvantaged areas where in any event public services are under pressure. The challenge for governments is to find the resources to address increased social needs in these areas and be willing to take affirmative action to address disadvantage.

Is wage inequality rising and has globalisation led to it?

The data is strongly suggestive of rising pre-tax inequality in many but not all member states. A comparison of 90/10 ratios of gross earnings among OECD members in the decade 1994 to 2003 shows a general trend to more inequality, with particularly large increases in the new member states (Czech Republic, Hungary and Poland). France, Ireland and Spain appear, however, to have stood out against this trend.

Germany has seen rising wage inequality since 1994,[14] with the gap widening mainly in the bottom half of the distribution, and for workers with low job tenure. For 25–54 year old males, wages grew by only 8 per cent in contrast to 23 per cent in the previous decade; in low-tenured jobs in the bottom four percentiles, wages actually fell. In Spain by contrast there is little overall trend to inequality despite an enormous growth in short-term contracts.[15] Between 1995 and 2002, the proportion of the workforce who had held their current job for less than three years rose from 35 per cent to 53 per cent; the proportion that had held their job for more than seven years fell from 46 per cent to 32 per cent.

There has been a steep drop in the share of wages in national income in the last quarter century – in continental Europe by up to 10 points, while it has been only 4 points in the Anglo-Saxon economies. It may be that the wage share declined so much in continental Europe because the profit share had become too low to incentivise investment and growth. Also many economists would argue that the slow growth of wages in Germany in the last decade was a consequence of the need for a slow and painful disinflation as the only available remedy for Germany's economic woes following the massive economic mistakes made at the time of unification. Wage shares in national income tell us nothing about how wages are distributed. In the US the wage share has fallen much less but there has been a massive rise in inequality.

There is a huge debate among economists about the scale and causes of rising wage inequality, mostly in the US and mostly based on US data. It is said that:

- Skill-biased technical change has reduced demand for workers with low skills, while demand for those with high skills has increased.
- Jobs in the middle are being hollowed out.
- People at the top are racing ahead.

How do these arguments relate to Europe? We have noted already the erosion of 'good working-class jobs' and the deteriorating position of the low-skilled: while this can mainly be attributed to occupational and skill shifts, globalisation reinforces the trends. Analysis of the UK labour market suggests a hollowing out of 'good working-class jobs' in the middle.[16] The share of jobs in the top 20 per cent of the 'job quality' distribution has increased hugely, but there has also been a significant increase in jobs in the bottom two quality deciles. By contrast, job numbers in the middle 60 per cent of deciles have declined.

This phenomenon of 'lovely and lousy' jobs is consistent with the thesis that the impact of technology is not so much to eliminate low-skilled jobs, as to eliminate routine jobs. Many routine jobs would in the past have been categorised as skilled, but technology is gradually replacing these jobs in the middle of the occupational structure. However, low-skilled workers such as shelf-stackers in supermarkets and care assistants for the elderly cannot easily be replaced and are in high demand. This hollowing out of good jobs is liable to be accentuated by globalisation with the potential for radical unbundling of economic activities which were previously considered as untradeable as a result of the increasing ability of companies to fragment their activities, slice up the value added chain, specialise vertically and off-shore many highly skilled jobs that would have once been regarded as part of a firm's irreducible core.[17]

As for racing ahead at the top, the explosion in salaries of top executives has been more or less evident throughout Europe, but to different degrees between countries. Apologists for this trend say that it is all due to more intense competition for top talent in a global market place. While this may explain the leap in earnings enjoyed by football stars and baseball players, the justification for top managers is open to question. First, the US evidence indicates a very weak association between top management reward and company performance. Second, some types of excessive management reward have been shown to offer perverse and economically damaging incentives, as many leaders of the financial services industry now accept. It appears high rewards at the top reflect an ideological shift in our societies, with top executives no longer caring about how large pay rises are perceived, rather than any structural shift in markets.

Tony Atkinson's recent work on the top 1 per cent of the income distribution in Europe bears out this view. He finds no common pattern.

The share of the top 1 per cent in France has remained more or less stable, while the UK has witnessed big increases in inequality at the top,[18] almost completely reversing the trend towards greater equality in top incomes since the Second World War. Inequality appears to have risen somewhat from low levels in Scandinavia and the Netherlands, but to have remained stable at relatively high levels in Italy. However, Atkinson judges that the rise in inequality looks more episodic rather than part of some longer-term trend. It came about in periods when governments pushed through tough reforms in the belief they were necessary to correct unsustainable public finances and restore competitiveness, and as a result of ideological choice to reduce taxes on top incomes.

Implications of labour-market trends for inequality in European societies

Studies of comparative income inequality[19] among different EU nations and the US find that levels of inequality are significantly related to choices made by national governments in their taxation as well as broader economic and social policies. Universal trends such as globalisation and deindustrialisation, and increased competition with the developing economies in Asia and China, are not enough to explain the dramatic contrasts in levels of inequality between the US and European nations, nor the existence of diversity within Europe itself. When one considers the differences in levels of income inequality between European countries, different public policy choices in taxation, welfare provision, education and health provide the most reliable explanation. Mediterranean and eastern European countries show the highest levels of inequality; the UK the highest compared to the rest of the rich EU members; continental countries are in the middle – just below the EU average – while the Scandinavian countries are the most equal societies in Europe and in the OECD as a whole.

The Nordic countries have for decades been more equal than the rest and still are, but there has been some upturn in inequality since the economic reforms of the late 1980s and early 1990s. By contrast the southern Europeans have tended to higher levels of inequality – but these have not shown any great tendency to increase over time. France, Germany and other continental European countries fall somewhere in between. In France the income distribution narrowed in the 1970s and '80s, and has remained broadly unchanged since. Germany witnesses a similar compression but the distribution now appears to be widening, though on nothing approaching a US scale.

Europe's nation-states still have considerable room for manoeuvre in relation to the political choices they make over distribution. Our societies are not hapless victims of global processes over which national politics can exert little control – or at least not yet: countries can choose to have more equal societies than the United States and still make an economic success of them, as the Nordics continue to prove. The Nordics benefit from efficient welfare states that appear to support rather than damage growth potential. Globalisation does not require a dismantling of the 'European Social Model' but it may require its modernisation. 'Modernisation' is an imprecise term that many critics see as code for erosion, but European experience suggests that modernisation can in principle increase the possibilities for social justice, if appropriate reforms are enacted.

The transformation of capitalism

In both Christian Democratic and Social Democratic thinking about Europe's post-war realities, it was axiomatic that the nature of capitalism had been transformed. Capitalism was no longer about the brutal pursuit of profit at the expense of human values. Capitalism had been transformed by the shift to a managerial capitalism where firms owed responsibility to a broad range of stakeholders, not just shareholders. Rhineland capitalism was the most admired example of this transformation and seemed consistent with securing high levels of economic growth. Britain was at the other extreme: managerial had replaced shareholder capitalism but failure to manage industrial relations led to Britain becoming labelled the 'sick man of Europe'.

For many Europeans structural shifts in the nature of modern capitalism appear disturbing.[20] In the heyday of the Rhineland model, labour guaranteed social peace, while capital offered jobs for life. This enabled firms whose competitive advantage depended on incremental improvement in product quality to invest in the firm's human capital through job-specific training for their staff. The separation of management from control enabled firms to take a long-term view and not be driven by short-term profit performance.

Today capital is once again mobile, as it was in the pre-1914 wave of globalisation. A more competitive market for corporate control is focusing managers much more sharply on meeting profit targets. Hedge funds are seeking to move in on situations where present profitability does not reflect the underlying value of the firm's assets and new, tighter and financially motivated management teams can deliver quick results. At the same time competitive advantage has in many sectors shifted from securing incremental product or service improvement to making a commercial success of innovation at the technological and knowledge frontier. Also the time horizons for capital investment have shortened. On this gloomy view, capitalism driven by these new imperatives increasingly focuses on profit at the expense of job security and long-term commitment to its employees. Financial performance and personal enrichment have been allowed to displace the values of mutual commitment and social partnership in the pursuit of enterprise.

The trade unions are in severe decline. Membership in the private sector has been hit by the decline of the old industrial economy, bargaining power by the advantage that capital mobility gives employers and by the rise of individualism at the expense of old collectivist values. Trade union density has fallen in the last decade – in Britain and Germany by about a quarter; in Italy and the Netherlands by over 10 per cent. In the new member states it more than halved. Only in the Nordics has union density been maintained. Trade unions remain strong in the public sector, but there is a huge issue for the unions in how they make themselves relevant to employees in private sector services, small- and medium-sized businesses, and among younger workers. In France only 3 per cent of private sector employees now belong to a trade union.

However, for all the focus on globalisation, it is important to remember that there have been massive structural reforms at EU level in the last twenty years. Europe has been transformed by the Single Market, capital mobility, enlargement with its implications for free movement of labour, and (for its members) the creation of the euro and its fiscal rules. Critics of the EU point to its sclerosis and resistance to reform: the truth is that the EU has seen massive economic change that will have long-term effects that are only now working their way through European economies and societies.

Jacques Delors' 1992 project was intended to allow companies to achieve economies of scale on a Europe-wide basis. The Single Market has made much more progress in goods than in services and this has facilitated the rationalisation of traditional manufacturing by multinational firms, with a heavy impact on traditional 'working-class jobs'. EU enlargement has facilitated a further round of supply-chain reorganisation in European manufacturing as semi-skilled assembly activities can be more efficiently carried out in the new member states where labour costs are a lot lower, but skill levels often as high.

European business argues that the widening and deepening of the Single Market has been very positive in giving European companies a strong home base to take advantage of the opening up of markets in the rest of the world. European companies are huge investors in Asia and use the region as a base for export to the rest of the world, including back to Europe. These dynamics have brought rich rewards for those involved in making them happen, not least the rapidly growing financial services and business support sectors of the European economy. But the whole process accentuates the divide between 'winners' and 'losers' within Europe itself.

There are political choices to be made here. Those who believe that markets promote economic efficiency should applaud what has happened in Europe and are likely to see little case for 'throwing grit in the wheels' of these dynamic processes. However, there are counter-arguments. For those who believe the present economic dynamics result in a waste of human capital and an unacceptably unfair distribution of rewards, there is an alternative: to use the EU decision-making processes that have driven these dynamics to shape them in a more socially efficient way. Today the EU is often spoken of as a 'model power' setting standards that the rest of the world should follow. If the EU has the power to do this, it is difficult to believe that it lacks the power to set standards that would shape its own model of capitalism.

A progressive reform programme at EU level could include measures to reform corporate governance, strengthen social partner rights to be consulted over key corporate decisions, embed a framework of employment rights that facilitate family-friendly practices and life-long learning, improve labour-market transitions and prevent the risk of a competitive downward spiral in corporate tax rates. There is huge room for debate and argument about the precise detail of such a programme. But the key obstacle is not the detail. It is a sovereigntist objection to 'ceding more powers' to the EU. There are of course legitimate concerns behind such objections, but to be weighed against them is the at least as powerful view that the nation-state is now too small to shape globalisation in these ways on its own. Europe's size matters – not just in terms of trade negotiations or effective action on climate change – but if one wants to transform a capitalism that is increasingly outside nation-state control.

Conclusions

At nation-state level, there is no evidence that globalisation precludes the adoption of policies designed to improve 'life chances' for its potential 'losers' – not on the basis of a one-off chance to succeed or fail in life, but on the basis of an effort throughout the life cycle to ensure that every individual has the opportunity not to be left behind. There are several key elements in this vision, including building new 'social bridges' by offering access to new ladders of opportunity throughout the different stages of the life cycle; actively facilitating change through better labour-market transitions that reduce the risks of polarisation between 'winners' and 'losers' from European economic integration and globalisation; and a comprehensive preventative approach to tackling social inequalities that seeks to address them at source rather than simply leaving the welfare system to pick up the bill for the consequences of social dysfunction and lack of economic opportunity.

This emphasis on life chances is far more than the old welfare state's offer of equal opportunity through education. Equality of opportunity offered by current education systems is more theoretical than real. What determines individual life chances is already set by the time a child reaches school. Disadvantages have their roots in family breakdown, parenting skills (or lack of them), ethnic background and discrimination, ill health and disability, unemployment and poverty, the character of the local neighbourhood or estate where children grow up. Finding ways to tackle these embedded disadvantages is extremely challenging for public policy. However, it will be a prerequisite if we are serious about eradicating poverty and social exclusion in our societies.

At the last, a comprehensive approach to improving life chances requires a strong commitment to social policy innovation. Existing welfare states have few ready-made answers. There is tremendous scope for effective mutual learning. Innovations need to be tested. The social returns on different forms of investment need to be assessed. Best practice needs to be rolled out at the fastest possible speed. Here, potentially, is a ready-made role for the European Union.

Notes

1 Held in November 2007.
2 Among Democrats, former Clinton Cabinet members of the seniority of Robert Rubin and Larry Summers, who in the 1990s were attacked as fiscal conservatives by liberal advocates of higher social spending, speak with remarkable openness and frankness about rising inequality in the United States.
3 Larry Summers' speech to Policy Network/Centre for American Progress Seminar, Washington, DC, October 2007.
4 Larry Katz, PN/CAP seminar, Washington, DC, October 2007.
5 Conducted for the launch in February 2007 of the Commission's Social Stocktaking Consultation.
6 A. Heath and S.Y. Cheung, *Unequal Chances: Ethnic Minorities in European Labour Markets* (Proceedings of the British Academy, Oxford: Oxford University Press, 2007).
7 R.J. Gordon, 'Issues in the Comparison of Welfare Between Europe and the United States', paper presented to the Bureau of European Policy Advisers, 'Change, Innovation and Distribution', Brussels, 4 December 2007: http://faculty-web.at.northwestern.edu/economics/gordon/BRU_071125.pdf

8 *Work and Health in the EU: A Statistical Portrait* (Luxembourg: Office of the European Communities, 2004).

9 European Foundation for the Improvement of Living and Working Conditions, 'Quality of Work and Employment 2006': http://www.eurofound.europa.eu/ewco/surveys/EU0609SR01/EU0609SR01.pdf

10 J.F. Kierkegaard, *Outsourcing and Offshoring: Pushing the European Model Over the Hill, Rather Than Over the Cliff* (International Institute of Economics, March 2005).

11 See R. Liddle and F. Lerais, 'Europe's Social Reality', Consultation Paper (European Commission, 2007). Comparing 1971 with 1999, the employment activity rate for 55–64 year old men fell from 73% to 39% in France, 77% to 48% in Germany, 79% to 49% in the Netherlands, 82% to 62% in Portugal, 83% to 52% in Spain, 83% to 67% in Sweden and 83% to 59% in the UK: in short, by a large amount in most EU15 member states and dramatically in some.

12 European Commission, Special Eurobarometer 261 (2005): http://ec.europa.eu/public_opinion/archives/ebs/ebs261_en.pdf

13 L. Chauvel, *Le Destin des générations: structure sociale et cohortes en France au XXe siècle*, 2nd edn (Paris: Presses Universitaires de France, 2002).

14 J. Gernandt and F. Pfeiffer. 'Rising Wage Inequality in Germany', DIW Berlin, SOEP paper 14, April 2006: http://www.diw.de/documents/publikationen/73/56584/diw_sp0014.pdf. In the former West Germany the 1994–2004 decade saw the 90/10 ratio rise from 2.1 to 2.5 for prime age males (25–54 year olds), and from 2.47 to 3.01 for all workers.

15 M. Izquierdo and A. Lacuesta, *Wage Inequality in Spain: Recent Developments* (Banco de España: Documentos de Trabajo 0615, 2006).

16 M. Goos and A. Manning, 'Lousy and Lovely Jobs: the Rising Polarisation of Work in Britain', CEP Discussion Papers, dp0604, 2003: http://cep.lse.ac.uk/pubs/download/dp0604.pdf

17 R. Baldwin, 'Globalisation: The Great Unbundling(s)', report prepared for the Prime Minister's Office – Economic Council of Finland, as a contribution to the project: Globalisation Challenges for Europe and Finland, part of Finland's EU presidency programme, September 2006.

18 The share of the top 1% in the UK income distribution rose from roughly 6% in 1980 to almost 14% in 2000.

19 S. Zartaloudis, 'Equality: A Political Choice', Policy Network paper (January 2008): http://www.policy-network.net/uploadedFiles/Publications/Publications/Equality%20a%20political%20choice%20-%20Policy%20Network%20essay.pdf

20 See for instance John Monks, General Secretary of the European Trade Union Confederation, 'The Challenge of New Capitalism', Aneurin Bevan Memorial Lecture, Brussels, November 2006: http://www.etuc.org/a/3052?var_recherche=%91The%20Challenge%20of%20New%20Capitalism%92

III

POLITICAL ECONOMY

7

Moving Beyond the National: The Challenges for Social Democracy in a Global World

Andrew Gamble

In its original forms as it emerged in the nineteenth century, social democracy was resolutely internationalist. Existing and established states were associated with the privileged orders of the ancient regime and the embodiment of property interests. The early social democratic movements in Europe saw themselves as operating outside existing forms of the state, creating new forms of co-operation and community beyond the reach of the state, and anticipating the overthrow of the existing forms of the state in a remaking of both politics and society. This transformation was expected to be international. A fundamental tenet of early social democracy was that the working class had no country.[2] The solidarity of the working class existed across all spatial divisions, whether national or regional, and the new world order which socialists wished to bring about would transcend national divisions.

For most of the period since the First World War, however, social democracy has been predominantly national in character, following the breakdown of the liberal world order in the two world wars of the first half of the twentieth century. The hopes for building an international solidarity of labour in the nineteenth century had been based on a world in which economic integration was proceeding apace, and in which connections were being established between all regions and all peoples of the globe. The old territorial political divisions were seen as increasingly irrelevant to this new world of freedom of movement of people, goods and capital, which by the first decade of the twentieth century was in certain respects more globalised than the contemporary international order.[3]

Much of this liberal order collapsed during the carnage on the western front and, after attempts to resuscitate it post-1918 failed, during the even greater political and military struggle for territory and resources which then developed. This collapse of the liberal economic order had a profound effect upon all forms of social democracy and socialism. The Second International fell apart in 1914 when the majority of the representatives of the workers in Germany, England and France discovered that they did have a country after all and backed their national governments in voting for the war. This willingness of organised labour to subordinate class solidarity to national solidarity was a defining moment in the evolution of social democracy, stamping it with a new national character, which it has never since lost.

The fragmentation of the global order meant a new emphasis upon the national, and the nation-state, both as the source of political legitimacy and as the instrument for protecting and advancing the interests of particular groups. The unity of the social democratic movement was broken beyond repair. The earlier schism between the supporters of reform and revolution was now eclipsed by the much deeper schism between two wings of social democracy – those who supported the October Revolution in Russia and the regime it established, and who thus formed parties which affiliated to the Communist International, and those who opposed the communists because of their disregard for democracy and their willingness to implement socialism through dictatorship, and who thus formed parliamentary social democratic parties, many of them, like the SPD in Germany, still Marxist in orientation.[4]

The other profound split in the ranks of the Socialist International came with the emergence of the Fascists and the National Socialists, many of them, like Mussolini, former socialists. They condemned cosmopolitanism, emphasising the priority of nation over class, and promulgating doctrines of racial purity, as well as advocating strong national states and the need for national solutions to political problems. The parties of the Comintern, although formally committed to internationalism, became increasingly wedded after Lenin's death to the national interest of the Soviet Union and the doctrine of socialism in one country. The most internationalist element of the old Second International remained the social democratic parties, but even here the focus shifted and national strategies became more important than protecting international solidarity.

The era of national protectionism left a profound imprint on social democracy, from which in recent decades it has struggled to emerge. The strength of this imprint derived both from the necessities created by the breakdown of the liberal world order, but also from the success of different social democratic parties in adapting to this new environment and devising strategies to build coalitions which brought them electoral success and the chance to use state power to implement their programmes. Socialism in one country became indelibly associated with Stalinism, Soviet planning and autarchy. Social democracy in one country had a longer life, because although few examples of it existed before 1939, it blossomed in the new circumstances of the post-war world, with the reconstruction of a liberal world order under the leadership of the United States. One of the main successes of this liberal world order in its struggle against communism was the emergence of successful social democratic regimes in many countries of the west, delivering high levels of welfare and social security as in the east, but combining it with economic efficiency, democracy and civil liberties. Social democratic regimes proved successful in providing new legitimacy for the established social order through their ability to reconcile organised labour to the existing state, by showing how it could operate in their interest.

Social democracy in one country reached its zenith in the three decades after 1945. Its achievements were vigorously contested by many on the left, who revived the old debate about reform and revolution in the Second International, arguing that the existing state could not be used as an instrument in the creation of socialism but only to shore up capitalism.[5] Social democrats maintained, however, that in many areas reforms could permanently improve the position of the working class and advance the cause of social justice, and that the pursuit of social justice and greater equality and fairness was the core objective of social democracy,[6] which mattered much more than the transfer of productive assets into the hands of the state. Although many social democrats continued to advocate nationalisation of key sectors as one of the instruments of a progressive programme, they came to see it as only one of a number of different instruments which were available to them, and not necessarily the most important.

This change reflected the experience of social democratic parties in government, which many of them acquired after 1945, allied to the persuasiveness of a number of new social and economic theories that pointed to the transformation which had been wrought in capitalism by the application of Keynesian techniques of economic management, and new concepts of universal welfare provision. The powers of the modern state were highly developed and capable of being extended in numerous ways, and social democrats embraced the idea that the state machinery was a weapon they could take hold of and employ. Many in the post-war generation of social democrats celebrated this innovative use of the state as the taming of capitalism, as employing the countervailing force of democracy to offset and reduce the pressures in a capitalist economy towards ever-greater inequality.[7] Capitalism represented the unregulated market which knew no national boundaries. The task of social democracy was to re-impose social and political priorities on the way in which the market distributed resources, using the power of the state to redistribute and regulate. This was often presented as a constant struggle to keep the raw power of capitalism caged and under control, and led to a celebration of the virtues of the public sector, public service, and the public ethos, in contrast to the market.

Each social democratic regime developed in rather different ways and became associated with different models of capitalism and national formations. The global economy, although reviving under the new liberal order agreed at Bretton Woods, remained unmistakeably an international rather than a global economy, composed of the different national economies and their separate jurisdictions. Out of the different national paths emerged distinctive types of regime, different worlds of welfare capitalism, for example, and noted differences in institutions, from corporate governance to industrial relations. What was common to all the social democratic regimes, however, were high levels of public spending and state involvement in managing their economies and societies.

Social democracy in one country

Even with the gradual restoration of a liberal economic world order after 1945, many features of national protectionism persisted. The balance between greater international economic co-operation from a secure base of national economic management worked extremely well during the years of the long post-war boom, which lasted through the 1950s and 1960s, only definitively coming to an end with the collapse of the Bretton Woods system in 1971 and the first generalised recession in 1974 and 1975. The 1970s and 1980s proved to be much more difficult decades for the international economy, and saw a number of major shifts in policies, ideas and institutions, which cumulatively produced the new era of globalisation.

Many social democratic regimes struggled to adapt to the new environment. Social democracy, which at its inception had been so international in its focus and so resistant to national ties, now found it difficult to shed its national carapace, with which its achievements were associated. The rediscovery by capital of the freedom and power of operating globally beyond the constraints of territorial division was not matched by social democracy, which as a result began to see many of the safeguards and restrictions which it had established being eroded and rolled back in the new liberal era.[8]

The extent to which national economic management in general and social democracy in particular as a form of political economy and political regime have been rendered obsolete by the changes introduced by the trends associated with globalisation has been much debated, and the picture that emerges is a complex one. National governments have been forced to adapt to new demands and pressures, but at the same time have retained important capacities to choose policies and to shape their environment rather than being shaped by it. Many of the wilder fears about neo-liberalism, for example that it would cause a race to the bottom, the dismantling of universal welfare programmes, a severe contraction in public spending and social protection, the sweeping away of all employment rights, have not been borne out by events.

That is not so say that nothing has changed. The new era of floating exchange rates and the relaxation of controls on international finance has had some dramatic effects, and has altered the constraints which governments have to face, making some of the instruments which they used to employ, such as exchange-rate controls, ineffective. The power of the financial markets to destabilise currencies and governments has been demonstrated several times since 1971 (Britain in 1976, France in 1982–3, Sweden in 1992). Governments have had to learn how to maintain international financial confidence in the way they conduct their affairs, or risk an exodus of capital. The price of openness, of remaining an integral part of the global economy, is an acceptance of the discipline which the financial markets impose. This has not prevented some economies borrowing very heavily to finance their domestic programmes, but they have had to find ways of doing it which do not endanger financial confidence, and they remain vulnerable to sudden changes of market sentiment.

The growth of trade from the 1950s onwards has created a high level of interdependence in the international economy which has made the cost of reducing ties increasingly prohibitive. In this sense there has been a reduction in the freedom of governments. A national protectionist strategy of severing ties with the global economy and promoting a much higher level of self-sufficiency in order to pursue policies free of concerns about international financial pressures has been recognised as no longer viable. Acceptance of the constraints of the global economy and the realities of economic interdependence is not, however, the same as being obliged to adopt particular neo-liberal prescriptions on domestic economic management. As many social democratic regimes have found, there is considerable variety in the policies that can be pursued.

The extent to which there was ever a pure form of social democracy in one country, free of any international pressures or obligations, and able to chart entirely its own course, relying on its own efforts and resources, is highly debatable; but it is a dream that still resonates because it suggests that no compromises are necessary, and that social democracy can be established free of all external constraints. But even while most social democrats accept that this was an illusion of the era of national protectionism, it is still emotionally and intellectually hard for many to reconnect to a new cosmopolitan vision of an international social democracy.

Two other changes have been important in the questioning of national models of social democracy. Both predate the globalisation era itself, but both are of increasing importance within it: the new international division of labour and the growth of migration. The new international division of labour reflected changing forms of comparative advantage and their exploitation by increasingly dominant global companies who organised the system of production transnationally, utilising the distribution of skills, resources and labour to best advantage. The policies of these firms threatened the maintenance of particular sectors and employment within many national economies, and therefore created major policy dilemmas for social democratic governments, particularly where the employment concerned was in manufacturing industry. One response was to subsidise and protect employment, sometimes through nationalisation, but the cost was often high, because of the long-term difficulty of sustaining a sector that was no longer internationally competitive.

Most social democratic governments therefore responded to these pressures by devising industrial strategies to raise the competitiveness and productivity of domestic industries and the skills of the workforce, and by trying to ensure that jobs were available which could be sustained without subsidy. There were very different records of success in this. But even the most successful economies still faced difficulties in maintaining traditional manufacturing, and managing the necessary move to an economy in which services, especially internationally traded services, were increasingly important. The communities that had grown up around traditional manufacturing were the natural electoral base of social democracy, so the decline of these industries and the trade unions associated with them presented not just an economic challenge but an electoral and ideological challenge. Social democratic parties had always had to reach out beyond the constituency of the industrial workers, to win the support of other groups, and create a progressive coalition for change, but in the wake of the restructuring of the 1970s and 1980s this became still more pressing.

The industrial workers are still a vital component of the coalition, but they also tend to be the part of the coalition with the most national protectionist instincts on jobs and industrial subsidies.

A further pressure associated with the trend to a more globalised economy has been the increase in migration. The freeing of labour markets has proceeded much more slowly than either the freeing of capital markets or the liberalisation of trade, but it has gathered pace, driven both by the need for the rich nations to increase their labour supply and by the desire of so many from poorer regions to get access to the employment opportunities and wage levels which the rich enjoy. The rich world is increasingly besieged by the hundreds of thousands who would enter if they could, but are denied the possibility of doing so. Fears of the effect of migration on living standards, employment and housing, although often exaggerated, have become potent in domestic politics in many of the rich nations, fuelling national protectionism and leading to increasingly draconian controls. In practice controls have often been ineffective, and unknown numbers of illegal immigrants have entered the rich nations. But it is another factor that reinforces the defensive and protectionist character of social democracy, seeking to uphold the standards and citizenship benefits that have been achieved in particular national economies.

The pressure towards a more global economy in terms of finance, trade, production and labour has undercut the arguments for social democracy in one country. But they have not rendered it obsolete. That is because, as critics of globalisation have urged, many of the trends are not truly globalising trends, but regionalising trends. The regions of the world have become much more interdependent, but the growth of interdependence between regions has been much less marked. This means that the defences which national governments have erected to protect themselves from global markets have proved more resilient than first thought, and the pressure on countries to conform to a global norm, or even to a regional norm, has so far been less than some of the protagonists of globalisation expected, reinforcing a tendency for national governments to remain defensive, holding on to what has been achieved rather than thinking about ways of building an international social democracy.

The problem for social democracy is that defensive positions cannot be sustained indefinitely. Important though nation-states remain to any substantive social democratic project, and however limited some forms of economic globalisation may in fact be, there are other aspects of globalisation which do suggest the emergence of a set of problems for which social democracy in one country is quite inadequate. These problems have not suddenly arisen. They are long-standing aspects of modernity, and they continually reappear, particularly during periods of rapid economic progress. They are the unintended consequences of the processes which modernity has unleashed. Chief among them are processes of scientific discovery and technological advance which, combined with the capitalist forms of production and exchange, have had profound environmental and social impacts, such as the huge disparities between the global rich and the global poor, and the effects on the planet biosphere, including global warming, which may prove irreversible. Amidst these great changes political authority has remained fragmented, with most political functions being exercised within quite sharply defined territorial jurisdictions. The governance of the various processes that form and sustain the modern world is notoriously uneven, and in the current era this is leading to many insoluble kinds of policy dilemmas, particularly over the distribution of resources and opportunities, the provision of security against crime, terrorism, the prevention of infectious diseases, population growth and environmental degradation.

Contemporary dilemmas of social democratic politics

Social democracy for much of the twentieth century was national in its formation and its preoccupations, but it now faces the need to become transnational and cosmopolitan again, applying social democratic principles to the problems of making the state more effective in a more global world. Social democratic government at the national level is constitutional government,[9] because it is conducted according to rules and principles that are binding on all political actors, and which therefore help to constrain the unfettered exercise of power by separating or dividing it. Constitutional government provides a framework in which government can be both responsible and representative – managing conflicts, protecting rights, promoting participation and maintaining the security of its citizens. There will always be dispute at any one time over the best rules and institutions for achieving this, as well as over the principles constitutional arrangements should express, and which ones should take priority over others. There will also always be debate over the extent to which constitutional government is frustrated or facilitated by the provisions of the constitution, and whether the impact of economic, social, cultural and political changes requires amendments to the constitution, or even different constitutional arrangements altogether.

A key challenge for social democrats is how to embed these principles in the global polity, creating the kind of public sphere and public space for debating policy, adjusting interests and evaluating decisions which characterise established democracies. But this has to take place at a time when national democracies are under considerable strain, facing challenges to their capacity to be representative, responsible and participative. There is a crucial difference, however, between the national and the global level. National constitutions traditionally seek to regulate and limit political power, and constitutional government by definition is limited government. But at the transnational level the need is not so much for limiting government as creating a capacity for government, and providing regulation of those agents who are currently able to exercise power without any scrutiny or account-ability. It is necessary to enquire not only whether the institutions and procedures for limiting national governments are still the right ones, and whether they can be improved, but also whether national governments have the capacities they need to meet the expectations of their citizens and deliver the services and the public goods that they want, and whether citizens have the means and opportunities to participate in determining policies and how they are being governed. The response to the last two challenges points towards the necessity for new transnational systems of governance.

This cannot be done, however, simply by replicating the national state at the global level. Social democrats in the past have been chiefly concerned with problems arising from the division of labour, the move away from self-sufficiency and the creation of extended and impersonal networks of interdependence. These trends have made possible huge increases in wealth and in population, along-side continual changes in the structure of occupations, services and lifestyles, and the application of modern science to create continu-ous technological innovation. But social democrats also need to be concerned with the division of knowledge. As the division of labour takes hold, so knowledge and information have become progressively more fragmented and dispersed. This has major implications for how contemporary societies and politics are organised and governed. Even while certain forms of knowledge, particularly modern science, have come to pervade and shape more and more areas of human life, this has not delivered rational control either of society or of the natural world, but has instead increasingly displayed the contingency and limited character of human knowledge.

Engagement and disengagement: where have all the citizens gone?

If social democrats are to make a contribution to the problems of con-temporary politics, then they have to move beyond the nation-state, and begin to think again in transnational and cosmopolitan terms about the conditions for ensuring that the global polity, and not just the national polity, is governed by social democratic values and norms. But this cannot be done successfully without at the same time engaging with the problems which threaten national social democracy. There are three particular problems – citizen disengagement, loss of accountability, and increasing complexity. Since the advent of mass democracy there has been a concern about how to engage citizens in politics. But today it has assumed a new urgency, driven by specific contemporary economic and cultural changes. The basic problem is this: do most voters still relate to politics as active citizens, concerned to share in collective decision-making as an important part of their self-identity, or have they become instead passive consumers of politics? Why should they exercise their options for voice in the political system rather than their options for exit – either by switching parties or by not bothering to vote at all? If they no longer regard themselves as citizens, then they may not feel the need to be represented by political parties, or to identify with any particular one, and will act instrumentally towards voting and participation, disengaging from it unless they have some direct interest in a particular election or decision.

The possibility that we may be witnessing a major change in the character of participation by citizens in representative democracies, as indicated by the trend towards declining participation in formal politics, has received a great deal of attention in recent years. The size of the problem is measured by falling turnout in national, local and European elections, and by the increasing unwillingness of citizens to join political parties or identify with them. The mass parties of the past have begun to wither away, and are finding it much harder to recruit members. The old idea of representative democracy was that more and more citizens would want to become involved in determining the policies of the party they identified with, and that in this way they would feel involved in shaping the policy of the government when their party was elected. The involvement that citizens have by voting for a party that presents a manifesto at the time of a general election, which very few read, is much less. The decline of the mass party and the political education it provided for a large number of citizens has been accompanied by evidence of increasing political illiteracy in the electorate and declining standards of journalism. Although there is more political information more easily available than ever before, fewer citizens appear willing to make use of it, so that opinion polls in the established democracies regularly report high levels of ignorance about how government works, the identity of leading politicians, and current political issues and events. Advocates of democracy had expected that rising levels of education would produce an electorate able and keen to make informed choices between political programmes and political leaders. But those in charge of contemporary political campaigns have found that treating voters as consumers, and campaigning as a branch of marketing, is generally more effective in winning elections than treating voters as informed citizens. This has made electoral politics increasingly a competition of brands, styles and personalities. In response, the parties have begun to shed their mass character, and much of their internal democracy, so as to make themselves more effective competitors in the political market place. The political career has been professionalised, and an increasing emphasis has come to be placed upon the presentation rather than the substance of policy. The ideological gap between the parties has substantially narrowed, and parties become instruments of the state rather than instruments of civil society. At the extreme they become cartel parties.[10]

This process is compounded by trends in modern media, which have seen the rise of more aggressive and intrusive journalism, alongside a decline in the capacity of the media to scrutinise and to inform. Instead, the media has assisted politicians in developing a style of politics based around celebrity and personality. Some analysts have spoken of the rise of a media democracy,[11] in which the media come to supplant the institutions of representative democracy, such as political parties and parliament, as the main intermediary between the voters and the government. The media have adapted to their new role by adopting for the most part a negative, cynical, sceptical stance towards government and politicians, and present politics and public policy in ways which reinforce and spread similar attitudes in their readers and viewers.[12]

The new media culture is sometimes associated with wider cultural changes towards greater individualism and choice, and a move away from deference and the unquestioning acceptance of authority and expertise. But it is also associated with trends towards trivialisation and entertainment, which reinforce the bias against understanding, accelerate the decline of the public sphere, and weaken interest in participating in institutions such as political parties that have played such a key role in representative democracy. This creates a major challenge for building a transnational social democracy even more than national social democracy, which depends upon an educated, informed and active citizenry.

There are other more positive changes. Studies of participation have pointed out that while certain indicators of formal participation, particularly turnout, have declined, other forms of participation have increased.[13] Disengagement, to the extent that it exists, seems to be largely disengagement from involvement in and identification with the existing parties and established forms of representation.

Many citizens have increasing involvement with organisations and campaigns outside formal politics, many of which are increasingly transnational in their organisation and concerns. Research has shown that young people still take a lively interest in politics; it is just that politics is not defined in terms of the conventional categories of parliamentary politics. This evidence is important, although it highlights the increasing problems with representative democracy at the national level. Many voters have become disconnected from the formal political process, and national constitutional reforms, or constitutional reforms at the European level, have done little to remedy this. A well-functioning constitution requires institutions and mechanisms that make it easy for citizens to participate and help to sustain a vigorous civil society and the concept of a public sphere, which is separate from both the family and the market.[14]

It is important not to exaggerate the change that is occurring, or to underestimate the life there may still be in existing national constitutional forms. Much of the evidence on falling turnout supports the view that the more certain the outcome, and the less that is perceived to be at stake, the lower the turnout is likely to be. In a severe political crisis, or if the choice at a future election became very polarised, citizens might once again participate in much larger numbers in voting, as happened in the Italian election in 2006 when turnout increased to over 80 per cent. But it is clearly disturbing that the formal representative machinery is becoming a last resort rather than a first resort for so many citizens, not least because of the disproportionately sharp fall in the proportion of young voters willing to vote.

Another feature of the problem of disengagement is that there is considerable uncertainty as to who the citizens are in contemporary democracies and what they want. There is an assumption that the main problems in democracy lie with the political class and the institutions of representative democracy, frustrating the desires of the people for involvement, participation and commitment.[15] This may be true for some groups, but there is less evidence that it is true for the majority. Rather, the problem is that it is very difficult for political parties, or political campaigns and pressure groups, to reach large numbers of citizens more than fleetingly, and to sustain their involvement. Most voters do not want to become deeply involved in politics, preferring to give priority to other things in their lives.[16]

For much of the twentieth century mass electorates were organised around a number of basic alignments, which determined social identity, and therefore voting preference and political partisanship. There were different alignments in different countries, and they were often cross-cutting, but in several countries the class alignment was particularly strong, and so was political partisanship. This gave a particular meaning to the left/right spectrum, and to the positioning of different parties along it. It also gave a particular meaning to citizenship. Citizenship could be understood as a cumulative progress from civil to political and then to social rights. There were many battles along the way, but the meaning of constitutional government on this model was the gradual inclusion of new interests within the political system, the emergence of new majority electoral coalitions, and a moving consensus around policies that promoted social justice and the welfare state, with party competition focused on the trade-offs between social equality and economic efficiency. Citizens were partisan and committed, but the outcomes of the process promoted a set of workable compromises for public policy.

The social justice agenda is still there, but the solidity of the class alignments and their organisations in civil society on which it used to depend are much weaker than before. The interpretation of social justice has also changed, with the emergence of a set of new rights and concerns, voiced by new social movements, by multiculturalism, and above all by campaigns for global justice which have highlighted the gap between the rich north and the poor south. This is the new context which social democracy needs to address, as a priority and not as an afterthought.

Accountability and sovereignty: do governments decide anything any more?

These problems of representation within national democracies are compounded by problems of accountability. Social democratic governments have become acutely aware that they must improve the delivery of services to their citizens; at the same time their capacity to deliver is being threatened by the trends towards an increasingly interconnected world and the need to provide public goods for the whole world, not just for a particular national economy. The traditional idea of responsible government in a nation-state is that the government takes responsibility for its actions and is accountable for them to its electorate. The government has the constitutional power to take initiatives and propose new measures, and it does so mindful of its overall responsibility for the public interest and public welfare. Can national governments any longer be held accountable for their actions, or to put it another way, are national governments becoming accountable for less and less?

As argued above, globalisation is not a new phenomenon but one of the principal effects of an expanding division of labour, which has existed at least since the rise of the modern industrial economy. It is also extremely uneven, between states, between regions, and between sectors and nation-states. Some of the smaller nations in particular have not been overwhelmed by globalisation, but, on the contrary, have proven very resilient in adjusting to it.[17] The contemporary global economy has national and regional foundations, and cannot be properly understood without them.

What is new is that the present phase of globalisation, which first appeared in the early 1970s, and became most fully established from the 1990s onwards, has been accompanied by new kinds of political fragmentation which have made the task of national government more complicated. There has been a proliferation of new supranational bodies, and overlapping jurisdictions. Nation-states have become less self-contained, as international regimes of various kinds have been established to cope with the problems arising from the growing economic and political interdependence of the world economy. There are now many issues which are settled by negotiations in transnational and supranational bodies, and which only come to national parliaments for ratification. The European Union is one of the most prominent examples of this. Under the Single European Act and other treaties there are now important areas of policy in which the majority of legislation originates at the EU level and is passed down to member states for implementation.

The more that matters are transferred to subordinate or superior bodies, the less national governments can claim to be responsible for what they do. This therefore tends to undermine their legitimacy in the eyes of voters. If there is no longer any very clear centre of decision-making, and if governments no longer seem to be in charge, then the danger exists that voters will react accordingly, and lose trust in the governments they elect to promote the public interest or to protect the private interests of the citizens. At the extreme this can contribute to increasing distrust of the formal mechanisms of representative democracy.

One of the most difficult issues for social democracy is how to adapt to this rapidly evolving world of multilevel and transnational governance, in which it is hard to pin down exactly where decisions are taken, and devise new ways of connecting citizens with the decisions which affect them. To some extent there has always been multilevel governance – federalist constitutions, for example, stipulate it – but in Europe, a new dimension has been added by accession to the EU and in some cases by internal devolution. There is widespread ignorance about who is responsible for which policy, and naturally numerous opportunities for ministers to absolve themselves of responsibility by claiming that the decision which is being objected to has come from somewhere else. This ability to put the blame on some other tier of government has become endemic, and is corrosive to the authority of national government, because national governments are still symbolically looked to as the protectors of the national interest and the public interest. Huge expectations about the competence and capacity of governments to deliver outcomes which voters want still abound, and politicians themselves, particularly at elections, do little to damp down those expectations. Since they are competing with other parties for votes, the temptation is always to claim much greater competence than really exists. Only in government do politicians find that the levers they need to achieve the things they have promised often do not exist.

In a system of multilateral governance, and still more of transnational governance, it can be hard for the voters to understand where a particular decision comes from, and who is imposing it. Decisions by the EU Commission, by the European Court, by the WTO, and by the numerous boards which are busy standardising such things as accounting rules and carbon emissions, often constrain what national politicians can do. Many matters are clearly no longer exclusively an issue for national decision-making. National politicians are increasingly forced to provide accounts that justify the arrangements of pooled sovereignty, but by definition this can make them appear weak, especially if they face any kind of populist challenge calling for the repatriation of powers and the withdrawal from international regimes. The framework of international governance which has been erected so far, and which is absolutely vital for developing coherent common responses to the problems the world faces, is quite vulnerable to these kinds of challenges, since it generally fails most tests of accountability, transparency and legitimacy. All that national politicians can do is to claim influence over decisions, but such influence often looks weak measured against full-blooded assertions of national interest.

The challenge therefore is how to bring greater transparency to the governing process. National government remains crucial to the way societies are governed, but the structures of accountability and the lines of responsibility have become blurred. A more precise definition of powers and where and how they are exercised has become necessary, with appropriate channels for scrutiny and reporting. Government has a solidity which governance lacks. There are now many forms of governance, including networks and markets, which cannot be controlled or corralled by governments. But this does not mean that government is dissolving into governance, only that to understand the new processes of governance, including globalisation, we need to see how they provide a new context for government, one which departs from the old bureaucratic, top-down, hierarchical models of government which were once so common.

Complexity and knowledge: can citizens participate in decision-making?

The disengagement of citizens has undermined representative democracy, and the shift to new patterns of governance has undermined responsible government. But an even bigger problem facing social democracy and progressive politics in the twenty-first century is the growth of complexity which threatens to undermine participative democracy, by taking many areas of policy out of politics altogether, as politicians divest themselves of the responsibility for making hard choices, encouraging the rise of a managerial and technocratic style of politics at national and at global level over which citizens can have no influence. Government in the past has, of course, often been secretive and opaque, and this still continues, if to a lesser extent. Modern governments are probably now more open than they have ever been, aided by freedom of information acts and a more intrusive media. The change does not arise so much from the amount of knowledge available to citizens, as from the nature of contemporary knowledge and the process by which it is produced.

As with the other trends already examined, the extent of this trend towards greater complexity is controversial, and certainly uneven, and some of the wilder claims made in regard to it need qualifying. There are, however, some solid grounds for thinking that complexity is increasing in contemporary societies, as a result of the processes that have extended the division of labour and the division of knowledge. It is not something that has suddenly occurred, but has gradually emerged over a long period. It is associated with new kinds of risk, and with new ways of managing risk, and creates some major new dilemmas for policy.

The rise in new forms and new levels of governance is one of the sources of complexity; so too is the greater cultural diversity of modern societies, and the consequences of individualism for the way people live. But the principal source of increased complexity and the new forms of risk lies in the technologies that have become available in recent decades. Industrial societies have reached the point where economic and technological developments have become so rapid and so continuous that they are constantly revolutionising lifestyles and behaviour.[18] Established political and constitutional processes provide politicians with little control over these developments, yet they have to deal with their unintended consequences, particularly the new risks and new dangers they create. But because of the trends towards citizen disengagement from representative politics and declining trust in politicians and in government, as well as the shrinking capacity of the state in relation to the tasks it faces, government appears increasingly ill-equipped to handle the problems that technological development throws up, not least because so many of these developments pose fundamental moral and political challenges to the way people live, and even to the fixity of some of the constants of human life itself (such as extending its span).

One of the obvious consequences of these developments is an increasing dependence on expertise of various kinds, since many of the issues – from climate change to nuclear energy, from GM foods to genetic selection and the effects of new drugs – are such that only experts could possibly offer an informed opinion. But the experts' own knowledge is limited, they often disagree, and science deals in probabilities not certainties – all of which contributes to the feeling of a growing number of problems which are insoluble, and yet which everyone agrees have to be solved. Since politics is a practical activity aimed at finding practical solutions to problems, this is not good news for politicians. The problem which social democracy now has to address is therefore how to open up new spaces for politics, how to rethink how a new kind of public domain can be created which would reinvigorate both representative and participative democracy, empowering citizens and enabling them to participate in policy discussion in new ways. The instinct of politicians is increasingly to 'depoliticise' decisions by setting up boards and committees of experts to take the decisions on their behalf, thereby removing them from any political process, whether representative or participative. But this means that increasing areas of public life are subject only to very indirect accountability to the people. Politicians retreat to dealing with those few areas where their decisions can make a difference, or where there is high symbolic value in them being involved. For the rest they invoke terms like governance and globalisation to suggest that there are no alternatives to the courses they are pursuing, and that the constraints on policy-making are so tight that there is only one possible course of action.

As politicians are blamed more and more for what goes wrong in government, and the media portrays every branch of government as incompetent, chaotic, indecisive and corrupt, it is not surprising that politicians increasingly seek to divest themselves of the necessity of actually taking decisions in difficult areas. These are devolved to the appropriate experts. But politicians still tend to get blamed for anything that goes wrong, and ignored when things go well, even though they have less and less control over what actually happens. This trend towards depoliticisation and charismatic, celebrity politics threatens to undermine attempts to create more participative forms of democracy, as well as schemes for empowering citizens, and for rebuilding trust in representative democracy. Clearly a healthy social democracy requires all three. But it needs to find ways to resist the present trends that are pushing citizens and politicians further apart, and creating policy structures that for all the talk of consultation often make it harder for genuine participation to take place.

Conclusion

The changes identified here are often presented in apocalyptic terms. A sense of proportion needs to be maintained. Political systems and constitutions are fairly resilient and are in any case always changing. Though some of the new developments appear to pose special prob- lems and dangers, they also present opportunities for new forms of politics and for constitutional experiments, particularly initiatives to imagine how the global polity we have might be improved. This cannot be done by neglecting the health of national social democracy; it will be the foundation on which a cosmopolitan social democracy will be built. But it is also the case that cosmopolitan social democracy will not simply replicate national social democracy. Many institutions will need to be different.[19] It is hard to see how political parties could play the role they once did in developing national social democracy. Other ways of ensuring that different interests and groups are properly rep- resented, and other ways for individuals to participate in the political process, need to be found.

Every means to create new public spaces for the global polity must be tried, because only a global civil society can provide the networks, associations, campaigning organisations and public discussion that can begin to sustain the kind of politics the global polity is going to require. The crucial requirement for all forms of social democracy is that politics continues to be regarded as an open process of delibera- tion and choice among alternatives. Its main enemy is the belief that outcomes are foreordained and that the struggle to maintain healthy representative and participative institutions at all levels of the global polity is therefore futile. Forging a new transnational movement will not be easy, but it is the only way that there will be a future for social democracy.

Notes

1 W. Lippmann, *The Phantom Public* (1925), cited in Bruce Ackerman and James Fishkin, *Deliberation Day* (New Haven: Yale University Press, 2004), p. 10.
2 'The workers have no country. We cannot take from them what they have not got.' K. Marx and F. Engels, 'Manifesto of the Communist Party', in *Selected Works*, Volume I (Moscow: Progress, 1962), p. 51.
3 P. Hirst and G. Thompson, *Globalisation in Question* (Cambridge: Polity, 1996).

4   D. Sassoon, *One Hundred Years of Socialism: The West European Left in the Twentieth Century* (London: I.B. Tauris, 1996).

5   P. Anderson, *Arguments Within English Marxism* (London: NLB, 1980).

6   T. Crosland, *The Future of Socialism* (London: Cape, 1956).

7   J. Strachey, *Contemporary Capitalism* (London: Gollancz, 1956).

8   D. Harvey, *A Brief History of Neo-Liberalism* (Oxford: Oxford University Press, 2005).

9   R. Bellamy and D. Castiglione, 'Constitutions and Politics', *Political Studies* 44:3 (1966), pp. 413–17.

10 P. Mair and R. Katz, 'Changing Models of Party Organisation and Party Democracy: The Emergence of the Cartel Party', *Party Politics* 1:1 (1995), pp. 5–28.

11 T. Meyer, *Media Democracy: How the Media Colonise Politics* (Cambridge: Polity, 2002).

12 J. Lloyd, *What the Media are Doing to our Politics* (London: Robinson, 2004).

13 C. Pattie, Patrick Seyd and Paul Whiteley, *Citizenship in Britain: Values, Participation and Democracy* (Cambridge: Cambridge University Press, 2004).

14 D. Marquand, *Decline of the Public* (Cambridge: Polity, 2004); Paul Ginsborg, *The Politics of Everyday Life* (New Haven: Yale University Press, 2005).

15 See www.powerinquiry.org/report/index.php

16 G. Stoker, *Why Politics Matters* (London: Palgrave Macmillan, 2006).

17 P. Katzenstein, *Small States in World Markets* (Ithaca N.Y.: Cornell University Press, 1985).

18 U. Beck, *Risk Society: Towards a New Modernity* (London: Sage, 1992).

19 D. Held, *Global Covenant: The Social Democratic Alternative to the Washington Consensus* (Cambridge: Polity, 2004).

8

Social Justice in a 'Shrinking' World: Beyond Protectionism and Neo-liberalism

David Coates

The formulation of the question relating to global social justice that underpins this volume is arguably compatible with a conventional 'third-way' understanding of post-war social democratic history, at least as that has manifested itself in the self-presentation of New Labour in the UK. Though individual political leaders have their own personal ways of presenting the third-way case, most of them share a sense of post-war UK history as a set of discrete policy decades informed by bodies of economic thought: initially Keynesian, then neo-liberal, and now what Gordon Brown once famously called 'post neoclassical endogenous growth theory' – that is, new growth theory.

The dominant paradigm in the age of Old Labour, so the conventional understanding goes, was Keynesian. Keynes's writings gave a generation of progressive politicians and their electorates a particular view of the role and capacity of states as economic managers. That Keynesian paradigm broke down under the onslaught of stagflation in the 1970s, and was famously abandoned in the UK by Prime Minister James Callaghan in the midst of the 1976 IMF crisis.[1] It was replaced in dominance, in London at least, by a neo-liberal orthodoxy to which Old Labour Keynesianism had no answer, and against which the Labour left could only initially offer the outright protectionism of the Alternative Economic Strategy.[2] The subsequent dominance of neo-liberalism kept the Labour Party out of power for almost two decades – and it kept the Conservatives in power until a fresh generation of Labour politicians found an answer to it in new growth theory. New growth theory gave that new generation the confidence to advocate a progressive role for the state that could address, as neo-liberalism could not, the social as well as the economic requirements of a new age of globalisation.[3]

New growth theory gave the state a bigger economic role – and potentially a more progressive one – than neo-liberalism ever could.

The third-way state was not a Keynesian one, managing industrial investment and picking national champions. But nor was it a privatising one, strengthening economic performance by cutting back on public provision where it could and deploying internal markets when it could not. The third-way state was instead a 'lubricating state' and an 'enabling' one.[4] Its job was to generate the improvements in human capital, and the expansion of R&D, which alone would enable already established capitalist economies to survive and flourish in a world economy that was genuinely, and for the first time, globalising: a world economy characterised by intensified international competition, faster means of communication, impatient and mobile capital, and new centres of industrial output in hitherto dormant economic giants – particularly China, India and Brazil. Gordon Brown put the case for the third way in his pamphlet on reform inside the European Union:

> There are some who argue that the only way Europe can retain its unique balance of prosperity and fairness is to retreat from globalisation into a new protectionism and act at the EU level to erect new barriers to global trade and investment. Others look at the rapid pace of change and argue that nothing can be done in the face of globalisation and technological advance, that it is impossible in the modern world to sustain prosperity and fairness together, and that individuals must be left alone to adapt to far-reaching change. We reject both. Protectionism cannot work in a global economy where production processes are increasingly spread across continents, and businesses and consumers depend on international trade and investment links. In a world of global capital flows, protectionism can only bring about higher unemployment and higher prices. At the same time, a laissez-faire approach leaves people defenceless against change when we should be enabling them to master that change. Instead, we need a strategy that delivers a full-employment Global Europe. The answer is not to restrict or retreat from global competition, but to meet and master global change through policies that promote openness and opportunity for all. This calls for greater flexibility in product markets, labour markets and capital markets to ensure that Europe's businesses and individuals are equipped to take advantage of new opportunities; and ensuring fairness through policies that expand opportunity and choice, provide security for the vulnerable, and help people adapt to change. Structural reform that promotes flexibility and fairness together is the key to success in the modern global economy.[5]

For the purposes of this chapter, the policy package being proposed by Gordon Brown will be treated as an example of 'progressive competitiveness': a strategy through which progressive goals – things like full employment, adequate social services, rising living standards and poverty reduction – are realised by a strengthening of the competitive position of the national/regional economy for which progressive politicians have political responsibility.[6] The issue before us therefore becomes this: is a resetting of state–market relations in a progressively competitive way the best response that the left can make to the arrival of the era of globalisation?

Globalisation and state–market relations as products of class settlements

To address this issue fully, we have to link our understanding of 'state–market relations' and 'globalisation' to a wider discussion about the social classes from whose interaction social democratic political forces emerged.

It is always possible to think of 'state–market relations' as a technical issue, asking how far certain policy instruments can work in modern competitive conditions. Is industrial policy now outdated? Can regional policy be allowed? Are capital controls impossible?, and so on. Indeed, answering those questions is vital to any progressive politics in the modern period. But such questions cannot be adequately answered at the technical level alone. For beneath technical issues lie social ones; and it is to the social that the political must ultimately relate. Beneath and beyond technical debates about policy options lie class settlements and the global social forces that frame the scope of possibilities. The technical debates are important, but it is the class settlements and the associated global balance of social forces that ultimately structure them. A discussion of 'state–market' relations abstracted from those underlying structural realities can only serve to obscure this deeper truth; and in that way help to conserve whatever global balance currently operates. But progressive politics are not about conservation. They are about change; which is why, for progressive purposes, an abstracted debate about 'state–market' relations is ultimately fruitless.

Talking in technicalities, and ignoring underlying class realities, is what conservatives do. The left must not do the same. On the contrary, we need constantly to remind ourselves that when right-wing political forces advocate the deregulation of economic activity – and talk of 'free markets' – they are not advocating the creation of a world in which no one makes economic decisions. They are not advocating a 'free world' of independent small-scale producers. Theirs is not some Jeffersonian democratic paradise waiting to be realised. They are seeking to call into existence a world in which economic decisions are entirely made by, and in the immediate interests of, the CEOs of major private companies. When, by contrast, the state regulates the market, political forces constrain the freedom of decision-making of those private actors. When left-wing political forces use the state to constrain that freedom, they also strike a new balance between social classes: between the various forms and manifestations of capital on the one side, and the various forms of paid and unpaid labour on the other. Social democracy in its 'Old Labour' form struck just such a balance – de-commodifying the provision of certain goods and services, and regulating the private provision of the vast majority of goods and services which remained to be bought and sold. Old Labour struck a particular social settlement, a particular class accord. The issue before us is whether, in the new glo-balised economy, that particular class compact has now to be replaced by one in which the freedom of business leaders to make decisions without regulation must increase again.

How we decide depends on how we understand globalisation as a process, and on what weight we give to the claim about its novelty. We will come to what is new here, and what is not, later in the chapter. But first we need to anchor globalisation, just as we did 'state–market' relations, in a wider discussion of class. Globalisation is also nor-mally discussed as a technical matter, a product of improvements in transport, communication and the production and dissemination of knowledge.[7] Or, if it is given a more social edge, it is discussed primar-ily in terms of capital: capital mobility, capital relocation, the rise of new centres of capitalist power, and so on. What is left off the table more often than it should be is the recognition that the dominant transformations in the global order currently are actually anchored not in the changing global conditions of capital so much as in those of *labour*. Capital is not suddenly globally mobile simply because of an IT revolution. Technological change of that kind facilitates and amplifies capital mobility, but does not create it. The enhanced global mobility of capital in the last three decades has social rather than technical roots. The thing that has changed most in the last generation is not capital mobility per se, though that mobility is striking, and politically significant. What has changed most is the size of the global labour force now seeking wage employment. It is that change which is truly novel. If the IMF is right, the effective size of the global proletariat has quadrupled since 1980, and its location has widened in qualitatively new ways.[8] We need constantly to remind ourselves that capital is more geographically mobile than it was in the past because it now has more workers on whom to land.[9]

A changed global context

The space for a progressive resettlement of state–market relations is always something that is simultaneously internally constructed and externally constrained. Progressive state–market relations have always to be fought for internally, and are always shaped by the global order surrounding the fight. Labour movements have to oblige local employing classes to make deals with them – the deals are never freely given – and the deals they make vary, depending on the strength of local labour movements. That was certainly the case immediately after the Second World War, in the heyday of old-style social democracy. The strength of northern labour movements varied even then – politically they were strongest in Scandinavian Europe, industrially they were strongest in the late 1940s in the north eastern United States – and so the settlements they struck varied. They negotiated, that is, not one but several *varieties of capitalism*.[10]

While that shared global order prevailed, different 'social structures of accumulation' could and did develop in different national capitalisms, and survive – even prosper – alongside each other because of their differences. For a whole generation, state actors, and their electorates, came to believe in the reality of national economic management, and of different national routes to a shared and increasing prosperity. The Americans did it one way: high wages but low worker rights; low taxes and the thinnest of welfare nets. The western Europeans did it another way: high job security and internal job flexibility; high taxes and a generous social wage. The Japanese did it differently again: long hours and guaranteed employment for core workers; big exports and only modest income growth at home. Even when they worked, each of these post-war settlements had its hidden side: rural (and increasingly urban) poverty among African-American workers and then among Hispanic migrants in the US; hidden female unemployment and exploited Turkish/Algerian workers in Germany and France; and massive job insecurity for the 75 per cent of the Japanese labour force denied lifetime employment. But at least these various models 'worked' when measured against their own pasts: no 1930s-type depressions, no world wars (just regional ones), and a significant increase in general living standards from one generation to the next.[11]

But though these class settlements varied internally, they were made possible by a *shared* global environment. The existence of global constraints on progressive politics is not new: what is new is the character of the constraints themselves. In capitalism's post-war 'golden age', a particular global order was in place, one that left a space for Keynesian-style welfare politics in advanced economies. That particular global order had at least three distinct features that have now gone:

• American economic hegemony within the capitalist bloc, with US dollars and production systems fuelling economic growth and maintaining job demand.

- Communism, splitting the world in two, hermetically sealing off vast swathes of Russian and Chinese labour from any participation in – and hence competition with – capitalist production and exchange.
- Colonial and neo-colonial control of the third world, locking labour there into subsistence agriculture or primary-producing export enclaves.

The internal result of that external global order was a temporary period of labour *shortage* in the first world, and the capacity of labour movements there to negotiate historically unprecedented class compacts. That is why Keynesianism had its moment. It is also why that moment has now gone, why 'Old Labour' no longer applies. Old-style social democracy is no longer viable, not because something called globalisation has arrived, but because a particular global order built on American leadership, colonial empires and a Cold War stand-off has been replaced by a global order of an entirely different kind. This is not globalisation as something new. It is simply one global order replacing another.

Neo-liberal globalisation as a class project

So, if we are properly to understand the space for a progressive resetting of state–market relations in the modern period, we must operate with a far more complex understanding of what is, and has been, involved in globalisation than is common in much of political commentary and popular writing these days. Genuine caution and precision are absolutely vital here, because there has always been a global dimension to capitalism as an economic system, and because that global dimension has always set limits on the autonomy of the national. We may indeed be in new times, but we would all do well to recognise that these new times are best seen as a new stage in an old story, not as the beginning of a story which is itself new. History did not begin in 1997 or in 1992, and we must avoid any form of argument that suggests the contrary.

Capitalism did not at some point *become* global. It *began* global: global in the sense of world trade, and global too in a more basic spatial sense. Capitalism emerged initially only in certain places. Indeed at first its capacity to develop depended on other places not being capitalist. Processes of unequal exchange between the capitalist and non-capitalist worlds were central to its emergence. Combined but uneven development was written into its global order from the outset. The capitalist world was always, to some degree, 'flat'.[12] It was also always, from the beginning, driven by powerful inner tensions:

tensions between capital and labour, over the rate and pace of work and the relative rewards accruing to each particular class; and tensions between capitalists themselves, and between different fractions of capital – tensions that drove each generation of capital holders perennially to search out new techniques, new markets and new sources of labour. The dynamics of spatial expansion in capitalism are not new. Globalisation is not a novel phenomenon. Marx described its core characteristics in *The Communist Manifesto* more than a century and a half ago. Indeed, if we are in a new phase of capitalist development, it is only because we seem at last to have reached the full flowering of the global reach of capitalism endemic to it from its inception.[13]

A sense of global history is important here, because global settlements in one stage of capitalist development frame the space for developments in the next. Certainly we need to remember that the centuries-long struggle within and between capitalism's core constituent classes had created, by 1900, a global economic order characterised by combined but extremely uneven economic development: a core of industrialising economies, surrounded by agrarian and subsistence societies as yet largely untouched by major capitalist penetration; with processes of unequal exchange between the core and more peripherally placed economies. Japan and bits of California and Brazil apart, industrial capitalism by 1900 had emerged only within an *industrial rectangle* that ran from, say, Chicago to Moscow in the north and from perhaps Baltimore to Milan in the south. Inside that rectangle, strong imperial nations flourished, colonising (directly or indirectly) the rest of the global surface, and drawing into their core area cheap supplies of raw materials and labour. Nineteenth-century capitalism may not have looked particularly global in scale and character to labour movements seeking some modest local control over wages and conditions of employment within the emerging industrial core, because so much of the rest of the world was still genuinely pre-capitalist in form; but nonetheless, global imbalance was as central a feature of early capitalism as it is of capitalism today. If we are in a new stage of capitalist globalisation now, it is a stage the novelty of which derives not from globalisation per se, but from the fact that we are witnessing the first significant expansion of that industrial core – the Asian tiger economies apart – since the end of the nineteenth century.

The 'Asian tiger' experience of the post-war period is all the more remarkable because, outside the core industrial rectangle of early twentieth-century global capitalism, industrial development after 1917 occurred on any scale only *beyond* the boundaries of capitalism itself – inside the Soviet Union – in a brutal process of forced modernisation imposed by Stalinist terror. Even there, in the post-war Soviet empire, living standards lagged behind the growth of productivity achieved in the capitalist west, and did so because the Soviets failed to match, after 1945, the capitalist bloc's generalised application of semi-automated production techniques across the consumer goods sector of each leading economy. As we have already noted, it was this post-war stand-off between capitalism and communism, the spread of Fordist production within the capitalist bloc, and the continued imbalance in terms of trade between the first world and the third, which alone gave post-war social democratic parties in western Europe the space for their 'Keynesian' moment. Keynesianism didn't fail in the 1970s because suddenly there was globalisation. As we have just seen, Keynesianism failed – and social democratic parties suddenly lost their way – because the productivity gains available through Fordism hit their limits, OPEC began to change the terms of trade between the first world and the third, and Cold War tensions began progressively to ease.

The modern global order now faced by progressive forces did not, therefore, fall out of the sky. Its current architecture of unrestricted capital mobility and global trade rules policed by the WTO is a created one – created in the main only recently, and created under the auspices of neo-liberal political leadership. The globalisation to which third-way politicians would have us subordinate all policy ambitions was actually designed by their political opponents – the newly ascendant conservatives in Washington and London. It was they – the Reaganites and the Thatcherites – who scrapped exchange controls, allowing capital to move freely across national borders. It was they who pushed, from one trade round to the next, for the opening of markets and the free movement of goods and services.[14] It was never a completely free market for which they pushed, and we need to remember that. Crucial political constituencies of the right – farmers and arms manufacturers alike – continue to this day to bask in protectionism, both overt and hidden; but progressive forces – the constituencies of the left – are now obliged to design their programmes of social reform in a global order in which national controls over the movement and development of productive resources have been progressively dismantled, and made illegal at the level of international/EU law.

It is not that the deployment of such productive resources is not now controlled – it is. It is simply that their deployment is controlled in the main by the senior executives of large private companies, who pay themselves handsomely for the burden of doing so. Those who were disarmed in the process of resetting the rules in this fashion were the labour movements of the core capitalisms – denied (by the construction of global trade rules that blocked state regulation) the instruments they had traditionally used to maintain at least a degree of control over the terms and conditions of their employment. That

disarming of the left was not some unexpected and accidental consequence of an unplanned expansion of world trade. There was agency
here – conscious design.

In the broadest sense, it is clear that leading elements within the
national state structures of a series of advanced capitalisms, far from
experiencing globalisation as an externally generated problem, have
in truth actively participated in the construction of the institutional
and legal frameworks within which this global capital mobility has
developed. They have competed with each other to lower exchange
controls, attract foreign direct investment and contain labour costs;
and they have done so with enthusiasm, in a determined attempt
to meet their own internally generated set of short-term electoral
requirements.[15]

'The era of globalisation' therefore is not best understood as something new, technically given to us from outside – a kind of *deus ex
machina* beyond question or control. The changing of the rules of
global trade is best understood as a class project: as a process designed
to alter the balance of class forces on a global scale. As the traditional
boundaries of the industrial rectangle were undermined by extensive
industrialisation in key areas of Asia and South America, the class
compacts institutionalised in each northern capitalist variety came
under challenge. Capital went to workers, not just workers to capital;
and capital went where labour was plentiful and cheap.[16] American
workers began to lose their pension schemes and their private health
benefits. British workers lost their national bargaining systems, and
saw their wage position in international league tables progressively
erode. Even Scandinavian workers found themselves in the 1990s
experiencing unprecedented levels of post-war unemployment. The
crisis of northern labour movements – both industrial and political
– was but a regional reflection of the changing balance of class forces
globally, such that its resolution, from a progressive point of view,
has to be anchored in a redressing of that global class imbalance.
Globalisation, that is, is not a thing – immutable because impersonal.
Globalisation is a social relationship – and like all social relationships,
it can be regulated. Indeed from a progressive standpoint, it must be
regulated, and soon.

A 'global order of layered exploitation'

So in class terms, what is the nature of the present global order? It
is a global order of layered exploitation – an entirely unprecedented
fusion of old and new labour conditions which, if not managed,
seems set fair to produce a cataclysmic 'race to the bottom' that will

destabilise both the old centres of industrial production and the new ones: the old ones because wages and employment will fall, the new ones because those wages and jobs are a vital source of demand for the mass commodity production now developing apace in the newly industrialising economies. Centre-left politicians inside the northern industrial rectangle have to operate for the first time in a global context in which *two* kinds of working class now co-exist: an 'old' northern working class with hard-won industrial and social rights to lose, and a new 'southern' working class without those rights but now beginning to seek them. The key task for northern progressive politics is to find policies that can protect and strengthen northern industrial and social rights without simultaneously undermining the spread of those same rights to workers in the newly industrialising 'south'. It will not be an easy task, but it is *the* vital one.

Historically, the extraction of surplus value – and hence profit – from paid labour in the capitalist world order has taken two broad forms.[17] Either people have been worked long and hard while being paid little and less; or they have been set to work alongside machinery, producing a larger volume of goods and being given back in wages at least some of the extra revenue generated. In classic Marxist terms, that is, labour under capitalism has been subject to processes of either *absolute* or *relative* surplus-value extraction: absolute rather than relative initially, but progressively relative rather than absolute, as machinery spread and hours of work went down. Certainly, inside the industrial rectangle after 1945, the wage–effort bargain eased as mechanisation spread. The arrival of machinery lowered hours. Trade unions negotiated better working conditions. Wages and profits even periodically rose together. But in the Asian tiger economies, and now in China and India, mechanisation did not produce any easing of the wage–effort bargain. On the contrary, new technologies were borrowed, but old labour conditions were retained. In the newly industrialising south, twenty-first century mechanisation and nineteenth-century working conditions have been fused together. Across vast swathes of India, China and Brazil, the labour conditions of early capitalism are being reproduced for new working classes using the technology developed in economies staffed by old working classes,[18] and in consequence an entirely new dynamic of global competition *within and between* working classes is now underway.

Early capitalism was all about taking people off the land – men, women and children, it made little difference – putting them into factories, making them work long hours in primitive conditions, and paying them as little as possible. The accumulation of capital in newly emerging economies required, and arguably still requires, that adverse effort–reward bargain.[19] Certainly in the nineteenth century, the early stages of industrial growth – in the UK and US no less than in Germany and Japan – required long working hours. It required intensive work routines (indeed the move from cottage to factory was largely prompted by that need to intensify the work process). It initially required the full mobilisation of all forms of labour (men, women *and* children); and it mobilised them as whole family units by paying wages at the very margin of human reproduction. Starvation wages, long hours, no relief from work and struggle: the early proletarian condition was truly one of unremitting toil, extensive exploitation and dreadful conditions of life and leisure.

The rise of organised labour movements, and the emergence of social democracy, was a belated response to the horror of those industrial conditions. As labour organised, and as states began to regulate labour markets and production processes – first through factory acts, then through the institutionalisation of bargaining rights – so progressively these absolute forms of surplus extraction gave way to relative ones. The resulting and eventually generalised mechanisation of industrial production broke the limits on productivity fixed by the limits of the human body. Capitalism moved into a managed phase in which northern labour at least could eventually win generalised rises in living standards, the generalised easing of working conditions, and the generalised spread of welfare systems. Level playing fields were created between competing national economies within the industrial rectangle at a higher and higher level of wages and with increased benefits for workers. This occurred because the vast bulk of industrial production took place in the industrial triangle, labour movements were similarly strong in all the main national economies, and the bar was systematically raised, generation by generation, either by governments of the centre-left or by governments of the centre-right keen to poach a centre-left electorate.

The resulting post-war class accords consolidated within the core industrial rectangle are now being challenged because of the reappearance, elsewhere in the global system, of an earlier form of capitalism. As each of us is doubtless all too aware, in parts of the global economy hitherto excluded from circuits of industrial production, new working classes are now being rapidly created whose current working conditions mirror those commonplace in the north in the nineteenth century, conditions from which northern workers have systematically escaped. So it is not just the fact that the *size* of the global working class has quadrupled in a generation to which northern centre-left politics now has to respond, though that huge expansion has certainly occurred. It is also that *working conditions* largely left behind in the north are back in full play in the industrialising south, with the labour conditions in the two spheres brought into direct relationship with each other through the centrality of northern wages to the export-led growth strategies of the globally 'southern' industrial owning classes.

Indeed there is now a growing sense that, as production spreads and trade flows thicken, the 'north' and the 'south' are increasingly merging together: retaining their capacity to illuminate as 'conceptual' distinctions as they lose their capacity as spatial ones. Certainly, as I write this in North Carolina, a part of my city is locked into competitive relationships and labour markets that are genuinely 'southern': textile firms and furniture makers obliged to compete with cheap-labour-based producers based in continents far away, and to do so either by cutting wages or by taking production out of North Carolina altogether. Yet another part of this same city – its high-tech and medical sectors – knows no such international competitive pressure: at least not yet. Employers and workers in those sectors know competition, but nothing of the intensity faced by their equivalents in furniture and textiles. Public policy in the geographical 'north' thus has to contend *internally and domestically* with a division of working conditions that once was purely *external and international*. A global system of combined and uneven development has come home to disfigure northern economies, where once it disfigured only the south. The task of the centre-left under those conditions becomes that of simultaneously protecting its own 'third-world' workers from super-exploitation while strengthening the competitive capacity of its own 'first world' ones. Doing these two things separately is never easy. Doing them together, particularly in present conditions, is especially difficult.

Why say 'particularly in present conditions'? Because globally, a classic contradiction of capitalism is also re-emerging: that of generalised over-production. Low wages in the newly industrialising south are eroding working-class wages in the already industrialised north, and yet those northern wages are central to the success of the southern growth process. Someone has to buy all that is produced, after all, and southern wage levels are insufficient for that purpose. It is a contradiction being held at bay for the moment, by the accumulation of unprecedented levels of personal debt, and major trade imbalances, in both the US and UK economies: America in particular remains 'the consumer of last resort' keeping the whole ship afloat. American consumers were certainly key to lifting the world out of recession in 2002 – but at a huge price to themselves: the price of spiralling debt, with more and more people buying goods now out of wages not yet earned, and adding to the cost of those goods over time by accumulating the cost of borrowing to pay for them. Debt practices of this kind must ultimately implode: which is why, until and unless the 'race to the bottom' implicit in this unregulated juxtaposition of old and new working classes is broken by policies that move 'southern' production processes from their 'absolute' to their 'relative' moment, all the gains so hard won by the northern working class in the twentieth century must be in serious jeopardy – and with them, the stability of the global system as a whole.

The progressive competitiveness impasse

So is the pursuit of a 'strategy of progressive competitiveness' by the political leadership of the US and UK labour movements the best way of reversing this race to the bottom? Gordon Brown certainly thinks so: he has presented his programme of European fairness and flexibility as a race to the top.[20] I remain unconvinced that he is right.

Even if a Brown-like combination of re-skilling and enhanced labour-market flexibility were to work, its consequences would hardly be progressive. Equipping people with skills doesn't guarantee them permanently rising wages. If history tells us anything, it is that wages rise when skills are in short supply, only to fall when they are not. In any case, globalisation is not just about new technologies: it's also – as we have seen – about a global increase in the supply of those willing to work. Competitive re-skilling to avoid unemployment simply shifts global unemployment around the Monopoly board, off the square on which we happen to be standing and onto that occupied by someone less educated than ourselves – and anyway, we're not the only players at the board. Everyone these days is busy re-educating and up-skilling its labour forces, and eroding hard-won trade union and worker rights. At most, all that a third-way 'progressive competitiveness' strategy can achieve is what we might call the treadmill effect: everyone running harder just to stand still. It is less a recipe for long-term economic success than for a perpetual intensification of the work process, and a steadily deteriorating trade-off between work and leisure.[21]

At worst, a strategy of progressive competitiveness simply camouflages a race to the bottom behind the language of a race to the top, as one centre-left government after another salami-slices away welfare programmes and business regulations in a desperate bid for fickle and impatient foreign capital. This is more the politics of the bordello than the politics of the left – whole labour movements standing around, displaying their wares, trying to attract passing business, credentialising themselves before transient foreign investors whose appetite for ever more concessions is only inflamed by concessions already consumed. Certainly in the UK case, a decade of the Brown strategy has so far failed to effect any significant regeneration of the industrial base. On the contrary, ten years of flexible labour markets and re-skilling initiatives have left the economy with a shrinking manufacturing base (the manufacturing sector now contributing less than 15 per cent of total UK GNP), a huge trade deficit, and unprecedented levels of unsecured personal debt. You get lots of hairdressers the progressive competitiveness way, and plenty of shops; but the goods you buy, and the money you buy them with, are increasingly foreign and borrowed.

No matter how compelling the rhetoric of a proselytising Gordon Brown can occasionally be, the consequences of his policies hardly constitute a viable base on which to sustain the long-term political dominance of third-way New Labour.[22] On the contrary, the electoral as well as the economic fall-out from deindustrialisation of this scale is likely to be considerable, as an overworked and over-stressed electorate eventually reject social democratic candidates who offer them only more of the same: more credentialising, more work flexibility, more job insecurity, longer and longer working hours.

Towards a global solution

Ultimately, the global dimension to economic activity under capitalism has always meant the same thing: that the conditions under which people labour in one part of the world system are intimately affected by the way people work in another part. That hasn't changed: what has changed is the proximity and visibility of the interdependence. Working conditions in different parts of the world are so intertwined now by the thickening of trade flows, and made so evident by the speed and quality of information flows, that conservative forces insist they constitute a new reality before which progressive forces are entirely impotent. You cannot tame the tiger, we are regularly told. You simply have to ride it. Unregulated markets may be tough, but they remain the only sure way to stay on top of the animal.

That cannot be the position of the contemporary centre-left. Production is a social process. It requires social relationships of production. Social relationships can and should be designed by those subject to them. Globalisation has not removed that truth. It has simply enlarged the canvas on which it must be pursued. To defend or extend economic and social rights in core capitalisms, progressive political forces now have to deal with class relationships in economies outside the core; but in truth they always did. The left used to turn a blind eye – leave those far-away relationships in their pre-capitalist, colonial or communist form – and pretend that the super-exploitation of second- and third-world labour made no contribution to its ability to be 'progressive' at home. The collapse of communism and the spread of industrial capitalism into hitherto underdeveloped third-world economies now make that blindness impossible. Being 'progressive' at home is therefore now harder; but what is required for effective progressive politics is also now clear. The conditions for effective progressive politics in core capitalisms are exactly the same as the conditions required for effective progressive politics in newly industrialising capitalisms: namely the resetting of the balance between capital and labour back in labour's favour. An insistence on human rights, and the pursuit of international labour standards, can therefore no longer be after-thoughts and add-ons to progressive policy packages in the twenty-first century. The design of progressive policies has to begin with them. *It has to start by addressing new questions created by new global conditions.* It has to start by asking: how do we strengthen the economic and social rights of labour in economies other than our own; how do we ensure that we do not salami-slice away gains made here by generations of workers before us; how do we keep alive the historic struggle to manage capitalism?

The progressive challenge: managing globalisation

In the early post-war period, it was possible for centre-left political formations in the core economies of the north to play the 'national card': to build programmes of economic growth and social reform that united an indigenous labour movement with locally based employers in common cause. The spread of production and the thickening of trade flows have rendered that alliance impossible: indigenous labour movements remain, but nationally focused employers no longer domi-nate production in key manufacturing sectors. Large-scale capital has gone global. What used to be a national bourgeoisie is now, at best, a dynamic small- and medium-sized business sector operating in the lee of multinational business. The centre-left has no choice – if it wishes to reproduce in this generation the fusion of interests that so civilised capitalism in the previous one – but to work at two levels at once: at the supranational level to re-impose constraints on global capital; and at the national level to strengthen locally focused businesses and the labour movements on whose purchasing power those smaller busi-nesses so heavily depend.

Managing global capitalism in this way will not be easy but it will be possible; made so because ultimately such management runs within the underlying grain of the global system as a whole. The intensifi-cation of pressure on wages, working conditions and job security is increasingly triggering workers' protests across this new global capi-talism, and building a base of shared experiences and interest between workers who were hitherto geographically and culturally scattered. What that intensification has not yet done is trigger a sufficiently extensive debate on the left on the content of the alternative economic strategies that global labour now requires. Ratcheting up wages and working conditions, rather than ratcheting down, will require robust and innovative policy stances on both the labour and capital sides of the economic equation. On the capital side, it will require at the very least the taxation of speculative capital, the democratisation of financial institutions, and the re-imposition of capital controls. On the labour side it will require, at the very least, the drafting and enforcement of global labour standards, and a significant extension of the role of workers and unions in corporate decision-making.[23] It will also require a new set of global trade rules. Free trade between economies with vastly different wage levels but common access to modern technologies can only spiral wages down everywhere. Fair trade, not free trade, must become the order of the day: fair trade between areas of sharply differing average incomes, and free trade within areas in which income levels have a greater degree of parity. Free trade within the north, fair trade between north and south.

Unregulated global markets are in no one's long-term interest. They hurt workers immediately, and they ultimately bring systemic instability in their wake. An earlier generation of progressives knew that. They used the state to regulate capitalism. They imposed controls on the deployment of capital, and demanded high and rising levels of worker remuneration and rights. They practised Keynesianism both globally and at home. They managed the global order. They did not surrender to it. It is time that we did the same.

Notes

1 James Callaghan said this to the Labour Party conference in 1976: 'we used to think that you could spend your way out of a recession and increase employment by cutting taxes and boosting government spending. I tell you in all candour that that option no longer exists, and in so far as it ever did exist, it only worked on each occasion since the war by injecting a bigger dose of inflation into the economy, followed by a higher level of unemployment as the next step' (Labour Party Annual Conference Report, 1976, p. 188).

2 On this, see B. Stafford, 'The Class Struggle, the Multiplier and the AES', in Malcolm Sawyer and Kerry Schott (eds), *Socialist Economic Review 1983* (London: Merlin, 1983), pp. 1–23.

3 On this, see D. Coates, *Prolonged Labour: The Slow Birth of New Labour Britain* (London: Palgrave, 2005), p. 34.

4 The phrase is Gordon Brown's: acting 'as the lubricant in the engine of the . . . economy' – speaking to the conference on 'New Policies for the Global Economy', London, September 1994.

5 G. Brown, *Global Europe: Full-employment Europe* (London: HM Treasury, October 2005), p. 11.

6 This characterisation of 'progressive competitiveness' is Greg Albo's, developed in contrast to what he termed the neo-liberal commitment to a strategy

of 'competitive austerity', viz: 'the neo-liberal view contends that unemployment is a specific, individual, voluntary problem of the labour market . . . in
this view, lowering the natural rate of unemployment depends upon lowering
inflation, so that capitalists can have more certainty about their investments,
and de-regulating non-market barriers which prevent real wages from falling
in the labour market and thus preventing new hires and higher levels of
productivity and investment'. This programme involves 'reducing trade union
power, minimizing welfare disincentives to work; improving information
flows and labour mobility; leaving investment in training to individual decisions on their "human capital" needs; and eliminating market restraints, such
as minimum wages and unemployment insurance, which limit downward
wage flexibility. . . . the spread [of these policies] has led to an unstable vicious
circle of *competitive austerity*: each country reduces domestic demand and
adopts an export-oriented strategy of dumping its surplus production, for
which there are fewer consumers in its national economy given the decrease
in workers' living standards and productivity gains all going to the capitalists,
in the world market. This has created a global demand crisis and the growth
of surplus capacity across the business cycle.' G. Albo, 'Competitive Austerity
and the Impasse of Capitalist Employment Policy', in R. Miliband and L.
Panitch (eds), *Between Globalism and Nationalism: the Socialist Register 1994*
(London: Merlin Press, 1994), pp. 146–7.

7   For an insightful discussion of globalisation as 'extensity, intensity, volume
and impact', see D. Held, A. McGrew, D. Goldblatt and J. Perraton, *Global
Transformations* (Cambridge: Polity Press, 1999), p. 15.

8   '. . . the effective global labor supply quadrupled between 1980 and 2005, with
most of the increase taking place after 1990. . . . East Asia contributed about half
of the increase, due to a marked rise in working age population and rising trade
openness, while South Asia and the former Eastern bloc countries accounted for
smaller increases.' International Monetary Fund, *World Economic Outlook 2007*,
Chapter 5, 'The Globalization of Labor' (Washington, DC, April 2007), p. 162.

9   'Globalization in its modern form is a process based less on the proliferation
of computers than on the proliferation of proletariats.' D. Coates, *Models of
Capitalism: Growth and Stagnation in the Modern Era* (Cambridge: Polity Press,
2000), p. 256.

10 The literature on 'varieties of capitalism' is now huge, most of it reviewed in
Coates, *Models of Capitalism*. Perhaps the best recent example of this literature
is J. Perraton and B. Clift (eds), *Where Are National Capitalisms Now?* (London:
Palgrave, 2004).

11 For this argument in more detail, see D. Coates, 'Capitalist Flattening or
Flattening Capitalism?', *Work Organisation, Labour and Globalisation* 1:2 (Summer
2007), p. 4.

12 The term is T. Friedman's, in his *The World is Flat: A Brief History of the Twenty-First
Century* (New York: Farrar, Straus and Giroux, 2005).

13 For a pithy overview of contemporary capitalism and its history, see J. Fulcher,
Capitalism: A Very Short Introduction (Oxford: Oxford University Press, 2004).

14 Not they alone, of course. Free trade agreements – especially NAFTA – have
been pushed by third-way elements within the US Democrat and UK Labour
parties, so demonstrating the closeness of the linkage between neo-liberalism
and third-way economic strategies. On the linkage for the UK, see D. Coates
and C. Hay, 'The Internal and External Face of New Labour's Political Economy',
Government and Opposition 30:4 (Autumn 2001), pp. 447–71.

15 Coates, *Models of Capitalism*, p. 261.

16 The ILO reported in 2004 that 2.8 billion people were employed globally in 2003. Nearly 50% of them survived on less than $2 a day; and 550 million of them earned less than $1 a day (*Guardian*, 8 December 2004).

17 For a more detailed exposition of this argument, see the unpublished paper 'New Class Forces, Old Class Realities': http://www.wfu.edu/politics/coatesd/index.html

18 The scale and speed of change in China is breathtaking. There were reportedly fewer than 22 million non-agricultural workers in China in 1978. By 2000 that figure stood at 151 million; and 151 million is bigger than the entire population of every contemporary nation-state bar five! Chinese real wages remain internationally extremely low and, until recently, also remarkably stable.

19 In Guangdong province, for example, 'where many export factories are based, base wages are reported at about $80 a month and working hours can be up to 80 a week', A. Glyn, 'Global Asymmetries', *New Left Review* 34 (July/August 2005), p. 21.

20 See, for example, Brown's article 'Open Trade is Needed Instead of Blocking Imports', *Financial Times*, 9 September 2005.

21 The strategy of 'progressive competitiveness' is 'neither socially progressive at the level of the world economy as a whole nor free of its own internal propensity to be undermined by similar initiatives elsewhere, whose cumulative effect is to leave individual economies persistently prone to the crises of competitiveness, unemployment and social retrenchment that re-skilling was meant to avoid. . . . You cannot get off the treadmill simply by running faster. All you can do by that mechanism is temporarily pass others, until they respond by running faster too, with the long-term consequence of having the whole field increase their speed just to stand still. The victor in such a race is not the runner, but the treadmill.' Coates, *Models of Capitalism*, p. 254.

22 On this, see L. Elliott and D. Atkinson, *Fantasy Island* (London: Constable, 2007).

23 'The Left needs to create a trade policy that, at the very least, privileges the protection of labour standards, introduces controls on capital flows, and encourages the bilateral negotiation of special trading terms with newly developing economies that pay higher wages. It needs one that replaces the economic maxims of free trade with the social concerns of fair trade, and one that actively manages Aggregate Demand at the global level – in true Keynesian style – in order to undermine the otherwise persistently reproduced inequalities that flow from the unregulated exchange of goods between unequal trading partners.' Coates, *Prolonged Labour*, p. 211.

9

Globalisation, New Technology and Economic Transformation

Robert Atkinson

For many, globalisation – the tighter and broader integration of product, service, financial and labour markets – is at the core of the economic and social transformation of the last quarter-century. To be sure, the nature and extent of globalisation is new and unprecedented and it is easy to view globalisation as the key mover of change.

But while the extension of markets beyond national borders has amplified and accelerated structural economic and social changes, the fundamental driver, not just of globalisation but of many of these changes in the economy and society, has been the information and communications technology (ICT) revolution. In just twenty-five years we went from a world of electric typewriters to one of laptop computers more powerful than the mainframe computers of that era; from dial pay phones to GPS-enabled cell phones; from 8-track cassette players to iPods. Without the ICT revolution, globalisation as we know it would not be possible.

In this chapter, I first argue that economic transformations of the kind we are in the midst of today have occurred on a regular basis over the last several hundred years, and at their heart they are driven by technological revolutions.[1] I then examine how the last great economic transformation from the regional factory economy to the national mass production corporate economy after the Second World War led to the same kinds of geographic restructuring of production that we are experiencing today, only on a national level, as opposed to a global one. I then discuss how the new technology-driven economy is driving not just globalisation, but many of the economic effects we commonly attribute to globalisation. In other words, while globalisation has had an impact on industrial change, economic dislocation and income inequality, these changes are driven more by a technology-driven transformation to a new economy, in particular by the ICT revolution, than by globalisation per se.

Finally, I argue that while progressives are right to push for a global economy that achieves the kind of goals that most post-war developed nation economies achieved – robust growth that is broadly shared – to achieve that goal today, we need to shift to renewed progressive governance. The most important aspect of this will be to advocate a new global growth economics that puts in place policies and incentives to shift nations' economic policies away from negative-sum mercantilism and towards a positive-sum growth economics focused, first and foremost, on boosting productivity.

Economic transformations

Why has ICT driven the recent economic transformation? In a nutshell, it is because IT prices have plummeted, performance has exploded, *and* usability has improved in parallel over the last decade. If just one of these had happened, the digital revolution would have been stillborn. If prices had fallen without performance improvements, the result would be cheap but not very effective technologies. If performance had improved without price declines, IT would have proven too expensive to put into everyday devices and applications. If both happened but the technology remained hard to use, adoption rates would be significantly lower. Luckily, all three happened.

Moreover, the technology is anything but static. As ICT continues getting cheaper, faster, better and easier to use, organisations continually find new and expanded uses for IT every day, as the recent emergence of *YouTube* illustrates. It has become pervasive in its use and its impact, going far beyond just the internet and personal computers. As some keen observers of the digital economy point out, 'at each point in the last 40 years the critical step in the transformation of technological potential into economic productivity has been the discovery by ICT users of how to employ their ever greater and ever cheaper computing power to do the previously impossible'.[2]

Today, information technology enables the creation of a host of tools to create, manipulate, organise, transmit, store and act on information in digital form in new ways and through new organisational forms. As a result, ICT has transformed the internal operations of organisations (business, government and non-profit), transactions between organisations, and transactions between individuals, acting both as consumers and as citizens, and organisations. ICT has been instrumental in enabling the emergence of much more globalised markets in goods, services and finances.

Indeed, it is hard to imagine how today's globally dispersed production systems would work without ICT to knit them together, whether it is computer-based logistics systems that enable companies to weave together multinational supply chains; e-mail and low-cost telecommunications systems that let managers communicate easily across the globe;[3] or software, Internet and digital telecommunications capabilities that enable the dispersed location of a whole host of information-based services, such as call centres, back-office processing and software production.[4]

The technology revolution has not only improved our communications system, but made it more economical to ship products. Not only is the cost of shipping a pound of pig iron from Australia to Zaire lower, but as the weight-to-value ratio of products has increased, shipping costs as a share of total costs have declined. When most of the value of the economy was made up of heavy things that did not cost much (e.g. cement, wood, fish, commodity steel), it made little sense to ship them very far. But as the economy has become increasingly made up of lighter things that cost more (e.g. computer chips, airplanes, drugs) it is now economical to ship them around the globe. This is one reason why the inflation-adjusted value of US trade per pound has risen by approximately 4 per cent per year on average over the last three decades.

Furthermore, the weight of an increasing share of the economy is zero, since many services (e.g. insurance, software, media, call centres) can be transported in bytes, as opposed to atoms. A host of products that we once thought were tied to the local community in which they are consumed are now footloose. Retail transactions can be conducted 5,000 miles away over the Internet sometimes more easily than they could be 10 miles away on a busy road. Local business functions like banking, insurance and securities brokering are now conducted by phone and net at a distance. An array of professional services, including law and accounting, can be conducted online.

Indeed, the ICT revolution has enabled an increasing share of information-based services to remain physically distant from the customer (e.g. e-banking) or the other parts of the production process (e.g. back-office operations) while staying functionally close. The new digital economy is transforming economic geography, enabling as many as 12 to 14 million once relatively immobile information-based jobs in the United States to now potentially be located virtually anywhere across the globe.[5] In the New Economy, someone in Japan can purchase stocks online from E-Trade or Charles Schwab just as easily as someone in the United States. It is almost as easy to locate a call centre in Hyderabad, India, as it is to put it in Hagerstown, Maryland.

By improving supply chains and information on potential economic opportunities and reducing communication costs, ICT is allowing businesses, and indeed most organisations, to rearrange inputs, labour and capital as never before. These new globalised production chains allow businesses to specialise in what they are good at, contract out what they do less well, and reach scales that minimise costs and maximise innovation.

Why has ICT had such far-reaching and profound effects? The short answer is that ICT is what economists call a 'general purpose technology'.[6] Unlike other technologies that may affect just one process or one sector, general-purpose technologies (GPTs) are used pervasively and in most sectors. Moreover, the performance and price of GPTs improve over time, often quite dramatically. Finally, GPTs make it easier to invent and produce new products, processes and business models.

GPTs don't just lead to new products; they often lead to fundamental societal and economic transformations. Technologies like the steam engine, railroads, electricity, the internal combustion engine and steel are all examples of general-purpose technologies that drove economic transformation and growth in the past. The modern industrial economy of the early 1890s would have been impossible without the emergence of GPTs like steel and electricity. The emergence of cheap steel in the 1880s and 1890s transformed not just the steel industry, but also almost all manufacturing, since a wide array of industries, such as those producing bicycles, sewing machines and machine tools, could now take advantage of high-strength steel.

Through studying these technology-fuelled revolutions, noted economist Joseph Schumpeter was led to argue that the process of economic change is not an incremental and linear one – as most neo-classical economists conceive it to be – but rather a process of revolutionary transformation. New technologies do not advance incrementally, but rather burst onto the scene irregularly with clusters of breakthrough technologies, and resultant transformations from one kind of society to another. Schumpeter noted that 'These revolutions are not strictly incessant; they occurred in discrete rushes that are separated from each other by spans of comparative quiet. The process as a whole works incessantly, however, in the sense that there is always either revolution or absorption of the results of revolution.'[7]

We've been there before

Today's rapid economic, social and political changes driven by ICT are by no means unprecedented. This series of transformations, occurring roughly every fifty years, from one kind of economy and society to another, has in fact been the dominant if underappreciated story of advanced industrial economies.

These technology-led revolutions are exciting, sometimes breath-takingly so. They enable the creation of inspiring and important new products and services. They revive and spur economic growth. They provide the grist for a host of new entrepreneurial opportunities. However, as Schumpeter noted, while they are creative, they are also destructive. They upset conventional ways of doing things. They force individuals, organisations and even whole regions to adapt or suffer the consequences of not doing so. They turn some industries and occupations into 'buggy whip industries', with little real purpose any-more. In short, they produce winners and losers. Indeed, it is because technology-led revolutions both create and destroy that they are so troubling to so many people.

However, this is not the first time that economies have been through such a large transformation involving a dramatic geographic expan-sion of markets. The same process of geographical expansion and reordering has occurred before, albeit at the national level. The last major technology-led economic transformation – the emergence of the corporate mass production economy after the Second World War – also led to a dramatic expansion of the scope of most markets and led to a shifting spatial locus of economies.

In the United States, companies that had largely bought and sold from suppliers and customers in a particular region now did so throughout the entire nation. The US west and south, which had hith-erto served as peripheral regions supplying natural resource inputs to the midwest and east, were transformed into thriving and competi-tive industrial economic regions. As a result, factories that were once concentrated in the midwest and northeast began to migrate to the south and west. National corporations could now more easily manage a nationally dispersed production network (being able to fly to the plants, communicate by telephone, and more easily ship products to markets throughout the nation); they moved facilities that didn't require the more skilled labour of the north and midwest to the south and west. Whole industries decamped from the core to the periphery.

Just as today's globalisation is enabled by ICT, that era's 'nation-alisation' was enabled by new technologies. Air travel, long-distance communications and truck transport began to recast regional rela-tionships, allowing interlinked economic activities to spread. With the building of interstate highways, metropolitan regions and finally the entire nation were tied together. Widespread electrification allowed industry much greater locational freedom. The development of air conditioning made living and working in hot southern and western climes more tolerable. Additionally, the spread of mechanisation and 'chemicalisation' to the farm drove agricultural productivity.

And just like today, these changes were driven, at least in part, by wage differentials. In 1938, the richest state in the south was poorer than any state outside the south. Even by 1960, the per capita income in the south ($1,754) was significantly lower than in the United States as a whole ($2,223). Also like today, there were widespread calls to develop national as opposed to regional labour standards, so that the firms would have less incentive to decamp the north and midwest in search of low wages in the south and west.

Could this post-war transformation from regional to national markets have been stopped? Surely not, just as today's transformation to global markets cannot be stopped. Even if Congress had made it easier to form unions, and if the south and west were unionised at the same rates as the rest of the nation, this would have only slowed the process of industrial migration and expansion, for non-labour factor costs (e.g. land, power) were lower, and these regional markets were growing and would be served by national producers who sought the kind of scale economies that serving a national market brought.

Just as the shift from regional to national markets was preordained by technological developments and by the forces of capitalist expansion, so today is the shift from national to global markets inevitable. As much as some might wish to slow down, contain, or even reverse globalisation, the trend is unstoppable. Travel and communications will continue to get faster and cheaper and supply chains will be tied together to an even greater degree by inter-operable software. And linking it all together is what will become an even more inter-operable operating system, the English language.

Is globalisation the cause or the result?

Given the pervasiveness of globalisation it is easy to view it as the major driver of the changes – good and bad – that have transformed developed nations. But if this is true, these changes should be largely concentrated in those sectors of the economy most exposed to globalisation. This, however, is not the case, and suggests broader causes for the changes we see.

Let us start with changes in the total number of jobs. Some critics of globalisation in general, and trade agreements in particular, argue that globalisation leads to fewer jobs for the United States. In contrast, globalisation advocates often argue the opposite, that trade creates jobs. The *Washington Post*, for example, asserts that NAFTA was responsible for the creation of several hundred thousand US jobs. Either view may actually be right in the short term.[8] In the short run, growth (or decline) in a nation's trade deficit can have a negative (or positive) effect on employment. If imports grow faster than exports and all else is constant, GDP falls. But while there can be employment effects (growth or decline) in the short run, in the moderate and long run, trade has no effect on employment. Employment levels are determined by the supply of labour on the one hand, and the demand for it on the other. The demand for labour – in other words, full employment – is determined largely by macroeconomic factors such as interest rates, and microeconomic factors such as whether nations pay able-bodied individuals to not work.

Hence, if trade has no effect on the total number of jobs, it may have an effect on the sectoral composition of the economy. The factor perhaps most often invoked to highlight the impact of globalisation is the decline in manufacturing employment. From its high-water mark of 21 million workers (23 per cent of the workforce) in 1979, US factory employment fell to just 14.3 million workers (10.8 per cent) in 2004.[9] But the United States is not the only country facing such a decline. Japan lost more than 2 million manufacturing jobs in the 1990s, as the economy shifted more to services, while manufacturing's share of GDP in Germany fell from 33 per cent in 1990 to 24 per cent in 2001. For the EU15, of 26 industrial sectors, only one (rubber and plastics) had greater employment in 2001 than in 1979.[10]

Is globalisation the culprit? For a nation like Germany with an increase in its goods trade surplus (or in the case of Japan, a small decrease), globalisation cannot be the cause. Globalisation has meant more, not less, manufacturing production.[11] The US, to be sure, is in a class by itself. It is running unprecedented goods deficits at over 5 per cent of GDP, up sharply from the 1980s. However, even in the US, the principal cause of manufacturing job loss has not been the growth in the goods trade deficit, but rather differential productivity growth. Since 1997 manufacturing productivity has grown approximately 75 per cent faster than the overall economy. This means that manufacturers can produce the same amount of output with fewer workers. The same process has been at work in Europe, where EU15 manufacturing productivity grew approximately 50 per cent faster than the overall economy from 1979 to 2001.[12]

As a result, even if the US trade deficit had not increased, manufacturing's share of jobs would have declined. However, in contrast to some who claim that the increase in the trade deficit has not hurt US manufacturing,[13] this does not mean that a growing goods trade deficit has not played some role in the relative decline in manufacturing loss. Simple logic suggests that it had to. If a nation is satisfying its demand for consumption of goods by increasing its relative consumption of foreign products, and goods exports are not growing a commensurate amount, this means by definition that domestic goods production will be less than it would be otherwise.

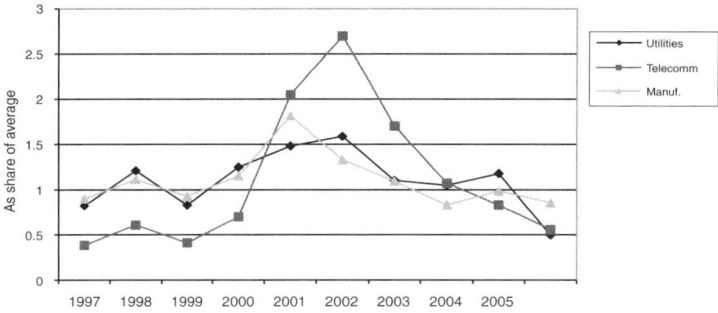

Figure 1   Job Loss by Sector, 1990 to 2006

Source: Authors' own compilation based on US Bureau of Labor Statistics 2008

The recent decline of the US dollar vis-à-vis most other currencies – a natural and welcome development, given that economic theory dictates that currency levels should fall (or rise) if a nation runs a large trade deficit (or surplus) – is already causing the goods trade deficit to shrink modestly and exports to grow. Continued decline in the dollar, especially against significantly overvalued Asian currencies, would lead to an even lower US goods trade deficit and a slowdown in the rate of manufacturing job loss. However, even if the goods trade deficit declines significantly, manufacturing jobs will likely continue to fall as a share of total employment, at least for the next several decades, since it remains easier to boost productivity in manufacturing than in services.

If manufacturing were the only sector that had seen job losses, and if the job losses from the increased trade deficit were large, the case for globalisation's impact would be stronger. But other sectors that are not traded internationally, such as electricity and gas services and telecommunications, suffered similar, and in some years actually had greater job losses than did manufacturing from 1990 to 2006 (see figure 1). Likewise, between 2000 and 2006 travel-agent jobs declined by 36,000, or 30 per cent, not because of trade, but because of the rise of online travel sites. Telemarketing jobs fell by 77,000, or 17 per cent, largely because of passage of the national 'do not call' legislation.

While trade is not the major cause of job loss at the major industry sector level, it has had greater impact on particular industries, with some sectors seeing job gains and others losses. A case in point is textiles and clothing. While manufacturing jobs fell 20 per cent from 1998 to 2006, textile and clothing jobs fell by 46 per cent, a loss of almost 700,000 jobs. In contrast, jobs in the aircraft industry, one of the few manufacturing sectors where the United States runs a trade surplus, fell by just 22 per cent over the same period. Regions and communities dependent on textile and clothing production have, not surprisingly, been hard hit by dislocations. For example, North Carolina, home to textiles and clothing production since the Second World War, has lost 27 per cent of its manufacturing jobs since 2000, compared to a loss of 18 per cent nationally.

Even if trade has not been the major cause of job loss in certain sectors, some argue that we have only experienced the tip of the globalisation iceberg and the worst is yet to come. Perhaps most widely known for holding this view is economist Alan Blinder, who presented a provocative and disturbing thesis: the off-shoring of service sector jobs is not just a routine extension of international trade, but a 'third industrial revolution' likely to lead to one in every three American jobs being shipped overseas.[14]

Yet Blinder's projections are vastly exaggerated. In overstating the number of jobs likely to be off-shored (probably by a factor of ten), Blinder makes three critical errors.[15] First, he overestimates the number of jobs that are tradeable.[16] Second, he overestimates the share of those jobs likely to be off-shored. And third, he omits the offsetting increase in service sector jobs from expanded exports. This last omission is particularly important since it is unlikely that the US trade deficit would grow by a factor of five or more, which is the level implied by Blinder's dire warnings, since other nations would surely tire of providing us with that amount of goods and services while receiving only Treasury notes in return.

Finally, even if trade were to have no impact overall on manufacturing employment or employment in particular sectors, trade could still lead to job losses (and gains) in particular companies and plants, leading to significant disruption for individual workers, and in some cases whole communities dependent on those plants. To be sure, such employment churning has increased. Overall, the rate of companies going out of business was at least three times greater in the boom years of the late 1990s than it was in the 1970s. And this risk is not just borne by workers (at least the risk of losing one's job). A CEO appointed after 1985 was three times more likely to be fired than one appointed before that date.[17] However, it is not clear to what degree this has been caused by globalisation.

Historically comparable data on layoffs are limited. But recent data paint a mixed picture. For example, in the early 2000s the rate of layoffs and discharges as a share of total employment in retail trade and manufacturing were about comparable. However, since then the rate in retail trade has been about 25 per cent higher than in manufacturing, even though very little retail trade is 'traded' internationally. Likewise, data on large layoffs paint a similarly mixed picture. In the second half of the 1990s (the most recent years for which data are available) mass layoffs were higher in manufacturing than in retail. However, in the last several years they are on average about 20 per cent lower in manufacturing, but about 20 per cent higher in retail.

This suggests that while churning and risk have gone up, the causes go beyond globalisation and extend to other factors, particularly more competitive markets, more dynamic business environments, and rapidly changing technologies. These changes mean that firms' competitive advantage can be lost very quickly. Harvard's Clayton Christensen popularised this notion with his best-selling book *The Innovator's Dilemma*, which showed how the new environment provided much less security for companies, even ones that did everything right.

If globalisation is not the major cause of increased risk and dynamism, surely it is at the root of declining wages. Many critics argue that the current process of globalisation drives down wages in either developing nations, or developed nations, or even in both. Former AFL-CIO economist Tom Palley argues, for instance, that globalisation and off-shoring 'have put U.S. workers in competition with two billion workers around the world, putting downward pressure on wages, benefits and working conditions'.[18] Statements like this lead many to believe that globalisation is reducing wages for everyone. In reality, this view mistakes changes in distribution of wages for overall wages. It simply doesn't matter how many workers join the global labour market. There will be no effect on average US (or European) wages or overall GDP for the simple reason that prices and wages are the flip side of the same coin.

While globalisation has not lowered average wages or output, it has contributed to growing income inequality. But the extent to which this has occurred is not clear. Some argue that globalisation is responsible for holding down the wages of most workers, while allowing a new global elite of managers and professionals, coupled with capital investors, to be the big winners.[19] Others have highlighted the stagnation of the middle class. Here, the starting point for relevant claims is the disjuncture between growth in productivity and growth in household income. Many point to the fact that GDP per person is up 63 per cent from 1979 to 2005, but real median household income has inched up a mere 13 per cent. If median household income had grown at the level of GDP per person growth, it would have been $20,656 more than it actually was. Surely this is rock-solid evidence of the middle-class squeeze, and it is not too far to the next step of laying the blame on globalisation.

Yet, upon closer examination, things are not quite that simple. Labour economist Stephen Rose has shown that the main reason for the large gap between productivity and median household income growth is that it is equivalent to comparing apples to oranges.[20] While it might seem natural to use GDP per capita growth as the basis of productivity growth, this is not appropriate if the goal is to link it to changes in household income. This is because changes in household size can have big consequences for median household income.

In this context, it is important to note that some groups below the CEO level have fared reasonably well. As Rose notes, women did particularly well, at least compared to where they were before. While many point to the fact that real median wages for males in the United States were unchanged between 1979 and 2005, they conveniently overlook the fact that real median wages for women were up 54 per cent. In fact, as recently as 1980, more than 60 per cent of women workers were in the lowest pay category, and only 3 per cent earned more than $50,000 a year. By contrast, today more than 36 per cent of new jobs for women pay more than $50,000.[21] Moreover, there was a significant rise in the share of male workers earning more than $75,000, thanks to growth in the managerial and professional sectors. The group that appears to have suffered the most is that of less educated men. Rose found that more than one-third of new jobs filled by men between 1979 and 2005 paid $25,000 or less.

So what is the impact of globalisation on this still troubling growth in inequality? Like the story in employment change, it appears that a number of different factors have contributed to the growth in inequality. The consensus among most economists is that trade has had only a relatively small impact on the increase in inequality within the United States.[22] To the extent that trade contributed, it is seen, along with technology, as driving inequality through fostering a fall in the relative demand for unskilled labour and an increase in that for skilled labour. According to this theory, trade and technology have increased the skill level of jobs, while at the same time the share of the workforce with a college degree has not expanded as fast, resulting in a labour shortage and an increase in these wages. Yet, while the skill-based explanation is appealing – it leads to a solution virtually everyone supports, namely more education – it alone cannot be the cause of the widening gap. If it were, then inequality among college-educated workers would not have increased.

But from 1974 to 1988 the 90/10 split among college-educated workers grew and then stabilised, while the 90/50 wage gap continued its upward trend.[23] As Autor et al. note, changes in education levels played some role in the growth of 50/10 and 90/10 inequality, but almost no role in the rise of 90/50 inequality.[24] This is reflected in the fact that the earnings of the top 0.01 per cent of taxpayers went from 50 times more than the average taxpayer's income in 1970 to 250 times by 1998.

An alternative and more satisfactory explanation is that changes in institutions and norms have played a bigger role.[25] The decline in private sector unionisation, while albeit related to globalisation, is one factor.[26] But other factors have little or nothing to do with globalisation. For example, the failure of policy-makers to increase the minimum wage as fast as inflation has contributed to increased inequality. This shortcoming has had nothing to do with globalisation, as jobs exposed to foreign competition usually pay above the minimum wage.[27]

Moreover, changes in social and institutional norms also seem to have played a more important role in this process than technology-based skill changes. In the old economy norms and practices limited large discrepancies in compensation, but these restraining norms diminished. What were once internal labour markets became external ones, with companies willing to hunt for the best talent and bid up their compensation to get them. Likewise, as the 'organisation man' became replaced by the 'free-agent man', individuals have become much more willing and likely to leave organisations in search of the best deal.[28] Globalisation may have increased the size of the prize, but norms and market conditions enable this phenomenon.

One of the implications of this is that the answer to modestly rising inequality is neither to limit globalisation and technology, nor to rely on the supposed silver bullet of education. In the 1990s, many progressives held out increased skills and education as the answer to inequality. While more education might help reduce the 50/10 split by helping the lowest-income workers gain more skills, it is not likely to do much to reduce the 90/10 split. The reason top CEOs, lawyers, doctors, entertainers, etc., get such winner-take-all salaries is not because there are too few college-educated graduates vying for their positions. It is because small differences in skill level result in large differences in performance and output and the market is willing to reward that. Thus, looking to means such as a higher minimum wage and higher top marginal tax rates are likely to be much more effective at reducing inequality.

Moving from populist resistance to renewed progressive governance

As each transformation from an old economy and old society to a new one was underway, each spread confusion and conflict, but each ultimately led to vast improvements in the quality of life for Americans. Defying economic transformations is a dead end – this insight remains as true today.

The rise of the new knowledge-based global economy has created both opportunities and challenges. Opposition and resistance to globalisation need to give way to a focus on managing it. Above all, the challenge is to shift to a progressive, rather than populist, agenda for the new global economy. While it is beyond the scope of this chapter to lay out in detail what this agenda should look like, it is worth highlighting two key components.

First, moving from new economy populism to new economy progressivism means abandoning the belief that globalisation is based on choices that individuals and organisations can make differently. John Kerry's attack on US corporate CEOs as 'Benedict Arnolds' in the 2004 presidential campaign was an example of this mistaken belief that individual choice is an important factor. While in theory CEOs have choices, the reality is that any CEO who does not take full advantage of global opportunities would be summarily dismissed by his or her board of directors. As a result, the issue is not about blaming individuals, companies, or the corporate community generally; it is about creating the kinds of incentives and environment that will bring about the economic results that benefit nations. For developed nations this means putting in place a much more robust domestic innovation and competitiveness agenda, coupled with a real effort to help individuals and communities better manage this new and riskier economic environment.[29]

Second, one reason why there is so much opposition to globalisation is the very real sense that there are no rules guiding the process. Indeed, globalisation will only work effectively – produce the most increase in wealth and ensure that the most people benefit – if all nations play by the right agreed-upon rules. Unfortunately, the global economy is increasingly characterised by zero-sum, or even negative-sum, beggar-thy-neighbour actions that lead to greater levels of disruption and lower levels of global growth, including tariff and non-tariff barriers to imports, subsidies to attract investment and promote exports, forced technology transfer, theft of intellectual property, and tax policies, like border-adjustable value added taxes, that subsidise exports.

However, the most prevalent and most damaging mercantilist practice is the rampant and widespread currency manipulation that many governments engage in today. In fact, currency manipulation is at the heart of the current problems with globalisation. One reason why ending currency manipulation is so important is that market-based currency adjustment is the way high-wage nations compete with low-wage ones. If a low-wage nation has an absolute advantage over a high-wage one, a falling currency in the high-wage one is the natural adjustment mechanism. This makes imports more expensive and exports cheaper, restoring equilibrium.

If we are to maximise global growth, the flow of goods, services and capital should be determined on the basis of actual costs and prices, not on implicit or explicit subsidies. Economists have long argued that subsidies produce inefficient results. Yet, mercantilist policies to keep currency prices below what market forces would dictate (either pegging to levels below true levels, as in the case of nations like China, or propping up currency by government purchases as in the case of many nations, including Japan) is as pure a subsidy as if the government wrote cheques to exporters. Ending currency manipulation would go a long way in easing opposition to globalisation and maximizing its benefits, even for the nations currently propping up their currencies.

This is not to say that nations should not be allowed to manage currency transitions so that they are not overly abrupt. However, systematic manipulation to gain competitive advantage by beggaring thy neighbour – a practice that violates IMF rules[30] – needs to stop, and the only way this will happen is if the nations who engage in it less than others (particularly the US, Canada and Europe), and international organisations including but not limited to the IMF, agree to co-operate to fight it.

As destructive as currency manipulation is, it is but a symptom of a broader problem, a misguided economic philosophy that many nations still maintain: mercantilist policies that see exports in general, and high-value added exports in particular, as the holy grail. This new mercantilism stresses high savings rates, low labour costs, technology policies to shift to high-value added manufacturing output, and export-led growth. Even if this strategy might have worked for some smaller nations like Taiwan and Korea in the past, it simply cannot work today. The markets of Europe and the United States are simply not large enough if nations like Brazil, China, India, Russia and other Asian nations continue to promote exports while limiting imports as their primary path to prosperity.

But there is a more fundamental problem with mercantilism. While it might lead to higher wealth in a few relatively small export-based industries, it does nothing to raise productivity in the rest of the economy. While the Indian ICT sector has created new opportunities for India, it accounts for only around 3 per cent of national value added. But productivity in India is just 8 per cent of US rates while Chinese productivity is 14 per cent. It is better but still problematic in more developed nations. Despite some extremely productive and innovative multinational firms, overall Japanese productivity is just 70 per cent of US rates and South Korea just 50 per cent.[31] Without higher productivity levels, it is impossible for these nations to raise their standards of living.

These anaemic levels of productivity in non-traded sectors do not occur by happenstance. They are a result in part of these nations concentrating their economic policies on supporting export sectors, including engaging in a host of unfair and mercantilist trade practices that are designed to limit imports and spur exports. These policies win the favour of powerful constituents (e.g. domestic producers seeking protection from foreign IT competitors; consumers who don't want to pay for software and other digital products; workers seeking policies to protect their jobs from competition) and only risk alienating some WTO officials, who seldom act to stop such practices.

This is a much easier political lift than engaging in the hard struggle of driving up productivity and dynamism in all sectors. Such policies would risk the opposition of powerful interests: unions and workers who may be displaced; domestic producers, including small businesses, who enjoy cosy relationships and low levels of competition; able-bodied individuals who are paid for not working; and government bureaucrats whose top-down control is challenged. But it is only by spurring competition and the use of the best production tools – often by increasing the use of information technology[32] – that these nations will see fast increases in standard of living.

As a result, over the last several decades the global economic system has become systematically distorted, with an increasing number of nations favouring beggar-thy-neighbour policies to attract and expand high-wage industries. Yet, it is worse than this. It would be one thing if nations were focused on boosting and expanding these technology-based industries through supportive policies like increased funding for research, government adoption of IT and e-government systems, educating highly skilled workers, and developing broadband infrastructure. These policies are not only fair but they enlarge the global pie by increasing productivity and innovation. They could erode US and European competitive advantage, but in our hyper-competitive global economy firms as well as nations routinely and legitimately compete to gain advantage. The real problem arises when countries resort to heavy-handed mercantilist negative-sum policies that end up lowering global economic productivity.

If export-led mercantilism is not the answer, what is? For most progressives the answer is to extend the post-war domestic demand-side Keynesian economic framework to the global arena. Just as progressives in the old economy saw the key economic threat as insufficient consumer demand, they see the problem of the global economy as one of too much production and too little demand. Accordingly, they favour a new global policy regime to boost demand in developed and developing countries alike. The Center for American Progress, for example, advocates an 'agenda of economic institution-building, including stronger safety nets and labor, environmental, consumer and investor laws and institutions that will enable the gains in national income brought by those countries' integration into the world economy to be shared more widely by their populations'.[33]

Progressives make a number of arguments for these reforms. The most important is the claim that they are the key to raising living standards in developing nations. But a fairer distribution of a small pie, while often helpful, is not the answer to solving developing-nation poverty; expanding the size of the pie is. Take the case of India. Any visitor to India cannot but be struck by the vast and desperate poverty. Yet, even if India pursued a radical redistribution programme so that every person received the same income, the average Indian would make just $3,800 (in purchasing-power parity), compared to $43,800 in the United States. The only sustainable answer for raising living standards for the vast majority of citizens in developing and developed nations is to raise productivity across the board, not to push exports or income redistribution.

Some progressives also argue that these redistributionist policies, including stronger enforcement of labour standards, won't just help developing nations, they will help developed ones as well. By raising wages and other business costs in developing nations, thereby reducing cost differentials between developed and developing nations, these policies will supposedly reduce imports by developed nations and spur exports from them. But while stronger labour and environmental standards are important to helping developing nations, implementing these would raise business costs in these nations by only a small margin. In addition, if currency prices are allowed to be set by the market, then wage differentials become irrelevant to export performance and competitiveness.

Like neo-mercantilists, global Keynesians also mistakenly equate growth in exports with economic growth. They believe that expanded trade and investment with developing countries drives strong increases in their living standards and consumption, which in turn generates additional demand for our own products and services, with the result of producing further improvements in our own living standards. But this is based on the view that living standards grow with more exports. Yet, as long as an economy is close to full employment, living standards are determined largely by domestic productivity rates, not by whether exports go up or down.

Conclusion: the need for 'growth economics'

Fortunately, the choice is not a stark one between neo-mercantilism and global Keynesianism. There is a progressive alternative which can be termed 'growth economics'. Growth economics is based on the view that the path to higher incomes entails raising domestic productivity by all firms in all sectors. It is also based on the view that it is not the amount of capital (financial or human) that nations have that is most important, but how that capital is used.[34] And it is based on the view that microeconomic factors (e.g. product and labour-market competition, technology policies, etc.) are more important to growth than macroeconomic ones.

Under a growth economics doctrine, the central task of global economic policy should be to encourage all nations to make raising domestic productivity a key priority. For example, Indian retail banking is just 9 per cent as productive as US levels and retail goods sector productivity is just 6 per cent. If India could raise productivity in these two sectors to just 30 per cent of US levels, it would raise its standard of living by over 10 per cent.

Doing this means working to develop a global consensus that domestic productivity growth should be the key focus of economic policy in every nation. Surprisingly, this is not the case, as many nations put redistribution or mercantilist trade policies first.[35] Global bodies like the WTO need to work more proactively against beggar-thy-neighbour mercantilist strategies. International development organisations like the World Bank and the IMF, and national development organisations like the US Agency for International Development, will not only have to stop promoting export-led growth as a key solution to development, they will also have to tie their assistance to steps taken by developing nations to move away from such negative-sum mercantilist policies, thereby rewarding countries whose policies are focused on spurring domestic productivity, not on protecting the status quo.

Progressives should take heart, however, from the fact that an effective growth economics agenda is quite different from a conservative's small-government agenda. Indeed, relying on the market alone and consigning government to a role of enforcing contracts and protecting property is a path to sub-optimal growth. All else being equal, economies that forge smart public–private partnerships will always outperform economies in which government abdicates its role and leaves most actions up to private actors. Markets get many things right and if forced to choose between an economy with strong markets and limited government, or one with limited markets and strong government, we should choose the former.

But in contrast to what supply-siders warn, that is a false choice – we can walk and chew gum at the same time. In other words, we can have policies that are both pro-market and pro-public policy intervention. And we can do this without defaulting to the supply-side mantra that lower taxes, especially on capital and the rich, drive growth. Indeed, in an economy powered by innovation, indiscriminate tax cuts on capital and the rich have no impact on growth. Rather, among other items, a growth economics agenda entails active public investments, especially in knowledge, in the form of both research and skills.

Even with this growth economics agenda, many progressives will still ask about redistribution. But just as we can have policies that are both pro-market and pro-public policy intervention, we can also have policies that are both pro-growth and pro-fairness, or at least that are not contradictory of one another. There is no reason why intelligent policies to promote fairness – such as higher minimum wages, stronger rights for workers, a stronger safety net, and more progressive taxation – should harm growth, as long as they are reasonable and not excessive.

Yet, at the same time, progressives also need to embrace policies that explicitly seek to boost private sector growth, and not hide behind the cloak that emphasis on redistribution policies, such as providing universal health care, is a growth policy. In short, it is false to say that a nation's economic policy must choose between growth and fairness. But, having said that, it is all too easy for progressives simply to ignore growth and assume that 'the market' will take care of that. It won't without smart growth economics policies.

Globalisation is a wonderful vision and can be an even more wonderful reality, but only if nations abandon negative-sum mercantilist policies and embrace growth economics policies focused on raising productivity for all sectors, and making sure that all individuals can benefit from this growth. If that happens, developed and developing nations alike will benefit greatly.

Notes

1 For a more in-depth discussion of these issues, see R.D. Atkinson, *The Past and Future of America's Economy: Long Waves of Innovation that Power Cycles of Growth* (Northampton, Mass.: Edward Elgar, 2004).

2 S.S. Cohen, J. Bradford Delong, S. Weber and J. Zysman, *Tracking a Transformation: E-Commerce and the Terms of Competition in Industries*, BRIE-IGCC E-conomy Project Task Force (Washington, DC: Brookings Press, 2001).

3 A three-minute telephone call between London and New York City cost $70 in today's dollars in 1964, but less than 50 cents today, and probably close to zero as we move to Internet telephony. Between 1987 and 1997 the cost of a US-to-London telephone call declined by 90 per cent. J. Burnham, 'The Growing Impact of Global Telecommunications on the Location of Work,' *Contemporary Issues* 87 (St. Louis, Mo.: Washington University, Center for the Study of American Business, October 1997).

4 The cost of a T-1 dedicated phone line between the United States and Manila has dropped from $30,000 a month to less than $10,000 in the past few years. Moreover, technology advances have allowed the number of voice channels that can be put on a T-1 line to increase about fivefold. See 'In a Global Economy, Competition Among BPO Rivals Heats Up', *Knowledge@Wharton* (9 October 2002): knowledge.wharton.upenn.edu/article.cfm?articleid=642

5 R. Atkinson and H. Wial, 'The Implications of Service Offshoring for Metropolitan Economies' (Washington, DC: The Brookings Institution, 2007): www.brookings.edu/~/media/Files/rc/reports/2007/02cities_atkinson/200 70131_offshoring.pdf

6   R.G. Lipsey, K.I. Carlaw and C.T. Bekar, *Economic Transformations: General Purpose Technologies and Long-Term Economic Growth* (New York: Oxford University Press, 2005).

7   Quoted ibid., p. 83.

8   'Trade Distortions', *Washington Post*, Editorial, 3 December 2007, A16: www.washingtonpost.com/wp-dyn/content/article/2007/12/02/AR2007120201588.html

9   Between 1992 and 2003 manufacturing employment declined by 2.6 million. About half of this decline was due to the fact that manufacturing productivity was higher than non-manufacturing sectors, meaning manufacturing could produce more with fewer workers. For example, jobs in the steel industry dropped from 400,000 to 180,000 between 1980 and 1992, yet we make about the same amount of steel today as we did then. About 25 per cent was due to slower growth in domestic demand for manufactured products relative to services. As we get richer, we tend to buy more services (e.g. health care, education, entertainment). Finally, one-quarter was due to an increasing trade deficit in goods. R. Atkinson, *The Bush Manufacturing Crisis* (Washington, DC: Progressive Policy Institute, 2003).

10 European Commission, *Fostering Industrial Change: An Industrial Policy for an Enlarged Europe* (Brussels: COM, 2004), Tables 3 and 4: eur-lex.europa.eu/LexUriServ/site/en/com/2004/com2004_0274en01.pdf

11 'EU, Euro Area and Member States' Trade with the Rest of the World' (Eurostat, accessed December 2007): epp.eurostat.ec.europa.eu/portal/page?_pageid=1996,45323734&_dad=portal&_schema=PORTAL&screen=welcomeref&open=/&product=Yearlies_new_external_trade_external_trade_by_products&depth=2

12 European Commission, *Fostering Structural Change: An Industrial Policy for an Enlarged Europe* (Brussels: COM, 2004), 274 final, Table 2: eur-lex.europa.eu/LexUriServ/site/en/com/2004/com2004_0274en01.pdf

13 D.J. Ikenson, 'Thriving in a Global Economy: The Truth about U.S. Manufacturing and Trade', *Cato Institute Trade Policy Analysis* 35 (28 August 2007): www.freetrade.org/files/pubs/pas/tpa-035.pdf. See also L. D'Andrea Tyson, 'Those Manufacturing Myths', *Business Week* (12 December 2005): www.businessweek.com/magazine/content/05_50/b3963177.htm

14 A. Blinder, 'Offshoring: The Next Industrial Revolution', *Foreign Affairs* (March/April 2006), p. 126.

15 R.D. Atkinson, 'Apocalypse Soon? Why Alan Blinder Gets it Wrong on Offshoring' (Washington, DC: The Information Technology and Innovation Foundation, 2006): www.itif.org/index.php?id=64

16 Atkinson and Wial, 'The Implications of Service Offshoring for Metropolitan Economies'.

17 R. Khurana, 'Transitions at the Top: CEO Positions as Open and Closed to Competition', MIT Working Paper (Cambridge, Mass.: Sloan School of Management, 2000).

18 T. Palley, 'The Economics of Outsourcing: How Should Policy Respond?' (Silver City, N.M. and Washington, DC: Foreign Policy In Focus, 2 March 2006): fpif.org/fpiftxt/3134

19 R. Kuttner, 'Survival of the Richest', *Boston Globe* (24 June 2006): www.boston.com/news/globe/editorial_opinion/oped/articles/2006/06/24/survival_of_the_richest/

20 S. Rose, 'Does Productivity Growth Still Benefit Working Americans?' (Washington, DC: The Information Technology and Innovation Foundation, 2007): www.itif.org/index.php?id=54

21 S. Rose, 'The Truth About Middle Class Jobs' (Washington, DC: Progressive Policy Institute, October 2007): www.ppionline.org/documents/MiddleClassJobs 100207.pdf

22 D.G. Blanchflower and M. Slaughter, 'The Causes and Consequences of Changing Income Inequality: W(h)ither the Debate?', Working Papers from Centre for Economic Performance and Institute of Economics (1998): econ papers.repec.org/paper/fthcepies/27.htm

23 The 50/10 ratio compares the income of people in the 50th percentile of income to those in the 10th (the lowest). Likewise, the 90/10 compares the highest quintile to the lowest.

24 D.H. Autor, L.F. Katz and M.S. Kearney, 'Trends in U.S. Wage Inequality: Re-Assessing the Revisionists' (Washington, DC: Brookings Institution, September 2005): www.brookings.edu/~/media/Files/rc/papers/2005/09labor_autor/200509kearney.pdf

25 See, for example, A. Singh, 'Income Inequality in Advanced Economies: A Critical Examination of the Trade and Technology Theories and an Alternative Perspective', Working Paper 219 (ESRC Centre for Business Research, University of Cambridge, December 2001): www.cbr.cam.ac.uk/pdf/WP219.pdf

26 R. Atkinson, 'Inequality in the New Knowledge Economy', in A. Giddens and P. Diamond (eds), *The New Egalitarianism* (Cambridge: Polity, 2005).

27 Autor et al. report that a simple regression of the 90/10 log hourly wage gap for the years 1973 to 2003 on the real minimum wage yields an R-squared of .71, a strong and positive relationship. Autor et al., 'Trends in U.S. Wage Inequality', p. 17.

28 A recent study of California workers found that four out of ten workers have been at their jobs less than three years. E. Yelin, *California Work and Health Survey* (San Francisco, CA: Field Institute, 1999).

29 R.D. Atkinson, 'Will We Build It and If We Do Will They Come? Is the U.S. Policy Response to the Competitiveness Challenge Adequate to the Task?' (Washington, DC: The Information Technology and Innovation Foundation, 2006): www.itif.org/index.php?id=62

30 Under rules established by the International Monetary Fund, each member country has agreed not to engage in 'protracted, large-scale intervention in one direction in the exchange market'. Unfortunately, the IMF has done next to nothing during the last two decades to enforce currency manipulation rules.

31 D.W. Jorgenson and K. Vu, 'Information Technology and the World Growth Resurgence', *German Economic Review* 8:2 (2007), pp. 125–45.

32 R.D. Atkinson and A.S. McKay, *Digital Prosperity: Understanding the Economic Benefits of the Information Technology Revolution* (Washington, DC: The Information Technology and Innovation Foundation, 2006): www.itif.org/index.php?id=34

33 T. Kalil and J.S. Irons, 'A National Innovation Agenda: Progressive Policies for Economic Growth and Opportunity Through Science and Technology' (Washington, DC: Center for American Progress, 2007), p. 36.

34 R.D. Atkinson, *Supply-Side Follies: Why Conservative Economics Fails, Liberal Economics Falters, and Innovation Economics is the Answer* (Lanham: Rowman & Littlefield, 2006), ch. 9.

35 W.W. Lewis, *The Power of Productivity: Wealth, Poverty, and the Threat to Global Stability* (Chicago: University of Chicago Press, 2004), p. xxiii.

IV

POLICY FRAMEWORK

10

Solidarity Beyond the Nation-State? Reflections on the European Experience

Maurizio Ferrera

Are social justice and solidarity possible beyond the nation-state? This question has been and continues to be at the centre of a long philosophical debate, which has highlighted the multi-faceted tension involved in opposing the universal and 'open' vocation of social justice on the one hand, and the particular and 'closed' vocation of the state on the other.[1] While primarily and fundamentally interested in issues of what is desirable, this debate has often touched upon the question of what is actually feasible. From a normative standpoint it is hard to justify the idea that the principles of justice should stop – as they typically tend to do in the real world – at the frontiers of the state. But even if it were highly desirable that they didn't, feasibility considerations allow us to modify our expectations, aware that the nation-state performs a host of other desirable functions.

The link between social justice, solidarity and state boundaries has been explored not only by philosophers but also by political scientists. Their prevailing focus has been on the political and institutional preconditions of 'sharing' practices such as forms of interpersonal and inter-group transfers of resources based on predetermined equity criteria. Also, the political science perspective has highlighted the strong nexus between state-national boundaries, on the one hand, and redistributive arrangements on the other. Whichever the specific content of the equity criteria, in the real world a just social order requires institutions for the pooling of resources and their selective redistribution over time. Such institutions can only exist within a space of interaction characterised by mutual trust and expectations of reciprocity. National boundaries are the most effective instrument for creating and stabilising such arrangements, ensuring that insiders cannot escape – except for lawful reasons – and that 'undeserving' outsiders cannot intrude.[2]

Positing a strong link between political and institutional phenomena does not rule out the possibility that they may well stand alone and be de-coupled under certain circumstances. We may thus legitimately raise the question: can we imagine forms of post-national solidarity, i.e. 'sharing' spaces that stretch beyond the boundaries of the nation-state? This chapter will explore that question in three subsequent steps. First, it will elaborate from a theoretical and historical perspective the link between boundaries and social solidarity. Next, it will offer a brief sketch of the process of 'nationalisation' of solidarity in Europe during the nineteenth and the twentieth centuries. Then it will show how the process of European integration has indeed opened a window of opportunity for the 'un-bounding' of solidarity and the experimentation with novel forms of open social citizenship. In conclusion, the chapter offers some speculative ideas on the relevance of the European experience for the development and promotion of what is described as a 'global sharing space'.

Solidarity as a form of social closure

Situated as it is at the crossroads between 'liberty' and 'equality', between 'self-interest' and 'altruism', solidarity is a somewhat elusive concept and a complex social good. On the one hand, it connotes a trait of whole social aggregates, that is, a high degree of 'fusion' or internal union, cohesion and commonality of purpose within a given group (the noun 'solidarity' comes from the Latin *solidus*, a firm and compact body). On the other hand, it connotes a particular set of ties among the members of such group: *sharing ties*, that is, transactions aimed at pooling (a part of) each member's resources for some common purpose. As is well known, modern welfare-state programmes pool resources (primarily financial) with the aim of countering the typical risks and adversities of the life cycle: from sickness to old age, from work accidents to unemployment. Such risks are combated by redistributing pooled resources both horizontally (from the non-damaged to the damaged) and vertically (from the better-off to the worse-off). Looked at from this perspective, the welfare state can be considered as a highly articulated and specialised form of institutionalised solidarity, serving both efficiency and social justice objectives.[3]

Solidarity became slowly institutionalised during the last two centuries in the wider context of state- and nation-building. The establishment of redistributive arrangements based on 'social rights' played a crucial role in stabilising the new form of political organisation (the nation-state) that gradually emerged in modern Europe. This stabilisation occurred through the anchoring of people's life chances to state-national organisations uniquely dedicated to social protection, reinforcing on the one hand those feelings of 'we-ness' that are a crucial underpinning of the nation-state construct, while on the other offering national elites new tools for acquiring and maintaining legitimacy and internal order.

People's life chances were 'anchored' by weaving social rights into the fabric of citizenship. As masterfully argued by T.H. Marshall, the evolution of modern citizenship involved a double process: of fusion and of separation.[4] The fusion was geographical and entailed the dismantling of local privileges and immunities, the harmonisation of rights and obligations throughout the national territory, and the establishment of a level playing field (the equal status of citizens) within state borders. The separation was functional and entailed the creation of new sources of nationwide authority and jurisdiction as well as new specialised institutions for the implementation of that authority and that jurisdiction at a decentralised level. In most European countries this double process of fusion and separation started with the establishment of civil and political rights that offered the new 'citizens' precious instruments for taking advantage of the opportunities available within state borders. But in a context of unfettered markets (and in particular of a purely 'self-regulating' labour market – the destructive utopia described by Polanyi),[5] civil and political rights were insufficient. Only the bestowal of certain material entitlements 'not proportionate to the market value of the claimant'[6] could keep ordinary citizens from falling into conditions of acute need, often jeopardising their very survival.

The incorporation of social rights into the space of citizenship was no easy task. In the economic sphere, the expansion of market capitalism produced a class society inherently built on inequalities, differential rewards and the 'commodification' of workers.[7] Classes and nations rose together: and even though the virtuous reconciliation between the meritocratic logic of the capitalist market and the egalitarian logic of national citizenship has been one of the greatest achievements of twentieth-century Europe, the path towards this destination was punctuated by marked social and systemic strains and clashes.[8]

Social rights had an enormous impact on social stratification and life chances. Marshall was certainly right when he pitted 'citizenship vs. social class', while the 'Swedish School' is equally correct in interpreting these rights as salient 'power resources' for wage-earners and labour movements.[9] But 'de-commodification' was not the only issue that shaped the forms and content of social rights in the various countries. Another important front, more pertinent for our line of reasoning, was the issue of *closure*: how far-reaching ought the new redistributive schemes to be? For which collectivities ought the new sharing ties to be defined and introduced? Such 'who' questions were as important as the 'what' questions emphasised by traditional debates about welfare-state formation.

Social rights are more demanding political products than civil and political rights. All rights have costs: enablement costs, to create the conditions for their actual exercise (such as free legal counsel for those people who cannot afford it), and enforcement costs. But, resting as they do on material transfers and services, social rights give rise to 'substance' costs as well. They require the availability of significant quantities of material resources that are not easy to extract from society, and of moral commitments to 'sharing with others' that are not easy to activate at the individual and primary group levels.[10] The definition of boundaries plays a critical role in the production of these rights. In the first place, boundaries are essential for constructing new 'special purpose communities' ready to pool certain risks. For welfare-state builders, boundary setting was a delicate balancing act between indulgence vis-à-vis the particularistic inclinations of pre-existing social categories and the self-defeating ambitions of redistributive 'stretching', that is, pushing the scope of solidarity beyond the limits which could be sustained by available material and moral resources. In the second place, boundaries are essential for enforcing affiliation to a sharing community. Now, compulsion is a prime component of citizenship in all its aspects, a fundamental instrument for assuring a correspondence between rights and duties. But in the sphere of social rights, which have precise, quantifiable costs, the matching of rights (entitlements) and duties (obligations to pay taxes and contributions) must be particularly accurate and stringent if fiscal bankruptcy is to be avoided. At least some civil and political rights can survive even without the full and constant exercise of the corresponding duties (contemporary democracy often functions with voting turnouts closer to 50 per cent than to 100 per cent). But social rights must be sustained by unrelenting sharing acts. This is why they rest on a specialised organisational form: that of compulsory social insurance. In most countries, the establishment of social rights meant the establishment of compulsory insurance schemes: against old age and disability, work injuries and sickness, maternity and unemployment. And, especially in the field of old age, the first implication for the members of such schemes was the payment of contributions (that is, the exercise of the duty), with benefits arriving only after long 'vesting' periods.

Defining and enforcing closure (in the form of obligatory affiliation and compulsory payments) remained a balancing act politically, but it conferred several economic advantages: less costly protection per insured person (thanks to the large, predictable, and reliable size of the sharing pool), the possibility of charging 'contributions' (flat-rate or proportional payments) rather than premiums (payments differentiated according to individual risk profiles, as in private insurance schemes) and the possibility of granting special treatment (such as lower or credited contributions, or minimum benefits) to categories of disadvantaged members. In contrast to private or voluntary insurance, compulsory (and public) social insurance could thus cover 'difficult' risks such as unemployment or family breakdown, and also produce not only horizontal redistributions (from the healthy to the sick, from the employed to the unemployed, and so on) but also vertical ones (from rich to poor). In this way, social citizenship could bring that 'general enrichment of the concrete substance of civilized life' through 'equalisation between the more and the less fortunate at all levels' that Marshall saw as its fundamental mission.[11]

Closure matters, then, for social rights (and thus for solidarity), and probably in a more direct and intense way than for the other rights of citizenship: 'bonding' can only build on firm 'bounding'. If observed from the angle of social citizenship, the European landscape appears today as a dense forest of compulsory spaces of 'social sharing', covering virtually 100 per cent of national populations, with very limited 'exit' opportunities (such as in the form of exemption from insurance). We may thus wonder: after more than a century of continuous deepening and expansion, has social solidarity reached its limits? Can scenarios of further deepening and expansion be imagined in Europe and beyond? To address these questions, a more precise understanding of the spatial nature of solidarity and of the historical process of 'bounding for bonding' is required.

The nationalisation of solidarity: a historical sketch

Solidarity is a 'sharing space' based on entitlements and demarcated by *two* distinct boundaries: territorial boundaries and membership boundaries. The former define the geographical scope of solidarity and link the eligibility and fruition of entitlements to forms of 'legitimate attachment' to a given territory on the side of claimants and beneficiaries. The latter define the scope of solidarity throughout the social structure based on various criteria (such as age, gender, employment status, need, and so on). Welfare-state formation can be seen as a lengthy historical process of boundary building, through which sharing collectivities were forged via territorial and membership demarcations.

In most European states, until the middle of the nineteenth century, external territorial boundaries were essentially of a military nature and had only a vague administrative-regulatory component.

The national territory was in its turn crossed by numerous internal barriers (e.g. in terms of labour and even physical mobility) as well as a high degree of legal differentiation. The very notion of a uniform legal code (in penal law, but especially in civic law) only made its appearance at the doctrinal level with the Enlightenment towards the end of the eighteenth century, and had a very slow take-off in practical terms throughout the century that followed.[12] The right to engage in a work activity of one's choosing only emerged with the dismantlement of the rigid guild systems and corporatist protections[13] – the other side of the coin being of course the rapid 'commodification' of workers in the capitalist labour market.[14]

The removal of barriers to free circulation as well as regulatory standardisation across the state territory proceeded at an increasingly rapid speed during the second half of the nineteenth century, and the establishment of social insurance schemes with a national scope constituted a sort of quantum leap for certain countries in this respect. As is well known, the first country to ever introduce compulsory insurance was Germany: in 1883 against sickness, in 1884 against work injuries, and in 1889 against old age. All industrial blue-collar workers were covered, regardless of where they worked within the Reich. The German reforms had a vast international echo. Austria–Hungary was the first country to follow suit (in 1887 as regards work injuries and in 1888 as regards sickness). Prior to the turn of the century came Denmark (means-tested national pensions in 1891), Norway (work injuries in 1894), Finland (work injures in 1895), France and Italy (work injuries in 1898). The other countries took off with subsidised voluntary insurance, but shifted to compulsory schemes in the first two decades of the new century. At the outbreak of the First World War, only Belgium was missing from the list (compulsory pension insurance arrived in this country in 1924). Even Switzerland – where cantons strenuously opposed federal interference in this field – succeeded in introducing compulsory insurance against work injuries in 1911.[15]

The alignment of redistributive boundaries with the territorial boundaries of the state added one extra spur for the adoption of those strategies of territorial closure and external boundary defence that gained priority in the political agenda of many European countries in the wake of 'nationalisation' processes. The definition of 'citizenship' and 'nationality' (i.e. of who belongs to the national community), and the issue of how to treat 'aliens', became a prime object of public policy and debates at the turn of the century, especially in the larger countries aspiring to consolidate or assert their status as great powers and experiencing at the same time significant immigration flows. France introduced a comprehensive law on citizenship (essentially based on the *jus soli* principle) in 1889.[16] After two decades of discussions and campaigns, the UK passed the first Aliens Act in 1905, and amended it in 1914.[17] The German Reich standardised rules on *Staatsangehoerigkeit* in 1913, establishing the *jus sanguinis* as fundamental criterion for the acquisition of German nationality.[18]

Some time elapsed, however, before these new legislative instruments became fully operative. In the two decades prior to the First World War, the European state system witnessed a period of increasing mutual interpenetration through international trade, foreign investment and labour migration. The new citizenship or alienship codes were not immediately and systematically employed as 'filtering' devices for inclusion/exclusion. The main goal of early citizenship policies was more the identification of nationals per se (citizenship as an object of closure) than the gating of access into domestic membership spaces (citizenship as instrument of closure). Even the British Aliens Acts of 1905 and 1914 were essentially aimed at empowering state authorities to deport 'undesirable aliens' for public order or national safety reasons rather than at discriminating against foreign workers. As noted by Carl Strikwerda, at the turn of the century workers could move freely across borders, passports were almost unknown, residence and work permits were not required and it was perfectly legitimate to own property and do business in other countries.[19] Each nation was creating distinct arrangements for social sharing that were territorially coterminous with state boundaries – but the latter were easily permeable. In Strikwerda's reconstruction, such context opened a window of opportunity for 'social internationalism', i.e. forms of transnational mobilisation for the production of basic rights of protection through a virtuous collaboration between national governments and international organisations.

At the beginning of the twentieth century the transnational links between national unions were surprisingly intense. A sort of advocacy coalition formed within this network, to promote international agreements on many delicate issues concerning workers' rights: from hours of work to women's employment, from judicial disputes to child labour and safety regulations. Frequent conferences on such themes were organised in Berlin, Brussels and Paris. In 1900 the International Association for Labour Legislation was created, which subsequently instituted the International Labour Organisation (ILO) in Geneva. Between 1900 and 1914 more than two hundred new international bodies were founded. A few conventions were signed on minimum labour standards and national governments agreed to stipulate bilateral agreements guaranteeing reciprocity in the new branch of social insurance that was emerging everywhere, that is, work injuries insurance. Even without reciprocity agreements, the prevailing legal tradition on labour disputes applied 'customary international law', so that workers operated de facto within a relatively homogeneous legal framework. In Strikwerda's words, in the early twentieth century, 'social citizenship was still being defined, and it could be either national or international or both'.[20]

This period came suddenly to an end during the Great War. The window of opportunity for any form of social internationalism closed off, and liberal nationalism – the readiness and willingness of European nation-states to entangle themselves in a web of mutual socio-economic relations – was replaced by nationalistic protectionism and in some cases outright chauvinist aggressiveness. It was during the war that the institution of citizenship and the new rules introduced in the previous decades started to be used as an instrument of territorial defence. Passports and entry visas became necessary for travel, residence and work permits were introduced almost everywhere, and the circulation of workers and capital became the object of restrictive regulation. During the great depression, the expulsion of foreign workers became a common practice in many receiving countries, e.g. France and Belgium.[21] In the UK, interwar legislation temporarily abrogated the *jus soli* principle and explicitly limited the social entitlements of aliens.[22] Originally involving cross-local regulatory standardisation and nationwide pooling of certain risks, during the interwar period mass social insurance planted deeper territorial roots, increasingly solid external boundaries were built around it and accurate filtering mechanisms were deployed in order to sort insiders from outsiders. A clear path had been chosen: social protection would be part and parcel of the 'bundle of territoriality' – a territoriality bounded and controlled by the authority of the nation-state.[23]

The definition of membership boundaries ('who shares what with whom' within each nation-state) was much more controversial and required much heavier political investment than the definition of territorial boundaries. The internal design of the European welfare state was significantly shaped by pre-existing or co-evolving structural constellations, in particular long-standing and newer cleavages such as state–church conflicts, ethno-cultural conflicts and ideological – primarily left–right – conflicts. However problematic and contentious, the drawing of internal membership boundaries gave rise to a web of redistributive collectivities and arrangements which became gradually 'crystallised' through dynamics of institutionalisation. The *Trente Glorieuses* (1945–75) were the apex of the *national* welfare state. The coverage of its schemes reached its 'natural' limits (that is, the whole citizenry, at least de jure) or got very close to it. The more localised systems of protection were progressively marginalised in their financial size and functional scope. Sophisticated techniques were invented and deployed in order to improve and rationalise the extraction of taxes and contributions, govern redistributive flows from the centre, and deliver benefits and services to the various clienteles. Finally, alongside the various insurance schemes for the standard risks, new non-contributory programmes of general social assistance were created, as well as increasingly complex health-care systems providing a wide array of medical services. The new programmes of social assistance differed from traditional public charity to the extent that they were based on rights rather than bureaucratic discretion. Health-care systems in their turn shifted the emphasis of social sharing from the provision of cash transfers to the provision of benefits in kind (pharmaceuticals, medical treatments, and so on). This shift made the institutional profile of the welfare state more complex because it bestowed a new role on service providers as relevant actors. It also made the welfare state more popular in general, and the European welfare state more distinct from its US counterpart, which remained much leaner in terms of public health cover.

Thus, in the first post-war decades – the 1950s and 1960s – the 'social citizenship' attached to state-national institutions achieved full flowering and also its greatest degree of both external and internal closure. For non-nationals, it was rather difficult to enter the solidarity spaces of other states, especially when it came to deriving benefits from them. Under certain conditions, foreign workers were admitted into the national labour markets and social insurance schemes. Bilateral treaties were agreed between various European countries concerning both the circulation of workers and their social rights.[24] But such treaties were typically designed to favour the labour-importing countries.[25] Imported workers were granted only temporary residence and work permits; the presence of 'vesting' rules concerning minimum contributory qualifications often barred them from the actual enjoyment of benefits (typically pensions). Moreover, a number of bilateral treaties maintained direct and indirect obstacles to equal treatment, such as residence clauses – which prevented benefits from being exported – and also displayed gaps in so-called 'material scope', that is, the range of accessible benefits such as unemployment benefits. Legal migrant workers were thus always obliged to pay contributions; but their chance of actually receiving benefits was far from guaranteed. The 'principle of territoriality' – a central tenet of international labour law[26] – meant that control over the most relevant aspects of social security was retained strictly in the hands of national governments, putting non-nationals in conditions of systematic disadvantage in dealing with issues of contribution accumulation, transferability, and the like.[27] More importantly, as a rule non-nationals were excluded from social and medical assistance benefits, either directly through explicit nationality requirements or indirectly via 'gainful residence' requirements (that is, the possession of legal work permits).

Nationals on the other hand were virtually 'locked in', obliged to be members of public schemes. Internally, the level of political debate or 'voice' around welfare policies tended to increase, but the expansion of these programmes contributed substantially to enhancing citizens' 'loyalty' towards their national variant of the welfare state. The availability of need-based benefits and 'social minima' linked to citizenship contributed to strengthening such loyalty and enhancing general feelings of collective solidarity. Welfare rights, legitimised through the electoral channel, made a fundamental contribution to nation-building, accentuating citizens' territorial identities.

Enter European integration: is post-national solidarity possible?

The process of European integration has gradually but irreversibly altered the compact national configurations which had consolidated during the *Trente Glorieuses*. When it was launched, the integration process was not meant to challenge the 'bounded' character of domestic social protection systems. On the contrary, the project was aimed at supporting the virtuous circle of economic modernisation and growth, political legitimation and stability, social cohesion and solidarity that started to operate in the early 1950s in each nation-state: a virtuous circle that Fritz Scharpf has aptly dubbed the 'democratic civilization of capitalism'.[28] European integration was intended to sustain the functioning of European-style 'welfare capitalism' by taking care of economic interdependence and by facilitating trade flows among the members of the EEC, thus securing higher rates of growth and higher fiscal dividends. And in its initial phase, the establishment of a common market did not endanger the autonomy of domestic authorities in setting the level and type of taxes and hence the level and type of social protection: national tax bases (including capital) and national consumers were largely 'captive' and thus the distributive and regulatory costs of the welfare state could be easily reflected in prices without jeopardising the profitability of capitalist production.[29]

With the passing of time, however – and especially since the mid 1970s – European integration started to gradually erode the 'boundary configuration' which served as a basis for national welfare regimes. The general story is well known and does not need to be recounted in detail.[30] Cross system boundaries have been extensively redefined, differentiated, reduced, or altogether cancelled. An internal market has been established, resting on the free circulation of goods, persons, capital and services. A common currency has been introduced, accompanied by rather rigid constraints on domestic fiscal policies. A tightly monitored competition regime has started to forbid national closure practices that are judged to be 'market distortions' by supranational authorities. Firms, capital and, more generally, 'tax bases' are no longer captive of the nation-state, thus weakening the traditional economic foundations of redistributive arrangements.

For our reasoning, the important part of the story is the specific impact of European integration on the boundaries of national citizenship spaces and of the institutional core of the welfare state, namely, compulsory social insurance. Through a series of binding regulations and court rulings, social rights (and the corresponding obligations) have been de-coupled from national citizenship within the EU and linked merely to work or residence status. The traditional link between rights and territory has become much looser: for most civic and social rights, the filtering role of nationality has been neutralised. A new political figure has emerged on the stage: the *denizen*, an outsider (in respect of the national space) who can enter (and of course re-exit), stay inside, voice, and even 'share' under certain conditions. While residence is still partly a matter of national sovereignty, the freedom to work anywhere in the territory of the Union is protected by the treaties and attentively policed by supranational authorities. On this front, it is clear that European integration has promoted an almost complete cross-local 'fusion' of what Marshall considered the basic civil right in the economic sphere: 'the right to follow the occupation of one's choice in the place of one's choice, subject only to legitimate demands for preliminary technical training'.[31] To be sure, the member states still retain very substantial prerogatives over the definition and operation of social rights within their borders. But the underlying and ultimate filtering function performed by national citizenship as the container of rights and the basic instrument of closure is no longer there.

In the field of social protection itself, co-ordination rules on the one hand (essentially, Regulation 1408/71) and competition rules on the other have severely restricted the exclusionary or discriminatory prerogatives of national governments vis-à-vis outsiders and have even launched an attack on the very 'sovereignty to bound' of the nation-state in the social sphere. Thanks to the principles of benefit exportability, national welfare states now must let in and out of their borders entire 'bundles of entitlements': import of entitlements matured under foreign schemes (as in the case of claims for the recognition of contributions paid abroad) or exports of entitlements to be redeemed in foreign territories (as in the case of claims to payments abroad). Although – as mentioned above – work-related insurance schemes had always envisaged the possibility of non-nationals participating as long as they enjoyed the status of legal immigrants, the institutional framework put in place by the 1971 Regulation represents a quantum leap in terms of 'opening', not only in its extremely wide personal and material scope but also in its degree of juridification, emblematically represented by the powers of a supranational court enjoying supremacy over domestic courts. The sovereign 'right to bound' is still there, but it is no longer an absolute right, subject as it is to the limits imposed by the EU competition and co-ordination regimes – which specify the conditions under which it can be legitimately exercised – and by the judicial review of the European Court of Justice (ECJ).

The development of the EU regime on social security co-ordination can be read as a new chapter in the long-term process of the expansion of social rights: referring to Peter Flora's metaphor, it can be read as a new phase of 'growth beyond limits', that is, of coverage and eligibility extensions beyond the limits of the domestic territory and beyond the reach of the nation-state. But does this also mean that Europe has unproblematically entered a new phase of post-national forms of social solidarity – a phase in which 'sharing ties' can stretch beyond state borders and reach out towards non-nationals? Is a new boundary configuration emerging in the EU, capable of reshaping the territorial and membership basis of redistributive communities? The short answer is: we are not there yet, and precisely as a consequence of boundary reconfigurations, many national welfare states have re-opened the classic debate about 'who can share what with whom' and have even taken some concrete steps of defensive 're-bounding' against non-nationals. But the seeds for a new phase of post-national solidarity have been planted and in due course – if appropriately 'gardened' – they may well reach full maturation. Let us articulate this diagnosis in more detail.

Slowly, but inexorably, over the last couple of decades the dismantlement of national boundaries around sharing spaces has elicited a growing politicisation of the 'opening' issue, and especially of the 'immigration' issue: questions of reciprocity and fairness regarding the access of 'foreigners' into national social protection schemes have emerged as increasingly prominent and contested topics in the political arena. Intra-EU cross-border flows remained relatively contained until the early 2000s, but have been rapidly increasing after the eastern enlargement of 2004–7. It must also be noted that even if not wholly assimilated to EU citizens, third-country nationals have come to enjoy virtually full access to social benefits in the member states where they legally reside: EU co-ordination rules apply to third-country nationals once they have legally entered the EU territory. In many EU countries the immigration issue has gained the potential of transforming itself into a basis for cleavage formation: an insider–outsider cleavage or even a fully fledged pro-integration/anti-integration cleavage, in parallel with the surge of 'ethno-regionalist' or 'right-wing populist' mobilisations. The negative results of the French and Dutch referendums on the Constitutional Treaty in 2005 have already proven that the emergence of such dynamics is not a purely academic speculation: a scenario of defensive re-bounding of national sharing spaces cannot be ruled out in the post-enlargement EU.

We can however envisage an alternative scenario, which may be dubbed 'incremental social transnationalism and supranationalism'. This scenario rests on three dynamics that are clearly at work in the current European social scene:

1. The gradual institutionalisation of a common membership space (in principle coterminous with the territory of the Union) by virtue of which all EU citizens and legal denizens have 'the right to have rights', including rights to 'share'. For the time being, the substantive contents of these rights vary according to the norms and rules which are in force in the portion of territory (national or even subnational) in which EU citizens freely choose to work and/or reside. But it is plausible to expect that the institutionalisation of such space will generate pressures for some form of standardisation, especially in the wake of supranational initiatives of monitoring and surveillance (including 'hard' surveillance through the European Court of Justice). In the fields of gender equality and fundamental rights, for example, cross-national 'fusion' has already produced (in Marshall's words) 'institutional separation', that is the emergence of new institutional structures at the EU level (the Institute for Gender Equality and the EU Fundamental Rights Agency) dedicated to the monitoring and assessment of national legal orders and social equalities. The ECJ has in its turn already shown that it intends to seriously enforce the principle that EU citizens have 'the right to have rights' and has even started to rule (and formulate doctrine) about the specific content of the rights (in the plural, including social rights).[32]
2. The gradual articulation and strengthening of the so-called EU social dimension, i.e. a set of schemes and programmes directly anchored at the supranational level, of a regulative and distributive nature, based on a variety of 'hard law' and 'soft law' instruments, including the Open Method of Coordination.[33] The strengthening of the social dimension of the EU is an important development not only per se, but also for the politics that accompanies it: a politics that has revived, in updated and amplified forms, those dynamics of transnational mobilisation and advocacy of 'solidarity across borders' which had made an early and unsuccessful appearance at the beginning of the twentieth century.

3. The emergence – and in some sectors, the actual flourishing – of
   transnational schemes and collaborative partnerships, in the wake
   of closer cross-border contacts and the specific regulative and financial incentives made available by the EU itself. Also, this front has
   witnessed a host of new political activities and the formation of new
   collective actors mobilising in the pursuit of shared objectives.[34]

Developments along these three fronts are less visible and certainly
less discussed than developments along the 'defensive re-bounding'
front. Although still rather scant, empirical research does indicate,
however, that the seeds are there and that the process of political and
institutional maturation has started: the scenario of an incremental
social transnationalism and supranationalism does not appear beyond
reach in twenty-first-century Europe. To paraphrase Strikwerda's
expression, within the EU social rights are now rapidly becoming
'national and supranational'.

   Speculating about the future is always risky and we should not get carried away by superficial forms of optimism. Reconciling 'solidarity' and
'Europe' – the logic of closure which underpins national dispositions
and practices of social sharing, and the logic of opening which typically
inspires the European integration project – is a daunting challenge and
it is certainly not easy for the European Union to find a balance between
these two opposite logics: a balance capable of sustaining the political
production of social solidarity under changed boundary conditions. But
if our diagnosis is correct, then finding this balance is not impossible and
the search for it is already underway. Institutional forms and options are
emerging, reforms proposals are being elaborated, and seeds of change
are visible at the grass roots of key social and political processes. The
nation-state still is, and probably will remain for a long time, the ultimate guarantor of entitlements and the prime legitimate space for the
exercise of social citizenship and for the delicate balancing of rights
and obligations. But in the wider space of the EU some institutional elements are emerging – citizenship rights, regulatory instruments, seeds
of a core of shared values and even identity traits – which if carefully
cultivated may provide a fertile ground for the 'nesting' of national
sharing traditions within wider membership spaces, thus containing
're-bounding' pressures and possibly activating cross-national dynamics
towards greater bonding between European citizens.

Conclusion

The unbundling of rights and territory, of citizenship and nationality, of political authority and state structures is not an exclusively

European phenomenon. According to some authors (e.g. Sassen),[35] the whole world is now witnessing a deconstruction of 'the national' and the experimentation of a wide range of spatial re-assemblages of various national functions and capabilities (including citizenship rights). Some global or regional economic regimes (such as the WTO or NAFTA) already foresee rules for the cross-border portability of rights and entitlements for certain occupational groups (e.g. managers) that already resemble those of the EU. And even within the US there seems to be a shift from the traditional doctrine of 'rights to individuals as nationals' to 'rights to individuals as individuals'.[36] A new window of opportunity for 'social internationalism' has again opened in the course of the last decade, as witnessed by the policy debates, the increasingly intense diplomacy, the transnational mobilisation dynamics and the (small) institutional advancements around the so-called 'social clause' within the WTO and the whole issue of the 'core labour standards'.[37]

Within the wider context of partial de-nationalisation trends, however, the European experience stands out as particularly significant for at least three reasons. The first reason is straightforward: historically, it was in Europe that the 'bundle of territoriality', i.e. the link between territory, rights and authority, made its first appearance during the modern era and reached its most intense and sophisticated institutional manifestation during the *Trente Glorieuses*. The fact that Europe is now clearly witnessing not only a reversal of the process (the 'unbundling'), but also that it is forging a novel institutional architecture which promises to generate a viable and balanced 're-assemblage' must be welcomed as good news by all those who subscribe to a 'universal' and open vision of social justice but are worried about its political and institutional feasibility.

The second reason is that the novel spatial architecture of solidarity which is gradually emerging in the EU and the 'incremental social transnationalism/supranationalism' scenario that we have outlined above can set a benchmark for other regions of the world, and in particular other experiences of regional integration such as North America, Latin America, South East Asia or even Africa. There is already a very well-articulated academic and policy debate which recognises the potential and promises of EU social developments and discusses possible emulations and institutional transfers.[38]

Finally, in due course the EU itself can become an agent of change at the global level by promoting its own 'model' in a host of direct and indirect ways. To some extent this has already happened, during the last enlargement process, and continues to happen through the so-called 'neighbourhood policy', and the EU external relations policy more generally.[39] The EU is often referred to as a 'civilian superpower'

– a notion which many dislike for its rhetoric and elusiveness. Being a pioneer of the new path towards post-national solidarity, developing and promoting a novel notion of *civitas universalis* (and not only *Europaea*) could be a concrete goal for such a superpower – one that should be supported and actively pursued by progressives around the world.

Notes

1 J. Cohen and C. Sabel, 'Extra Rem publicam Nulla Justitia', *Philosophy and Public Affairs* 34 (2006), pp. 146–75.

2 For a review of this literature see M. Ferrera, *The Boundaries of Welfare* (Oxford: Oxford University Press, 2005).

3 N. Barr, *The Economics of the Welfare State* (Stanford: Stanford University Press, 1993).

4 T.H. Marshall, 'Citizenship and Social Class', in T.H. Marshall and T. Bottomore, *Citizenship and Social Class* (London: Pluto Press, 1992).

5 K. Polanyi, *The Great Transformation: The Political and Economic Origins of Our Time* (Boston: Beacon Press, 1957).

6 Marshall, 'Citizenship and Social Class', p. 28.

7 See Polanyi, *The Great Transformation* and G. Esping-Andersen, *The Three Worlds of Welfare Capitalism* (Cambridge: Polity Press, 1990).

8 See R. Bendix, *Nation-Building and Citizenship* (New York: Wiley, 1964) and M. Mann, *The Sources of Social Power* (Cambridge: Cambridge University Press, 1986).

9 See W. Korpi, *The Democratic Class Struggle* (London: Routledge, 1983) and Esping-Andersen, *The Three Worlds of Welfare Capitalism*.

10 K. Offe, *Politica sociale, solidarietà e stato sociale*, in M. Ferrera (ed.), *Stato sociale e mercato mondiale* (Turin: Fondazione Agnelli, 1993), pp. 169–81.

11 Marshall, 'Citizenship and Social Class', p. 33.

12 G. Tarello, *Storia della cultura giuridica moderna. Assolutismo e codificazione del diritto* (Bologna: Il Mulino, 1998).

13 J. Alber, *Von Armenhaus zum Wohlfahrtsstaat* (Frankfurt: Campus, 1982).

14 See Polanyi, *The Great Transformation* and Esping-Andersen, *The Three Worlds of Welfare Capitalism*.

15 See Alber, *Von Armenhaus zum Wohlfahrtsstaat*, for a full picture and discussion of the sequence of introduction of compulsory schemes. Alber's analysis does not include Spain, Portugal and Greece, which also made their first steps in social insurance after the First World War.

16 On the French case see P. Weil, 'Nationalities and Citizenships: Lessons from the French Experience for Germany and Europe', in D. Cesarani and M. Fulbrook (eds), *Citizenship, Nationality and Migration in Europe* (London and New York: Routledge, 1996), pp. 74–87, and R. Brubaker, *Citizenship and Nationhood in France and Germany* (Cambridge, Mass.: Harvard University Press, 1992).

17 On the British case, see D. Cesarani, 'The Changing Character of Citizenship and Nationality in Britain', in Cesarani and Fulbrook (eds), *Citizenship, Nationality and Migration in Europe*, pp. 82–105.

18 On the German case, see Brubaker, *Citizenship and Nationhood in France and Germany*; J. Breully, 'Sovereignty, Citizenship and Nationality: Reflections on the Case of Germany', in M. Anderson and E. Bort (eds), *The Frontiers of Europe*

(London: Pinter, 1998), pp. 36–67; C. Lemke, 'Crossing Borders and Building Barriers: Migration, Citizenship and State Building in Germany', in J. Klausen and L. Tilly (eds), *European Integration in Social and Theoretical Perspective: From 1850 to the Present* (Lanham, Md.: Rowman and Littlefield, 1997), pp. 85–102.

19 C. Strikwerda, 'Reinterpreting the History of European Integration: Business, Labour and Social Citizenship in Twentieth-Century Europe', in Klausen and Tilly (eds), *European Integration in Social and Theoretical Perspective*, pp. 51–70.

20 See ibid., pp. 51–7.

21 G. Cross, *Immigrant Workers in Industrial France: The Making of a New Labouring Class* (Philadelphia: Temple University Press, 1983).

22 Cesarani, 'The Changing Character of Citizenship and Nationality in Britain'.

23 Originally suggested by J.G. Ruggie, this metaphor refers to the close association between territory and various forms of authority structures (including social rights) that emerged with the consolidation of the modern state system. The latter is characterised by 'territorially defined, fixed and mutually exclusive enclaves of legitimate domination'. J.G. Ruggie, 'Territoriality and Beyond', *International Organisation* 47 (1993), p. 147.

24 The first bilateral treaties were already signed prior to the First World War (for example, between France and Italy in 1904). The number of such treaties grew rapidly during the 1920s and 1930s. At the end of the Second World War, 133 bilateral agreements were in place, also thanks to the activism and expertise of the ILO. This net of bilateral agreements, however, had some significant gaps: for example in the late 1940s no treaty existed between Germany and Luxembourg or between Germany and Belgium. For a detailed reconstruction, see J. Holloway, *Social Policy Harmonization in the European Community* (Westmead: Gower Publishing, 1981).

25 F. Romero, 'Migration as an Issue in European Interdependence and Integration: the Case of Italy', in A. Milward et al., *The Frontiers of National Sovereignty: History and Theory 1945–1992* (London: Routledge, 1993), pp. 33–58.

26 F. Pennings, *Introduction to European Social Security Law* (The Hague: Kluwer Law International, 2001).

27 See V.R. Cornelissen, 'The Principle of Territoriality and the Community Regulations on Social Security', *Common Market Law Review* 33 (1996), pp. 13–41, and Holloway, *Social Policy Harmonization in the European Community*.

28 F. Scharpf, 'Economic Changes, Vulnerabilities and Institutional Capabilities', in F. Scharpf and V. Schmidt (eds), *Welfare and Work in Open Economies*, Vol 1. (Oxford: Oxford University Press, 2000), pp. 21–124.

29 See F. Scharpf, *Governing in Europe* (Oxford: Oxford University Press, 1999), and Scharpf, 'Economic Changes, Vulnerabilities and Institutional Capabilities'.

30 M. Ferrera, *The Boundaries of Welfare* (Oxford: Oxford University Press, 2005).

31 Marshall, 'Citizenship and Social Class', p. 10.

32 O. De Schoutter and S. Deakin (eds), *Social Rights and Market Forces: Is the Open Coordination of Employment and Social Policies the Future of Social Europe?* (Brussels: Bruylant, 2005).

33 J. Zeitlin and P. Pochet (eds), with Lars Magnusson, *The Open Method of Coordination in Action: The European Employment and Social Inclusion Strategies* (Brussels: PIE-Peter Lang, 2005).

34 For a bibliography on transnational and in particular cross-border co-operations, see the website of URGE: http://www.urge.it/cooperation.html#focus

35 S. Sassen, *Territory, Authority, Rights: From Medieval to Global Assemblages* (Princeton: Princeton University Press, 2006).

36 S. Sassen, 'The Bits of a New Immigration Reality: A Bad Fit with Current Policy' (2007): www. borderbattles.ssrc.org

37 See P. Alston, 'Core Labour Standards and the Transformation of the International Labour Rights Regime', *European Journal of International Law* 15:3 (2004), pp. 457–521, and G. Hansson, *Labour Standards, Development and Trade* (London: Routledge, 2008).

38 See T.A. Novitz, 'The European Union and International Labour Standards', in P. Alston (ed.), *Labour Rights as Human Rights* (Oxford: Oxford University Press, 2005), pp. 214–41; J. Zeitlin and C. Sabel, 'Learning From Difference: The New Architecture of Experimentalistic Governance in the EU', Eurogov papers no. C-07-02 (2007), and R. Walker and M. Wiseman, *Opening Up American Federalism: Improving Welfare in the European Way* (Washington, DC: George Washington University, 2006), Institute for Public Policy: http://home.gwu.edu/~wisemanm/OpenUp_060104_.pdf

39 See A. Clapham and J.B. Martignoni, 'Are We There Yet? In Search of a Coherent EU Strategy About Rights and External Trade', in V.A. Leary and D. Warner (eds), *Social Issues, Globalisation and International Institutions* (Leiden: Martinus Nijhoff Publishers, 2006), pp. 233–310, and E. Tulmets, 'The Introduction of the Open Method of Coordination in the European Enlargement Policy: Analysing the Impact of the New PHARE/Twinning Instrument', *European Political Economy Review* 3:1 (Spring 2005), pp. 54–90.

11

Spatial and Gender Inequalities in the Global Economy: A Transformative Perspective

Diane Perrons

Globalisation is a 'concept metaphor'[1] or 'trope of our times'[2] used to encapsulate the contemporary transformation of economic, social and political relations across the globe arising from the increased intensity, frequency and speed of interconnections between people and places through the organisation of work, the flows of goods and services, and the exchange of ideas. Even so, the contemporary world is characterised by difference rather than uniformity, and inequality on a global scale is stark and largely undisputed, despite unparalleled wealth, advances in human ingenuity, and a vast array of policies to promote development and redress regional and gender inequalities. Interestingly, some of the widest regional and gender gaps exist in countries experiencing the highest rates of economic growth.

The central argument of this chapter is that the processes generating current inequalities are so profound and embedded that it is necessary to move beyond marginal adjustments to the current orthodoxy and begin to specify what more inclusive growth and development would entail. Rather than thinking about political and redistributive solutions to economic problems, the chapter proposes a more inclusive model that would render such policies less necessary. The chapter does not add to the many recipes for regional development such as 'clusters',[3] implementing 'ICT4D',[4] or establishing 'cultural quarters' and 'creative' cities.[5] Neither does it add to the wealth of information provided by the UNDP, the European Commission or the many national, regional, or local planning agencies with respect to tool kits and training for gender mainstreaming, though all these can assist in ameliorating current inequalities.[6] Rather it argues that an effective challenge to inequitable regional, gender and socio-economic integration requires a deeper analysis of the processes generating uneven development and inequality together with a political will and capacity to transform them, including a willingness to reconsider the efficacy of the current neo-liberal model of globalisation. In this respect the chapter aims to add to the growing sense of unease with the current inequitable model of global capitalism, which can even be found within the supranational institutions.[7] More specifically, it makes some tentative suggestions regarding future research by drawing on alternative measures of regional well-being[8] and feminist economics with respect to engendering macroeconomic analysis.[9] The conclusion provides some tentative indications of the distributive implications of these alternative concepts. Given that life is an unrepeatable experiment and marginal changes can enhance well-being, the conclusion indicates some possibilities for more equitable social arrangements.

I begin by situating regional and gender inequalities within overall global trends before outlining some explanations for uneven spatial development and continuing gender inequality. Various problems with conventional approaches towards analysing and redressing uneven development and gender inequality are identified. In particular, questions are raised with respect to the current narrow understanding of the 'economy', in addition to the possible non-correspondence between measures of economic growth, economic inclusiveness and human welfare.

Economic growth and inequality in the contemporary global economy

Society as a whole has never been more opulent.[10] In the last 25 years world income has doubled and for an unprecedented number of people the economic problem – in Keynes's terms: provisioning basic survival needs for food, shelter and clothing – has been resolved. Nonetheless, at a global level the inequality gap between nations is wide and, depending on the measures used, is increasing.[11] Using GDP per capita, Branco Milanovic shows that inequality has increased steadily from 1950 if each country is taken as a single unit, but if weighted by population, has declined over the same period.[12] This reduction is largely due to the dramatic growth in post-reform China, because when the latter is excluded from the calculation, inequality has been fairly stable, if anything increasing slightly in the last decade. Danny Quah reports similar findings and also highlights how the reduction in 'world' poverty between 1981 and 2004 (measured by the number of people living on less than $1 a day) is entirely attributable to change in China, poverty elsewhere remaining the same or even increasing slightly.[13]

Both Milanovic and Quah highlight how inequality has increased within countries. Milanovic uses an emerging set of household panel data to show that interpersonal inequality on a global scale is substantially higher than inter-country inequality, which means that caution needs to be exercised before assuming that international redistributive policies are necessarily progressive in outcome.[14] They also find that the fastest-growing countries have experienced high levels of interpersonal and regional inequality.

Quah points out that China's economic growth has been associated with rising internal inequality, with the Gini coefficient increasing dramatically between 1981 and 2004, and to a greater extent in urban regions.[15] The fastest-growing urban regions are in the east which hosts 85 per cent of national trade by volume, and the majority of FDI and private sector enterprises.[16] Milanovic confirms this pattern in a study of internal inequality in five major world regions, finding rising levels of regional inequality in India, China and Indonesia during the 1990s.[17] In India the fastest-growing regions are in the southern and western states, and interpersonal inequality is greater within these regions, especially in the urban areas, although inequality is less marked if measures of human development rather than GDP per capita are used.[18] Further evidence of widening regional inequalities comes from the UNU-WIDER study which analysed regional disparities in fifty-eight developing and transition countries and found that while there are variations in the degree and the extent of inequality in the twenty-six countries for which temporal data was available, spatial inequalities were high and rising.[19] This study also found that on balance these increases were associated with increasing integration in the global economy through trade and exports, meaning that it is not exclusion from the global economy that is the source of inequality but rather the form of inclusion.

Within the EU15, where structural funds have been used to foster cohesion between member states, there has been some rapid convergence at the national level – especially with respect to Ireland, Portugal and Spain – since the mid 1990s. Within the EU25, regional inequalities have recently begun to narrow marginally but remain particularly wide between large city regions and between new and old member states.[20] In the revised policies for 2007–13 these trends are likely to continue, as funds have been made available to support projects fostering competitiveness in all regions, including those already rich, owing to concerns about economic growth and maintaining competitiveness with the US and Japan, in addition to continued aid for less developed regions. With respect to the US, while regional inequalities are more moderate, interpersonal inequality has been rising, with the earnings of the elite expanding dramatically while those of ordinary workers have stagnated.[21] In Silicon Valley, perhaps the iconic or superstar region of the new economy, the average earnings of corporate executives increased by 2,000 per cent between 1991 and 2000 while those of production workers declined by 7 per cent; the earnings ratio between them moving from 41:1 to 956:1.[22] More generally in the US, the college to high school wage ratio increased and while median earnings have fallen between 1973 and 2005, the mean has increased – indicating a clear increase in the share taken by higher earners.[23] Likewise in Europe earnings inequalities have been growing and are particularly marked in the fastest-growing regions such as London where the degree of polarisation is higher than in other UK regions.[24]

A further source of inequality that is not directly picked up in household or regional data is gender inequality. It cannot be assumed that incomes are shared within households; indeed the limited evidence that exists suggests the opposite, with men retaining a higher share of household income for personal use.[25] While gender earnings differentials are shaped by regional and interpersonal inequalities, typically being higher in the faster-growing and more affluent regions, there is no one-to-one correspondence; there are additional discriminatory practices and deeply rooted social processes driving gender inequality that require specific attention.[26]

The expanding international/global division of labour in manufacturing, principally in garments, electronics and toys – and more recently, in agri-business and the internationalisation of services, especially call centres, data entry and care work – is associated with rising female employment, and suggests that gender equality is increasing. Indeed, the proportion of women in non-agricultural employment formed one of the indicators for Millennium Development Goal 3 (to 'Promote Gender Equality and Empower Women').[27] On this measure, women have already achieved parity (a figure of between 45–55 per cent) in high-income economies, Eastern Europe and Latin America.[28] Nonetheless, aggregate trends cannot be used to make inferences about social change, which is likely to be complex and varied. Employment outside the home brings a range of opportunities including individual income and opportunities for socialising away from the watchful eyes of mothers, fathers, brothers and husbands, but the work can be hazardous and insecure and not all female workers retain control over their earnings.[29]

Gender inequality is also reproduced within paid employment. Almost universally there is a gender pay gap, employment is horizontally and vertically gender-segregated, and there are gender differences in contractual status and working times.[30] With respect to China, for example, there is a clear gender dimension to rising interpersonal inequality of earnings that can be disguised in household income data. In Socialist China women and men were 'guaranteed' equal rights including equal pay for work of equal value and as a result the wage dispersion was relatively low.[31] Initially there was some narrowing of the gap as the economic reforms strengthened competition, but as enterprises and local authorities secured greater autonomy, including control over wage-setting, the gender gap has widened, indicating a rise in gender-discriminatory practices. Thus for all regions men earned more than women even when controlled for personal and job characteristics, with the greatest gap being in the eastern, more 'reformed' region.[32] Likewise in all countries in the European Union there is a gender pay gap to male advantage and overall employment continues to be highly segregated by gender, though the extent of the inequality varies between states.[33]

More generally, just as women's share of paid employment is increasing the character of paid work is becoming more precarious and, especially in the global south, more likely to be found in the informal sector even though countries are increasingly integrated into the global economy.[34] As Diane Elson has argued:

> There is a paradox at the heart of contemporary restructuring as far as many women are concerned. On the one hand, their bargaining power in relation to the men in their households, their communities, their networks, and the organisations of their civil society may often (though not, as we have argued, inevitably) be increasing as a result of their greater participation in labour markets. But at the same time their households, communities, networks, and the organisation of civil society are increasingly at the mercy of global market forces that are out of control.[35]

All these trends indicate that economic growth has been extremely uneven in the current phase of neo-liberal globalisation with some countries, especially China and India, and some regions within these countries, growing extremely rapidly while others have fallen behind. It is also important to note that overall at a global scale the levels of growth have been lower in the recent neo-liberal decade than in the boom years between 1950 and 1973 when the distributive pattern was more even.[36] The next section looks at some of the processes underlying these trends in more detail.

Processes generating spatial and gender inequalities

Uneven development is something of a paradox in the global economy, where the development of ICTs and dematerialised products might suggest that geographical distance no longer matters. Yet at every spatial scale – the globe, the nation, the region, the city or locality – economic activity is clustered, generating a spatially uneven pattern with booming cities and city regions on the one hand and decaying industrial regions and rural regions with low levels of development and generally lower well-being on the other. In the past it was simply the lack of integration between the less developed regions and the centre that was considered problematic; now however it is increasingly recognised that this form of connection also matters as it profoundly influences development possibilities.[37] Similarly, it was once assumed that women's incorporation into paid work would resolve gender inequality, but the enduring gender differentials within paid employment nullify this expectation. Regional and feminist economists have analysed the clustering of economic activity and processes generating wage disparities for some time, but the prevailing neo-liberal growth model predicts convergence and temporal tendencies towards equalisation of factor returns. For this reason policies for redressing such inequalities are not prioritised and are often considered to be detrimental to optimal long-term efficiency and growth.

The model of equalisation of factor returns

The essence of neo-liberalism is that development and modernisation are enhanced by open markets and free trade. Free markets are said to allow the factors of production, labour and capital to flow to where they are most efficient. Labour and capital are predicted to move from areas of surplus to areas of deficit, stimulated by higher returns resulting in an efficient and balanced pattern of development in which the returns to the factors of production are equalised across regions. Technology should also move from capital-rich to capital-poor regions as diminishing returns set in, allowing the less developed regions to catch up. Similarly the model predicts that wages reflect the marginal product of labour and that employers with preferences for discriminating in favour of men (or women or any particular racial or ethnic group) would be eliminated in the competitive process. Within this perspective the role of the state should be confined to providing a stable framework within which free markets and private capital can flourish. It should not therefore regulate or subsidise prices or wages, as this would distort factor flows, and neither should it be involved in productive activities, which should be privatised if not already in the private sector.

There are clearly important disparities between the assumptions underlying the pure market model and the enduring regional and gender inequalities outlined in the previous section. These disparities are also well documented in economic texts dealing with market imperfections; nonetheless these analyses seem to have been overlooked by IMF technocrats and others influential in informing macroeconomic stability policies. In the context of globalisation what were once regarded as market failures, or exceptions to the norm of market optimality, have perhaps become the rule, owing to increasing interconnectivity between states and the seismic impact of systemic outcomes that perversely counter the rationality of micro decision-making at the local or particular level. Nonetheless, within the main policy discourse the neo-liberal orthodoxy remains paramount, in contrast to Schumpeterian, Keynesian or Marxist economics that offer alternative analyses of economic processes with potentially more equitable outcomes. Some contrasting approaches towards uneven development and gender inequality are reviewed below before tentative suggestions are made towards more inclusive models in the final section.

Models of divergence and inequality

First-order or basic geographical characteristics of relative location and usable resources are strongly influenced, if not over-determined, by second-order effects linked to cumulative and dynamic growth processes that lead to the geographical clustering of activities and corresponding uneven development. The idea of cumulative and divergent growth stems from the work of Alfred Marshall (1961, first published 1890) and economists working within a Keynesian perspective, such as Nikolas Kaldor.[38] This approach has been given renewed emphasis in the new economic geography/spatial economics associated with Paul Krugman,[39] the business economist Michael Porter,[40] and those following the cultural or institutional turn in economic geography.[41] While some theorists see unevenness or clustering as temporary others see it as an inherent characteristic of contemporary capitalism, unless redressed by policies for economic and social cohesion.

Formal spatial economics models the relationship between centripetal and centrifugal forces – in other words, the relationship between forces that tend towards spatial concentration and those that tend towards spatial dispersion – which are in turn dependent on the relative significance of economies of scale and transport costs.[42] Centripetal forces include: market size (the larger the market, the more powerful its attraction to firms); functional linkages between firms (the higher the number, the greater the clustering); thick labour markets (that is, the presence of a pool of labour with diverse skills); and finally pure external economies, including knowledge spillovers. Centripetal forces are opposed by centrifugal forces, which include: immobile factors such as labour (which may be unwilling to move); land rents (which may be lower outside the existing concentrations);

and pure external diseconomies such as congestion. In general the greater the economies of scale and the lower the transport costs the greater will be the tendency towards spatial clustering. As transport costs have fallen with contemporary ICTs, geographical concentration will tend to increase as firms are able to supply a wider range of markets from a single location. The limited internal markets in less developed regions together with the distances from external markets clearly limit their development potential in these respects.

The more positive aspect of Krugman's analysis for the less developed regions is the recognition that clusters can evolve accidentally and having done so economies of scale and external economies can lead to cumulative growth as a consequence of 'lock-in', or path dependency. Thus competitive advantage can arise from past humanly located economic activity, rather than natural resources, and appropriate policies can potentially stimulate such a process. Krugman himself does not dwell on policy implications. In this respect Allen Scott's approach is useful as he combines the quantitative relations addressed by Krugman with a qualitative analysis of the social and contextual aspects of economic behaviour, including the intangible costs of communications between buyers and sellers, such as trust and reliability.[43] Figure 1 presents a schematic model representing the outcome of these interactions and indicates their different potentialities for expansion.

Regional motors, global city regions or global cities, that is, large and dynamic clusters – or, drawing upon an analogy with Quah's work on social divisions, superstar regions[44] – emerge where spatially dependent transaction costs are heterogeneous, i.e. where direct transport costs may be low but where costly face-to-face contacts and external economies are high (figure 1, point 5). These superstar regions are typically the largest and wealthiest regions in the countries concerned and have a wide range of industries and services associated with modern economies as well as the living spaces of their employees in addition to high-level producer services. The existence of high transport costs or low externalities constrains development potential elsewhere.[45]

One of the problems with these models of clustering is that they focus very much on connections between firms within the cluster or region and pay less attention to the flows of value between regions and the way that firms within clusters are integrated into the global economy. Yet the manner of integration also has profound implications for the development possibilities of the firms and by implication for employment in and development of the regions where they are located. Combining the industrial district/clusters perspectives with value chain analysis offers a way forward in terms of analysing regional development within the contemporary global context.[46]

Externalities	Spatially dependent transaction costs		
	Uniformly low	Heterogeneous	Uniformly high
Low	1. Spatial entropy	2. Random dispersal and emerging hierarchical landscapes	3. Hierarchical landscape – small market centres – dispersed activity
High	4. Small interconnected clusters	5. Super clusters or superstar regions	6. Small disconnected clusters

Figure 1   Formation of Different Types of Clusters

Source: Adapted from A. Scott, *Regions and the World Economy* (Oxford: Blackwell, 1998).

Inequalities within growth regions

Global value chain analysis traces the amount of value added produced in the stages of a commodity's life from direct production through to final sale and so highlights the uneven locational distribution of the gains from economic activities. While much of the literature focuses on the governance relations between firms and their potential for upgrading to higher value added activities, the model can be extended to consider differential employment forms and their potential contributions to the development of the region where they are located.[47]

With respect to the superstar regions what makes them so different from metropolitan centres of the past is precisely these global interconnections and the ability of the firms present to appropriate such a large share of value added. In addition there are high-level producer service functions such as accountancy, law or public relations, together with key financial institutions supplying new financial products, whose economic significance has grown in recent years. These regions house the strategic control and command points of the global economy – that is, in part, they represent the outcome of the asymmetry between the spatial dispersal of production and the continued centralisation of control within large corporations.[48] These firms supply global markets and have branches or affiliates in many countries leading to transnational networks of cities in both poor and rich countries, leading in turn to new divisions in the global economy between places in and outside of the global network, with those not included in the network losing power and position relative to cities that are connected.[49] Global city regions include areas such as New York or London, Los Angeles within the context of southern California, Kuala Lumpur, with the multimedia super-corridor and Hsinchu-Taipei in Taiwan, Hyderabad (Cyberabad) and Bangalore in India, or the Pearl River Delta area in China. While all countries seek to have a global city region within their territories, and many regions aspire to this role, the feasibility is clearly questionable as is their normative desirability given the internal inequalities discussed below.

The leading firms may form only a relatively small volume of the total activity in the booming city regions but have a profound impact on its economy. One dimension of this impact, which contributes to the internal polarisation, is the demand that they, together with their highly paid, but time-pressed employees, generate for a wide range of services typically provided by low-paid workers.[50] The polarised wage structure partly relates to the contrasting economic properties of the services provided. Producer services have the economic properties of knowledge goods: being non-rival, with economies of scale, infinite expansibility and a global reach allowing the highly profitable firms to pay high wages.[51] By contrast, services such as catering, cleaning and care have limited economies of scale and are delivered personally often on a one-to-one basis in a discrete location. Baumol refers to these different characteristics respectively as technologically progressive and unprogressive, and argues that the real costs of the latter will tend to rise with the activities disappearing or being subsidised by the state as a consequence.[52] In today's neo-liberal and global world however, private firms employing a disadvantaged workforce – women, ethnic minorities or migrants, indeed often ethnic minority migrant women – increasingly provide these services.

Gendering of inequality

The technical explanations can account for tendencies in wage dispersion, but not the magnitude of the wage differences or their gendered, migrant and ethnicised forms. Maids and nannies, for example, form part of a global care chain which takes a hierarchical form on the basis of nation, gender, race and generation. Women from poorer regions of the world care for the children and elderly relatives of people in richer regions, and 'mothering is passed down the race/class/nation hierarchy, as each woman becomes a provider and hires a "wife"'.[53] The UNU-WIDER study recommends migration (in addition to infrastructure provision in less developed regions) to resolve regional inequalities, but it is important to recognise that migration is an individual solution to the structural problem of uneven development which it could easily reinforce given the prevailing cumulative rather than equilibrating growth tendencies. In addition, while migration is largely voluntary it takes place within an uneven context that constrains choice and involves significant social costs. Rachel Parreñas' ethnographic study of the long-term impact on the children left behind by migrant workers in the Philippines highlights some of the tragic human costs associated with these flows.[54]

These low-paid workers play a vital role in sustaining the city regions but are connected only indirectly via subcontracting arrangements to the firms drawing on their services. People working directly for the high-paid employees (such as nannies and cleaners), or indirectly in restaurants and ironing services, are likely to be in the informal sector. This work plays a crucial role in supporting these high-level activities but the workers either do not share in the fortunes of those for whom they work or do so only marginally. Their consumption is not central to the current pattern of globalisation, in marked contrast to more nationally oriented models of growth in the Fordist/Keynesian era where expansion depended on rising working-class consumption norms. Nonetheless, the migrant workers' remittances play a vital role not only for their families but also in sustaining the economies of low-income countries. Indeed workers', remittances have become a major source of foreign funds in low- and medium-low-income countries and form a significant component of GDP (for example 10 per cent in the Philippines and 16.7 per cent in Jamaica).[55] The magnitude of these flows is such that governments have developed special mechanisms and agencies to facilitate migration (in addition to the less scrupulous operators of illegal migration) and for managing the financial flows, possibly fossilising uneven development despite the gains that can accrue to participants.

Migration certainly plays a role as a survival circuit for governments and workers of low-income countries and sustains the fast-growing cities and regions through the elastic supply of low-income workers.[56] Given the social costs involved and the way that growth processes tend to be cumulative, the final section addresses the question of moving towards more equitable models of development that might make movements of this kind less necessary.

Transformative understandings and measures of regional well-being

The strategies for redressing regional inequalities proposed in the UNU-WIDER study – infrastructure provision for the less developed regions and free migration – are typical of what might be termed affirmative policies, in the sense that they seek to redress the adverse outcomes of market imperfections but not the underlying market tendencies towards uneven development. Similar to the UNU-WIDER study, the European Union also tends to favour policies that promote long-term competitiveness rather than providing direct aid that is believed to distort competition, leaving assistance to the socially excluded to come from retraining and the social policies of member states. Nonetheless the European Union's stated objectives have always sought to combine growth with cohesion at national and regional levels and for this reason Chinese researchers are looking at European policies, though the 2007–13 Structural Funds suggest something of a retreat from this position.[57]

Even so, the understanding of cohesion within the European Union is confined to narrowing GDP per capita differentials, despite concerns as to what GDP really measures, and whether a one-to-one positive relationship can be assumed between GDP and well-being.[58] In addition there can be a large difference between the GDP produced and GDP retained in a region when development is externally controlled or financed. This understanding can be contrasted with a more trans-formative approach which seeks a broader understanding of regional cohesion and a model of development that directly produces more balanced outcomes rather than relying on ameliorative policies. These issues are addressed in turn first by decomposing GDP per capita into its constitutive elements and second by examining an alternative, more holistic model of the economy proposed by feminist economists.

Measuring regional well-being

With respect to measuring regional well-being one possibility would be Amartya Sen's capability approach and its empirical manifestation in the various human development indices developed by the UNDP, but this is likely to exceed data availability at the regional level for some time.[59]

Figure 2 maps the European Union at the NUTS 1 regional level.[60] The 00.0 axis marks the European Union average, so regions in the top right-hand quadrant have above-average productivity and employ-ment rates. What is immediately clear from the diagram is the extent of differentiation both within and between states. In particular the comparatively low levels on both measures for some of the new member states – Latvia (lv0), Lithuania (lt0), Estonia (ee0) and Slovakia (sk0) (recorded as whole countries) together with some of the Polish regions (pl). Likewise the (de) regions that are below average formed part of the former DDR. By comparison The French ultra-peripheral regions, Guadeloupe (fr91), Martinique (fr92), French Guiana (fr93) and Réunion (fr94), have comparatively low employment levels but close to average productivity levels (output per person). Redistributive income transfers from the French welfare state boost GDP, making it similar to regions of the Italian south (itf) and Sicily (itg) likewise supported by state transfers. Other French regions, while much closer to the average on both measures, have higher productivity but lower

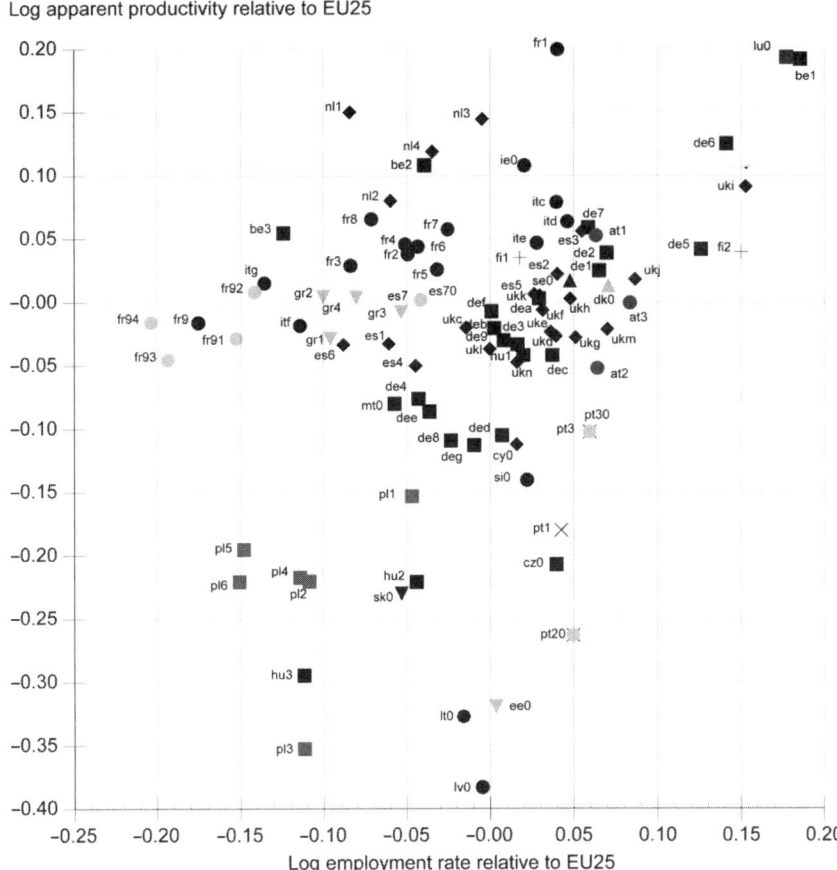

Figure 2 Regional Inequality in the European Union (NUTS 1 regions)

Adapted from Scott, 1998.

Note: To make Figure 2 manageable most regions have been plotted at the NUTS 1 level but the EU ultra-peripheral regions have been plotted at NUTS 2. This is an acceptable comparison because the ultra-peripheral regions form distinct territorial units in a similar way to NUTS 1 regions.

employment rates reflecting French policies with respect to retirement but also the more secure labour-market conditions that make labour-market entry difficult for young people. The exception is the Île de France (fr1) (Paris), which is above average on both measures, especially productivity, but similarly to other City regions – Luxembourg, (lu0) Brussels (be1), London (uki), Bremen (de5) and Hamburg (de6) – these productivity rates can be inflated by commuters who are not included in the population measure. These measures of regional well-being do not take into account the inequality within the region, which tends to be higher in richer regions, and there is no reason to suppose that richer regions automatically provide a favourable environment for those on low incomes.[61]

In addition to well-being as measured through employment, a broader model of regional development might also pay attention to the existence of value derived from the cultural or spatial identity of the region. In their analysis of the European Union's ultra-peripheral regions, Fortuna et al. ask: 'What would become of the Canaries without tourism and sun; of the Azores without milk and green fields; of Guadeloupe without sugar cane and white sand beaches?'[62] Clearly, this is an issue for the people of the remote regions to decide. Ireland is also renowned for its tranquillity and beauty (though with Irish 'mist' rather than sun),[63] and has a degree of peripherality though of a much lower order. Nonetheless it has moved from 63 per cent of the EU15 GDP per capita average in 1987 to 120 per cent in 2000 (131 per cent of the EU25 in 2003 and 146 per cent of the EU27 in 2007), and yet arguably the culture and landscape remain intact. Just as China and India have pursued controlled forms of integration with the global economy, this Irish 'miracle' did not take place through the market alone or simply through infrastructure provision and free emigration, though the European Union provided infrastructural support and Ireland was a country of emigration from the mid nineteenth century until the mid 1990s.[64] The Irish state provided considerable support for Foreign Direct Investment, including very favourable tax policies over a number of years. On a more negative note this 'miracle' is associated with widening interpersonal and regional inequalities – the majority of growth being concentrated in and around Dublin – and there is a considerable gulf between GDP and GNP as some of the value associated with the inward investment in Ireland flows away from the country.[65]

Recognising the productive contributions of the reproductive work

Decomposing GDP in this way enhances understanding of well-being but it is still focused on the productive economy and pays insufficient attention to the less tangible and more hidden factors which make life possible and worth living. This partial understanding of the economy, that associates well-being with output and considers the private sector the sole generator of wealth, overlooks all the productive work performed by the state and domestic sectors. Such neglect reflects a gender bias in thinking and constitutes a major source of gender inequality given the uneven and unequal responsibilities between women and men for this work. With respect to the European Union this neglect is somewhat surprising given that gender mainstreaming requires all EU policies, including regional policy, to be assessed from a gender perspective at all stages, including design, implementation, monitoring and evaluation.[66]

Feminist economists have analysed gender biases in macroeconomic policy, especially neglect of the reproductive sector and the unequal gender impact of structural adjustment and conditionality policies on poorer countries.[67] In response they have identified a broader understanding of the economy that in principle could produce more balanced and gender-even growth.[68]

Neo-liberalism, with its tight monetary policies including pressures to reduce taxation and privatise the production and distribution of services, affects women and men rather differently. Cut-backs in public expenditure tend to fall more heavily on sectors referred to as consumption- rather than investment-dependent, that is, health, education and childcare rather than roads and infrastructure. In the UK, for example, state-subsidised childcare is financed from current rather than capital expenditure which means that it is constrained by the Treasury 'golden rule' of balancing the books annually. These practices – treating one as investment and the other as consumption – reflect gender-biased thinking by neglecting to consider that good quality childcare could be seen as investment in the sense that it contributes to the formation of human capital and a sense of citizenship. Given the segregation of employment and the uneven division of domestic labour these restrictions affect women more than men in restricting employment opportunities and by their having to make up the deficit of state provision through their own labour. More generally within neo-liberalism individuals become increasingly dependent on the market for their livelihoods and, given enduring gender inequalities within paid employment, the consequences tend to fall more heavily on women.

Diane Elson addresses these biases by proposing amendments to the conventional circular flow of the income model to recognise the productive contribution of the household/domestic sector to human capital, trust and social values; all qualities that are necessary to sustain the economy.[69] What she terms the circular flow of output model similarly consists of three sectors. The private sector, focused on cost recovery and profit; the public sector, concerned with developing and implementing the regulatory framework (infrastructure/social rights and regulations) necessary to sustain the private sector; and the domestic sector, concerned with the dynamic provisioning of values, that is, the provision of labour and people with ethics, communicative and caring skills. Elson argues that all three sectors are necessary for sustainable development.[70] In this model the productive contributions of reproductive work are recognised. Such recognition might assist in redressing the low valuation of this work which in turn could prompt a more lateral division of labour between women and men with respect to care work and in so doing remove some of the constraints that women experience with respect to fuller participation in the labour markets. More generally, recognising the costs and productive contributions of reproductive work together with the negative externalities associated with growth might contribute to a fuller discussion of the kind of economy that would enhance well-being – rather than assuming this automatically follows from increased GDP.[71]

Conclusion

Disaggregating inequality statistics draws attention to the very complex geographical patterns of contemporary development. No longer is there a simple one-third–two-thirds world of 'haves and have nots' corresponding geographically with a north–south divide. Rather, development is characterised by a complex mosaic of fast-growing 'superstar' regions found in both north and south, where the super rich as well as the highest levels of interpersonal inequality are found, set within a slower-growing periphery, typified by lower average incomes but lower inequality. Regional patterns of inequality are laced with interpersonal inequalities by gender, race, ethnicity and social class. Both uneven spatial development and rising interpersonal and gender inequalities are associated with the neo-liberal growth model.

As spatial, interpersonal and gender inequalities are found alongside high economic growth perhaps they do not matter, or form a necessary stage in the process towards greater affluence – along the lines of Deng Xao Ping's 'get rich first' strategy. Following the above discussion there are a number of reasons for rejecting this view in addition to normative equity goals. Given cumulative tendencies towards spatial concentration there is little evidence that trickle-down works, and discretion in wage settlements is invariably associated with gender discriminatory practices, as for example with the Chinese reforms, or university pay in Sweden.[72]

Despite globalisation and the structures of supranational institutions the existence of cross-national variations in the extent of interpersonal, regional and gender inequalities indicates that states retain some capacity to organise their internal affairs including patterns of distribution. Higher levels of equality are generally found in countries which least follow the neo-liberal pathway. These contemporaneous variations in inequality together with past epochs of greater equality indicate that alternative models of economic and social regulation are possible.

Social consensus in Europe from the late nineteenth century rejected the idea that the market could produce optimal quantities of goods such as health, education or housing, or manage the economy in a socially acceptable way, leading to the formation of the Keynesian welfare states throughout much of Europe in the mid twentieth century.[73] Keynesian macroeconomic and welfare policies represented a new mode of economic and social regulation which raised working-class living standards and reduced the claims on social wealth by rentiers (dismissively termed by Keynes as 'coupon clippers').[74] Likewise Roosevelt's New Deal policies in the US led to the ending of the Gatsbyesque Gilded Age and the onset of the Great Compression,namely a period of narrowing differentials. [75]

Today social values have changed again, rentiers or shareholders have resurfaced and their claims on social wealth, together with the high earnings of finance workers that make them possible, are socially sanctioned, indeed celebrated. While profitability has always been important, in contemporary times maintaining share values increasingly influences the strategy of firms, leading to short-term investments and flexible employment rather than innovation and training. Failure in this respect renders firms vulnerable to takeover and aggressive bidding from private equity firms. Finance and private equity firms have a reputation for being dynamic, innovative and central to the competitive restructuring of firms. Julie Froud and co-authors point out that in practice this is not the case, as the majority of private equity initiatives buy existing companies and make significant profits simply by restructuring their financial architecture,[76] more specifically by expanding the debt and reallocating the equity and liabilities of the companies to their own advantage, i.e. not by creating anything new or innovative.[77] If correct, this analysis questions the social value of these activities and the high incomes of the perpetrators. In the UK, the top 1 per cent of earners are disproportionately male, middle-aged, live in London or the south east, and work in finance, property or law. Their relative position has improved in recent years, though linked to the fortunes of the stock market.[78] It is their earnings that provide the market for conspicuous consumption such as the £35,000 cocktail reportedly on sale in a London bar,[79] while childcare workers in private nurseries in the same city are unlikely to be able to afford the services they are supplying. Indeed, Krugman suggests 'we are living in a new gilded age as extravagant as the original'.[80] It is difficult to see how this extravagant consumption performs a role in maintaining competitiveness that could not equally be played by consumption patterns derived from a more equitable earnings distribution.

There are historic precedents for an alternative system of redistribution or mode of social regulation, and contemporaneous examples such as the Nordic countries make it clear that the distributive arrangements within states are a matter of political choice. Given the 2008 crises in the banking, private equity and financial markets this may be the moment in which to press for such an alternative model.

The question of securing greater gender equity is more complex as it is universally present and enduring, but even so there are significant cross-national variations in its extent. Countries with lower overall inequality tend to have lower gender gaps, both secured through more regulated labour markets and stronger employee rights – including rights to parental leave as well as childcare support.

At present, when women enter the labour market their domestic roles are often transferred to other women which, given the low pay of care work, perpetuates inequalities between women – within and across countries, as illustrated with respect to the gendered, raced and nation structure of the care chain. An alternative model, and one that might encourage higher financial returns to care workers, would be to effect a lateral re-division of labour between women and men. In this regard the designated 'daddy leave' in Norway and Sweden has had some impact. The Norwegians found that flexible leave between parents was disproportionately taken by women. Only effective compulsion on a 'use it or lose it' basis led to men taking leave.[81] The extent of this designated period is very limited – originally just a month. Even so it will be interesting to see whether it has any longer-term impact on the domestic division of labour and whether more knowledge of the character of care work will create support for increasing its remuneration.

Parental leave and childcare support may require higher taxes. Taxation policies and social provision shape social behaviour, but all choices are constrained in some way, and what is clear from the Norwegian model is that only with the non-flexible daddy month did the male share of leave increase, suggesting that free choice tends to reinforce the status quo. If, collectively, people have a view about what is desirable with respect to gender equity, then it seems reasonable to expect social policies and expenditure to be oriented towards that goal.[82] With respect to regional issues, higher taxes are also more likely to lead to more balanced patterns of regional growth. The spatial consequences of a progressive tax system can be far more effective in generating transfers of income regionally than all of the tailor-made regional development strategies.

In a global context, thinking about a modified Keynesian strategy is clearly a complex issue, owing to the interconnectedness of economies such that increasing the wage share and being attentive to the requirements of reproductive work could reduce competitiveness. However, this argument is premised on the acceptance of a profit-led model of growth. As Stephanie Seguino and Caren Grown have pointed out, the economy could equally be viewed as a 'closed wage-led economic system'.[83] This view of the economy suggests that in principle it would be possible to develop a more inclusive and co-operative model on a global scale. When Keynesian policies were first introduced they required a redirection of priorities and resources from capital to labour within the nation. Likewise, as in the Keynesian/Fordist era, a new mode of social regulation could be introduced to allow contemporary productivity gains to be shared more widely. This may require some form of global governance, to ensure genuinely progressive redistributions of social value, and ideally one that would rest upon participatory forms of democracy at different spatial scales in order to overcome the weaknesses of the current supranational institutions and the unequal representation of states within them. Addressing inequality would also require lateral changes in the division of labour between women and men, which would contribute to tackling some of the deeply rooted gender inequalities that currently seem to be immune to all policy initiatives. Transformative remedies along these lines would potentially allow society to take control over rather than be led by the market/economy, with the likelihood of less unequal outcomes at all levels and a greater likelihood of more even development spatially and between women and men.

Notes

1 H.L. Moore, 'Global Anxieties: Concept-Metaphors and Pre-theoretical Commitments in Anthropology', *Anthropological Theory* 4:1 (2004), pp. 71–88.

2 J. Comaroff and J.L. Comaroff, 'Occult Economies and the Violence of Abstraction: Notes from the South African Postcolony', *American Ethnologist* 26:2 (1999), pp. 279–303.

3 M. Porter, 'The Economic Performance of Regions', *Regional Studies* 37 (2003), pp. 549–79.

4 WSIS, *World Summit on the Information Society* (2003): http://www.itu.int/wsis/index.html

5 R. Florida, *The Rise of the Creative Class: And How It's Transforming Work, Leisure, Community and Everyday Life* (New York: Basic Books, 2002).

6 UNDP, *International Cooperation at a Crossroads: Aid, Trade and Security in an Unequal World* (Oxford: Oxford University Press, 2005), and European Commission, *Gender Mainstreaming: Tools in Support* (2007): http://ec.europa.eu/employment_social/gender_equality/gender_mainstreaming/general_overview_en.html

7 See J. Stiglitz, *Making Globalization Work* (London: Allen Lane, 2006); World Bank, *World Development Report: Equity and Development* (2005): http://siteresources.worldbank.org/INTWDR2006/Resources/WDR_on_Equity_FinalOutline_July_public.pdf; UNDESA, *The Inequality Predicament, Economic and Social Development: Report on the World Social Situation* (2005): http://www.un.org/esa/socdev/rwss/media%2005/cd-docs/fullreport05.htm; UNDP, *International Cooperation at a Crossroads*.

8 M. Dunford, 'Disparities in Employment, Productivity and Output in the EU: The Roles of Labour Market Governance and Welfare Regimes', *Regional Studies* 30:4 (1996), pp. 339–57.

9   See D. Elson, 'The Economic, the Political and the Domestic: Business, States and Households in the Organisation of Production', *New Political Economy* 3:2 (1998), pp. 189–208; and D. Elson and N. Cagatay, 'The Social Content of Macro Economic Policies', *World Development* 28:7 (2000), pp. 1347–64.

10 A. Sen, *Development as Freedom* (Oxford: Oxford University Press, 1999).

11 World Bank (2007), *The 2005 International Comparison Program: Preliminary Results*: http://web.worldbank.org/WBSITE/EXTERNAL/DATASTATISTICS/ICPEXT/0,,pagePK:62002243~theSitePK:270065,00.html

12 B. Milanovic, *Worlds Apart* (Princeton and Oxford: Princeton University Press, 2005).

13 D. Quah, 'Global Imbalance, Global Inequality' (Policy Network, London, 2007) and D. Quah, 'Life in Unequal Growing Economies' (2007): http://econ.lse.ac.uk/staff/dquah/p/lug-1pr.pdf

14 Milanovic, *Worlds Apart*.

15 Quah, 'Life in Unequal Growing Economies'. In percentage terms the Gini coefficient increased overall in China from 29.1 to 44.9 between 1981 and 2004. For urban regions this increase was from 15% to 34% while for rural regions 23 to 34.

16 See L.C. Lu and Y.D. Wei, 'Domesticating Globalisation, New Economic Spaces and Regional Polarisation (Guangdong Province, China)', *Tijdschrift Voor Economische en Sociale Geografie* 98:2 (2007), pp. 225–44; Y.C. Ng, 'Gender Earnings Differentials and Regional Economic Development in Urban China (1988–97)', *Review of Income and Wealth* 1 (2007), pp. 148–66; and X.B. Zhang and K.H. Zhang, 'How Does Globalisation Affect Regional Inequality Within a Developing Country? Evidence from China', *Journal of Development Studies* 39:4 (2003), pp. 47–67.

17 B. Milanovic, 'Half a World: Regional Inequality in Five Great Federations', World Bank Policy Research Working Paper No. 3699 (2005): http://ssrn.com/abstract=647765

18 N. Singh, L. Bhandari, A. Chen and A. Khare, 'Regional Inequality in India: A Fresh Look', UC Santa Cruz Economics Working Paper No. 532; UC Santa Cruz Center for International Economics Working Paper No. 02-23 (2002).

19 R. Kanbur and A. Venables, 'Spatial Disparities and Economic Development', in D. Held and A. Kaya (eds), *Global Inequality* (Cambridge: Polity, 2007).

20 European Commission, *Growing Regions, Growing Europe: Fifth Progress Report on Economic and Social Cohesion* (Luxembourg: European Commission, 2008).

21 B. Milanovic, *Half a World: Regional Inequality in Five Great Federations*.

22 C. Benner, *Work in the New Economy: Flexible Labour Markets in Silicon Valley* (Oxford: Blackwell, 2002).

23 P. Krugman, 'Globalisation and Welfare' (James Meade Memorial Lecture, LSE, 14 June 2007): http://www.lse.ac.uk/collections/LSEPublicLecturesAndEvents/pdf/20070614_Krugman.pdf (podcast available through LSE website). See also T. Piketty and E. Saez, 'Income Inequality in the United States', *Quarterly Journal of Economics* 118:1 (2003), pp. 1–39.

24 See G. Esping-Andersen, 'More Inequality and Fewer Opportunities? Structural Determinants and Human Agency in the Dynamics of Income Distribution', in Held and Kaya (eds), *Global Inequality* for a discussion on European earning inequalities. For Britain see I. Kaplanis, 'The Geography of Employment Polarisation in Britain' (IPPR, 2007): http://www.ippr.org.uk/publicationsandreports/publications.asp?title=&author=Kaplanis&pubdate=&policyarea=&search=search

25 S. Chant, *Gender, Generation and Poverty: Exploring the Feminisation of Poverty in Africa, Asia and Latin America* (Cheltenham: Edward Elgar, 2007), and J. Pahl, *Money and Marriage* (London: Macmillan, 1983).

26 One reason why gender inequality in earnings tends to be higher in richer regions arises from the wider dispersal of male earnings found in such regions. This in turn is linked to the presence of jobs across the entire employment hierarchy, and the continued existence of a glass ceiling for women. That is, despite some fracturing as more highly educated women enter the upper echelons of employment, entry to the very top is still rare.

27 See UN Millennium Project 2007: http://www.unmillenniumproject.org/goals/index.htm

28 This measure is designed to reflect the more empowering effect of paid work in the non-agricultural sector where women are more likely to receive wages directly and less likely to be regarded as family helpers.

29 N. Kabeer, 'Marriage, Motherhood and Masculinity in Globalisation: Reconfigurations of Personal and Economic Life', IDS Working Paper 290 (Sussex: Institute of Development Studies, 2007).

30 ILO, *Global Employments Trends for Women Brief* (Geneva: ILO, 2007): http://www.ilo.org/public/english/employment/strat/download/getw07.pdf

31 Ng, 'Gender Earnings Differentials', p. 148.

32 Ibid.

33 Overall, women are over-represented in activities relating to nurturing, care, clerical work and sales, while men are over-represented in sectors and occupations involving money, management and machinery. Only 21% of the workforce have a woman as their immediate superior while 63% have a man, the remainder having no immediate supervisor. Women managers and supervisors are much more likely to be supervising other women, and less than 10% of employed men have a woman manager (European Foundation, 'Quality of Women's Work and Employment. Tools for Change', Foundation Paper no. 3 [Dublin: European Foundation, 2002]).

34 S. Chant, and C. Pedwell, 'Women and Gender in the Informal Economy: An Assessment of ILO Research and Suggested Ways Forward', International Labour Organisation Discussion Paper (Geneva: ILO, 2008).

35 D. Elson, 'Labour Markets as Gendered Institutions: Equality, Efficiency and Empowerment Issues', *World Development* 27:3 (1999), p. 618.

36 A. Maddison, *Monitoring the World Economy, 1820–1992* (Paris: OECD, 1995). Maddison compared the growth rates in seven world regions for two periods – 1950–73 (Fordist) and 1974–92 (neo-liberal) – and found a significant decrease in the rate of growth in the second period in all regions except Asia where there was a small increase. Maddison's calculations were updated to 2004 by M. Weisbrot, D. Baker and D. Rosnick, *Scorecard on Development: 25 Years of Diminished Progress* (Washington, DC: Center for Economic and Policy Research, 2005: http://www.cepr.net/documents/publications/development_2005_09.pdf) and they reached a similar conclusion. See also M. Dunford, 'Growth, Inequality and Cohesion: A Comment on the Sapir Report', *Regional Studies* 39:7 (2004), pp. 972–8.

37 R. Kaplinsky, 'Globalisation and Unequalisation: What Can Be Learned From Value Chain Analysis?', *Journal of Development Studies* 37:2 (2000), pp. 117–46.

38 N. Kaldor, 'The Role of Increasing Returns, Technical Progress and Cumulative Causation in the Theory of International Trade and Economic Growth', *Économie Appliquée* 34:4 (1981). Reprinted in F. Targetti and A. Thirlwall (eds), *The Essential Kaldor* (London: Duckworth, 1989), pp. 327–50.

39 P. Krugman, 'What's New About Economic Geography?', *Oxford Review of Economic Policy* 14:2 (1998), pp. 7–17.

40 M. Porter, 'The Economic Performance of Regions'.

41 See A. Amin and N. Thrift, *Globalization, Institutions, and Regional Development in Europe* (Oxford: Oxford University Press, 1994), and M. Storper, 'The Resurgence of Regional Economies, Ten Years Later: The Region as a Nexus of Un-traded Interdependencies', *European Urban and Regional Studies* 2:3 (1995), pp. 191–222.

42 See Krugman, 'What's New About Economic Geography?', and M. Fujita, P. Krugman and A. Venables, *The Spatial Economy: Cities, Regions and International Trade* (Cambridge, Mass.: MIT Press, 1999).

43 A. Scott, *Regions and the World Economy* (Oxford: Blackwell, 1998).

44 D. Quah, 'The Invisible Hand and the Weightless Economy', Centre for Economic Performance Occasional Paper No. 12 (London: LSE, 1996); D. Perrons, *Globalisation and Social Change: People and Places in a Divided World* (London: Routledge, 2004).

45 For more details see Perrons, *Globalisation and Social Change* or Scott, *Regions and the World Economy*.

46 J. Humphrey and H. Schmitz, 'How Does Insertion in Global Value Chains Affect Upgrading in Industrial Clusters?', *Regional Studies* 36:9 (2002), pp. 1017–27.

47 See S. Barrientos, 'Gender, Codes and Labour Standards in Global Production Systems', in I. van Staveren, D. Elson, C. Grown and N. Cagatay (eds), *The Feminist Economics of Trade* (London: Routledge, 2007).

48 S. Sassen, *The Global City* (New York, Tokyo, London (second editions), Princeton: Princeton University Press, 2001).

49 Ibid.

50 For a more detailed explanation of the wage polarisation see Perrons, 'Globalisation and Social Change: People and Places in a Divided World', and Kaplanis, 'The Geography of Employment Polarisation in Britain'.

51 See Quah, 'The Invisible Hand and the Weightless Economy'.

52 W. Baumol, 'Macroeconomics of Unbalanced Growth: The Anatomy of the Urban Crisis', *American Economic Review* 57:3 (1967), pp. 415–26.

53 A. Hochschild, 'Global Care Chains and Emotional Surplus Value', in W. Hutton and A. Giddens (eds), *On the Edge: Living with Global Capitalism* (London: Jonathan Cape, 2002), p. 137.

54 R. Parreñas, 'Long Distance Intimacy: Class, Gender and Intergenerational Relations Between Mothers and Children in Filipino Transnational Families', *Global Networks: A Journal of Transnational Affairs* 5:4 (2005), pp. 317–36.

55 International Migration Outlook, 'International Migration Remittances and their Role in Development' (2006): http://www.oecd.org/dataoecd/61/46/38840502.pdf

56 S. Sassen, 'Global Cities and Survival Circuits', in B. Ehrenreich and A. Hochschild (eds), *Global Woman* (New York: Metropolitan Books, 2003).

57 See Dunford, 'Growth, Inequality and Cohesion', for a discussion of the Sapir report.

58 See H. Jarvis, 'Home Truths about Care-less Competitiveness', *International Journal of Urban and Regional Research* 31:1 (2007), pp. 207–14, and R. Layard, *Happiness: Lessons from a New Science* (London: Allen Lane, 2005).

59 Sen, *Development as Freedom*.

60 See http://ec.europa.eu/eurostat/ramon/nuts/basicnuts_regions_en.html.

61 Jarvis, 'Home Truths about Care-less Competitiveness'.
62 M.A. Fortuna, T.P. Dentinho, J.C. Vieira and R.G. Luis, *Evaluation of the European Policies in Support of Ultra Peripheric Regions* (part of the project 'European Regional Development Issues in the New Millennium and their Impact on Economic Policy', Zagreb, Croatia, 29 August–1 September 2001), p. 26: http://www.ersa.org/ersaconfs/ersa01/papers/full/95.pdf
63 Irish 'mist' being a euphemism for fairly persistent light rain.
64 As recently as the late 1980s, Ireland was experiencing net outward migration of over 40,000 a year but from 1998 to 2004 there was an annual average net immigration figure of 36,000 (58,000 immigrants less 22,000 emigrants).
65 In 1999 GNP for Ireland was 13% less than GDP owing to the profits earned by foreign-owned enterprises, which can leave the country thus making GDP per head greater than GNP per head.
66 There has been some progress in examining the impact of policies on women and men separately but less in terms of recognising how the formulation of the policies includes gender bias.
67 Elson and Catagay, 'The Social Content of Macro Economic Policies'.
68 See Elson, 'The Economic, the Political and the Domestic'.
69 Ibid.
70 Ibid.
71 See Layard, *Happiness: Lessons from a New Science*, for a critique of the one-to-one association between GDP and happiness, and Jarvis, 'Home Truths about Care-less Competitiveness' (p. 208), for a discussion of the contrast between the 'good life' and the good city or region for everyday life.
72 L. Gonas, A. Bergman and K. Rosenberg, 'Equal Opportunity and Unwarranted Pay Differences: A Case Study of Gender-related Pay Differences in a Knowledge Based Society', in D. Perrons, C. Fagan, L. McDowell, K. Ray and K. Ward (eds), *Gender Divisions and Working Time in the New Global Economy* (Cheltenham: Edward Elgar, 2007).
73 See K. Polanyi, *The Great Transformation: The Political and Economic Origins of Our Time* (Boston: Beacon Press, 1957).
74 I. Ertuk, J. Froud, S. Johal, A. Leaver and K. Williams, 'The Romance of Agency and an Alternative Problem Definition' (Centre for Research on Socio-cultural Change, Manchester, 2006): http://www.ipeg.org.uk/papers/hallsworth_papers/k_williams.pdf
75 P. Krugman, 'For Richer', *New York Times*, 20 October 2002: http://www.pkarchive.org/economy/ForRicher.html
76 J. Froud, A. Leaver, K. Williams, 'New Actors in a Financialised Economy and the Remaking of Capitalism', *New Political Economy* 12:3 (2007), pp. 339–47.
77 This works by financial arrangements which expand the share of debt in the company that is acquired by the private equity firm but then restricting the returns to the debt holders and making the majority of gains accrue to the minority of equity holders (Froud et al., 'New Actors in a Financialised Economy').
78 M. Brewer, L. Sibieta and L. Wren-Lewis, 'Racing Away? Income Inequality and the Evolution of High Incomes', IFS Briefing Note 76 (London: Institute of Fiscal Studies, 2007): http://www.ifs.org.uk/bns/bn76.pdf
79 The cocktail served at the Modiva nightclub in London 'consists of a large measure of Louis XII cognac, half a bottle of Cristal Rose champagne, some brown sugar, angostura bitters and a few flakes of 24-carat edible gold leaf . . . at the bottom of the crystal glass is an 11-carat white diamond ring' (A.

Chakrabortty, 'What Credit Crunch? Club Launches £35,000 Cocktail', *Guardian*, 8 December 2007).

80   See Krugman, 'For Richer'.

81   B. Brandth and E. Kvande, 'Care Policies for Fathers in a Flexible Time Culture', in Perrons et al., *Gender Divisions and Working Time in the New Global Economy*.

82   In Rousseau's terms: to secure the General Will rather than the Will of All; in other words, recognising that the summation of individual rationality does not always lead to collective rationality. J.J. Rousseau, *The Social Contract*, trans. Maurice Cranston (Harmondsworth: Penguin Classics, 1968).

83   S. Seguino and C. Grown, 'Gender Equity and Globalisation: Macroeconomic Policy for Developing Countries', in van Staveren et al., *The Feminist Economics of Trade*, p. 306.

12

Addressing Adverse Consequences of Globalisation for Workers

Anke Hassel

In the debate about globalisation – the changes in the international economy towards creating one world market for finance, goods and labour – many economists argue that the overall balance of globalisation is positive: that the negative effects of non-trade-liberalisation outweigh the negative effects of liberalisation, and that negative distributional effects within countries affecting employment and wages can be addressed by smart policies on education and welfare.[1] They point to extraordinary growth rates in the developing world, trends towards economic prosperity in those countries that participate in trade, and the general success of open economies.

Others, however, regard globalisation as a dilemma: on the one hand, it induces downward pressures on social spending by constraining governments' ability to tax or engage in deficit spending. On the other hand, globalisation increases the demand for social protection because of the economic insecurity it produces.[2] For them, the effect of globalisation is 'to increase social dislocations and economic insecurity, as the distribution of incomes and jobs across firms and industries becomes increasingly unstable'.[3]

Public opinion is even more sceptical. Surveys show that while in most countries a majority think that globalisation has a positive effect, the minority who think the opposite is pretty substantial. A survey of public opinion in eighteen countries by the Chicago Council on Global Affairs and WorldPublicOpinion.org, published in April 2007, concluded that 'majorities around the world believe economic globalisation and international trade benefit national economies, companies, and consumers. But many think that trade harms the environment and threatens jobs and want to mitigate these effects with environmental and labour standards'.[4] Opposition to globalisation tends to be strongest in wealthier countries such as the US and

Europe and weakest in fast-growing countries that have only recently integrated into the world economy, such as China. The populations of developing countries who have been recipients of foreign direct investment for a long time tend to be more sceptical too. Similarly, a recent study by the German Marshall Fund found only slight majorities in the United States (52 per cent) and Europe (53 per cent) in favour of globalisation.[5] Thirty-four per cent of Americans and 38 per cent of Europeans view globalisation unfavourably. Where do citizens get their views on globalisation? Studies on trade preferences show that those sceptical about globalisation tend to belong to certain socio-economic groups. The type of people's employment as well as their income bracket determines what they think about trade. Opinions about trade and globalisation are closely correlated to skill and educational levels. Workers with only a high school education are almost twice as likely to support protectionist policies as workers with a college education.[6]

The attitudes of respondents cannot be called ill-informed or cowardly, nor are they necessarily nationalist. Rather, they simply reflect the worries of low-skilled workers in wealthy economies, who have reason to believe that while the economy and society as a whole might benefit from increases in globalisation, they themselves might fare less well. And these worries are backed up by current research on the effects of globalisation. Without knowing anything about trade theory, factor equalisation or sophisticated statistical analyses, low-skilled workers are largely correct when they assume that globalisation might increase overall wealth, but will not fill their bank accounts or improve their job opportunities.

The *Employment Outlook* of the OECD, for example, states that there 'is some evidence that deepening trade over the past few decades has increased both earnings inequality and insecurity for OECD workers'. The report goes on to state that it is difficult to separate the impact of globalisation from that of technological change or structural reform and that the impact is not as great as is popularly understood. But it does point out that the effect of globalisation on workers varies, and is determined in part by their skill levels: 'While offshoring has no real impact on the overall numbers of workers in employment, it can reduce demand for low-skill workers, probably because businesses tend to move the most routine production stages overseas.'[7]

As a consequence, globalisation is likely to have contributed to slow wage growth in the US and Europe in recent years, and is also partly to blame for rising income inequality. Over the last two decades or so, a majority of advanced industrialised economies have experienced increasing economic inequality and economic insecurity as well as rising gaps in employment and unemployment rates between high-skilled and low-skilled groups on the labour market.

The gist of the problem that governments of advanced industrialised countries have to deal with when addressing globalisation is this: low-skilled workers in high-productivity countries have reason to worry that they are among the groups that will be increasingly squeezed between rising prices, falling or stagnating wages, and benefits for those not in employment. At the same time, such workers constitute a large proportion, if not the majority, of the electorate in these countries. A further increase in economic insecurity among the lower middle classes will have political implications, in particular for left-of-centre politics.

In terms of policies, governments have generally faced the dilemma of accepting either rising inequalities and low wages along with high employment rates or higher wages for the low-skilled with high levels of unemployment. As recent studies have demonstrated, the liberal Anglo-Saxon countries favoured high employment at low wages while many of the continental European countries chose the protection of pay over employment. Only the Scandinavian countries have seemingly escaped the dilemma and have achieved both high employment and high egalitarian wage distribution, but under the condition of a strong role of the state in employment creation. In the last decade – encouraged by the OECD's *Job Study* – many governments have moved more towards an Anglo-Saxon liberal approach of employment creation by making labour markets more flexible. This approach has been successful in the sense that employment levels overall have increased, but it has not solved issues of income volatility and economic insecurity.

Therefore, the question is now whether employment creation alone is the complete and satisfactory response to the worries of the low-skilled in a globalised world. From a progressive perspective the answer should be no. Workers and their families are looking also for economic security – reliable income levels and social protection combined with jobs. What turns the Scandinavian economy (and some other small European economies) into model cases of economic openness, social cohesion and full employment are complex and comprehensive systems which combine activation measures through active labour-market policies, training, public employment and childcare, a strong inclusion of trade unions and workers' representatives, and high levels of social spending. This combination has been successful in limiting economic inequality and insecurity. The complexity and comprehensiveness of national systems, however, also makes policy transfers and learning very difficult.

The issue is politically salient, as we know that economic openness and volatility increase demands for social security. An increasingly skewed distribution of economic gains in democratic societies raises a perfectly legitimate formation of political preferences for policies that either strengthen redistribution or protect the losers from further losses. As the median-wage earner moves down the income ladder and further away from average income, and as more service sector workers and middle-class families experience processes of economic insecurity and volatile income fluctuation which in the past had only affected some of the working-class strata, social and economic protection will become an increasingly important policy field for sustaining further globalisation. This will, however, only be politically feasible if the middle classes are convinced that they will equally benefit from redistribution.

Globalisation, pressure on the low-skilled, and national variations

Many of the developments that make workers feel insecure about their jobs and people uneasy about globalisation are only partly due to the process of globalisation itself. The way we work and live has changed tremendously over the last three to four decades. Much of this is due to the expansion of communication technology and technological progress in general, and to the increase of women's employment and the growth of the service sector. In many cases all these factors have come together. Technological progress in the manufacturing sector is likely to have led to more job losses in advanced industrialised countries than has the relocation of production to low-wage countries. Today, on average no more than 20 per cent of employees in OECD countries are employed in the manufacturing sector; this share has almost halved over the last thirty years. Moreover, the expansion of service sector employment has gone hand in hand with the expansion of female employment. Office work and personal services in education, health and household services have increased dramatically, with major effects on the world of work.

Even if there had been no international economic integration, today the working world would still look different from how it did three decades ago. Many of the worries we are now facing about economic insecurity and equality, as well as the employability of the low-skilled, would probably have been just as pressing as they are under the effects of globalisation. Workers would still have lost jobs, as they did when new technologies were introduced. Some skilled trades would still have disappeared. For instance, bitter battles over the replacements of skilled craftsmen in the printing industry by new machinery occurred when newspaper publishers moved out of Fleet Street in London in the 1980s. These changes had nothing to do with globalisation. There is no positive role model of an economy or society that has flourished in isolation and without increasing international exchanges of people and goods. This is regardless of what we might assume would have happened to the developing world if there had been no spread of technology, finance and manufacturing across the globe.

For this reason, it is time to move beyond the question of whether and why globalisation works. The debate on globalisation is too often depicted in black and white, with the proponents of globalisation mobilising all their data and statistical analysis to prove that globalisation has an overall beneficial effect for virtually everyone, in order to condemn any policy move that might slow down trade or regulate the world economy. On the other hand, anti-globalisation activists very often do not have practical suggestions on how to deal with the effects of globalisation. Little is known and understood about how to regulate trade and financial flows without causing detrimental effects on economic gains, particularly for developing countries.

For instance, much of the debate on global labour standards is dominated by the concern that any increase in labour standards will hurt developing countries disproportionately, while protecting jobs in the developed world. If the only competitive advantage of poorer countries is their relatively low wages and poor working conditions, any government of a developing country is bound to protect these low standards when fighting for investments, and will not be persuaded to increase standards if this means a loss of investments.

Nonetheless, the move towards a global market place, in the context of vast discrepancies in living standards, costs and wages in different parts of the world, has had a distinct impact on employment in the industrialised world as well as developing countries. The fundamentals of the effects of globalisation on workers can be summarised as follows.

Pressure on wages and employment

If there were a global market place, wages for a particular job should be the same, wherever the job is done. We are obviously still far away from such a scenario, as wages even within the EU cover a wide spread. Unskilled manual workers in Germany, for example, are still five times as expensive as their counterparts in Romania. Wages in the suppliers firms of the textile and garment industries in South East Asia, in turn, are only a fraction of the Romanian wages. Given the choice and the decrease in transportation and communication costs across the globe, we should not be surprised that firms aim to exploit these cost differences in order to remain competitive in the market. Companies which relocate primarily argue that they do so in order to reduce labour costs.[8] But to what extent will this be the case? And what is the effect on wages and employment in the high-cost countries?

The recent *Employment Outlook* by the OECD has looked into the matter and comes to the conclusion that the deepening of the trade and international production network is a potentially important source for the vulnerability of (low-skilled) workers. The report particularly points out that:[9]

- Foreign competition tends to reduce employment in the most exposed industries.
- Off-shoring has no or a positive effect on employment. Jobs lost due to off-shoring are generally compensated by new jobs due to the stronger competitiveness of firms. These new jobs are usually at a higher skill level than the ones that were lost, which leads to a lower demand for low-skilled workers.
- Off-shoring might be responsible for the increasing sensitivity of labour demand to wages.
- Foreign competition might contribute to the erosion of long-term employment relationships for the low-skilled.

While it is difficult to estimate precisely the scope of these effects, they generally support the view that globalisation is beneficial to economies as a whole, but can be detrimental for those at the lower end of the skill distribution, who find it difficult to get a new job, once the job they held in a manufacturing firm has been relocated abroad.

These findings are in line with empirical studies by labour economists on wage inequality and economic insecurity.[10] While real wage growth on average in the industrialised world has been below productivity growth, increasing wage inequality has meant that the bottom half of wage earners have seen very low wage increases, if not real wage decreases, over the last ten years. Wage inequality has increased sharply over the last decade, particularly in the Anglo-Saxon countries. The effect was stronger in the upper half of the income distribution. While in the bottom half of the income distribution relative wages remained largely the same, the upper middle classes saw a relative increase in their wages.

Moreover, low-skilled workers tend to have higher unemployment rates and longer unemployment spells than high-skilled workers, with the gap between low- and high-skilled workers becoming wider rather than narrower. In other words, high-skilled workers tend to be the beneficiaries of the increasing opportunities presented by globalisation; the low-skilled are facing not only job losses, but also stagnating real wages and difficulties in finding new jobs.

Less is known about the effects of globalisation on those who are in between low and high skills, in particular those who have specific skills at the medium level. While the OECD suggests that those who have skills potentially benefit from restructuring, because more high-skilled jobs are created, there is also some indication that intensified restructuring increases the income volatility of the middle classes. Activation policies and the need to find new employment very quickly might devalue existing skills and force skilled workers into lower-skilled occupations. In the United States, there is now a substantial risk of a drop in income when changing employers. This has created widespread feelings of income and job insecurity, which had already begun to grow during the 1990s.[11]

Diversity of national institutions and company strategies

Suzanne Berger and her team at the MIT have investigated the processes of the globalisation of firms and the emergence of a global economy. They were interested in the question of whether relocation to cheap-labour countries was the only option companies had when facing global competition and whether one could observe a convergence in firms' strategies when dealing with global markets. In her book *How We Compete* she shows that companies' strategies vary widely, even in the same industry facing the same problems. She found that for most firms, the exploitation of low-wage labour is a dead-end strategy, since firms have no chance of gaining a durable advantage which is tied to long-term sup-plier relations, brand names, intellectual property, specialised skills and reputation.[12] She also argues that there is no single best model for how business can successfully transform itself to deal with globalisation.

There is a diversity of successful decisions by companies about relocation and production models, even in the most globalised and cost-pressured industries such as the clothing industry. Clothing companies in northern Italy continue to compete successfully despite high-cost pressure from low-wage countries. The suggestion that a firm must respond to the expansion of global markets by following the route of relocating to cheap labour locations, and thereby increas-ing economic insecurity for those in high-wage countries, is therefore not warranted, even though we observe an overall trend towards off-shoring and the effect that has on low-skilled workers. For instance, only 20 per cent of cases of firm relocation in Germany were job moves abroad; all other relocations took place within Germany.[13]

A similar argument can be made when we look at the effect of globali-sation on specific countries or regions. Very general conclusions about the impact of globalisation for each and every corner of the world are often misleading, since the effects vary enormously by countries and regions. One example is the different dynamic of global sourcing of services in North America and western Europe. Global sourcing of services is lower in Europe than in North America, which has partly to do with language competencies and the role and regulation of services in different economies. Public ownership of services such as health and education also tends to limit the potential off-shoring of services from Europe to the developing world.

Additionally, best-practice role models on how to succeed in a globalised world have changed over time. When facing inflationary shocks following the oil crisis of the 1970s, Germany and the small corporatist countries, particularly Scandinavia and Austria, were hailed as positive examples, since they were able to command their labour-market institutions for controlling inflation. In the 1980s, the Japanese approach of lean production was seen as revolutionising the world and leading the way towards global success. In the 1990s, the rise of shareholder value strategies in the Anglo-Saxon world, combined with policies of deregulation and decentralisation, brought back the liberal model at a time when both Germany and Japan were heading for trouble. Post-socialist transformation countries as well as the European continent were advised to liberalise and follow the Anglo-Saxon approach. Today, the liberal approach is still dominant, but the acceptance of diversity is more prominent than in the past.

As a consequence, the way globalisation affects a country like Germany, whose economy is specialised in high-quality engineering, is likely to be very different from the way it affects the UK, which has specialised in the financial sector. The Finnish economy is dominated by one company which is the leading supplier of mobile phones, while the Danish economy mainly consists of small to medium-sized firms, many of which specialise in transport and logistics. In other words, different economic structures and types of specialisation in various countries are responsible for the different effects of, and adjustment mechanisms to, globalisation.

Hence, depending on the way a national economy is integrated into the world economy, there might be good reasons for it to specialise further in its most competitive industries, even though this might increase the country's openness and dependence on the world market. It is the diversity, rather than uniformity, of what globalisation means for different countries which is central to understanding the transformation of the global economy that we are witnessing. Even though there are general effects on low-skilled workers, the patterns of transformation vary in different regions. Globalisation deepens patterns of economic specialisation. Economic specialisation is based on the availability of specialist knowledge and infrastructure, which again is embedded in highly diverse institutional settings of labour-market regulation, firms' finances, training and social provisions, even among the group of industrialised countries. Each national economy will aim to protect its competitive advantages and use its competitive edge for managing the long-term transition towards a service economy. While in the long run employment in manufacturing tends to shrink, national economies will develop different types of service sectors, depending on their economic specialisation. Understanding these diverse economic settings is key to developing a policy agenda to tackle the common challenges presented by globalisation.

The policy agenda: how to achieve economic security for all?

The printing unions which tried to stop publishing houses from moving out of Fleet Street could not prevent that change taking place; and protests against globalisation are unlikely to succeed either. This does not mean that globalisation cannot or should not be regulated or that its impact on the low-skilled cannot be abated. Nor does it mean that the unions – when protesting against change – do not have a point when highlighting the social effects of what is about to happen to their members. Innovation and new technology pose risks for workers who have invested in a specialised trade. These investments have to be taken care of in order to offset high income losses by off-shoring.

Good public policy should not try to stop globalisation, but needs to think in terms of the protection of and investment in skills and human resources when dealing with economic insecurity and inequality. Trying to stop firms from moving and relocating, imposing stricter labour standards on developing countries, or erecting trade barriers, is unlikely to solve the problems of helping workers to deal with structural changes. This is not an argument against raising labour standards. They are valuable for setting the standard for decent working conditions in general, and have positive repercussions for the protection of skills and long-term human resources. Moreover, the pressure for raising labour standards in the developing world will intensify as the regions become wealthier. They do not however present a solution for dealing with off-shoring and foreign competition in industrialised countries, which are ongoing.

Therefore, the aim must be to enable workers to move between jobs without risking a major loss in income, status or skills. Among economists, the flexibility part of this approach is generally welcomed and supported. Where there is much less agreement and a lack of policy debate is over the extent and provision of insurance and protection against losses.

Workers' concerns

Workers' concerns about losing their jobs vary between countries (see figure 1).[14] Generally speaking, Scandinavian countries do better than liberal countries. Workers are most concerned about losing their jobs in continental and southern European countries. Christopher Anderson and Jonas Pontusson have looked into the reasons for the discrepancy. As we might expect, higher unemployment levels in different countries lead to greater worries. Also, lower-skilled, younger workers and women tend to worry more than the higher-skilled, older workers and men. Interestingly, worries about losing one's job are not related to job stability. There is no correlation between worries about losing one's job and job tenure rates. Job tenure rates have generally been stable. In eighteen out of twenty-one OECD countries, the average number of years in one job even increased between 1995 and 2005.[15]

There are, however, three policy-related instruments which have an effect on workers' concerns:

> First, government legislation restricting the ability of employers to fire workers and/or imposing costs on employers who do fire workers appears to have a quite significant impact on individuals' assessment of how secure their jobs are (cognitive job insecurity). Second, government spending on labour market programmes designed to improve the employability of unemployed workers and to help them find new jobs reduces labour market insecurity. Third, generous unemployment

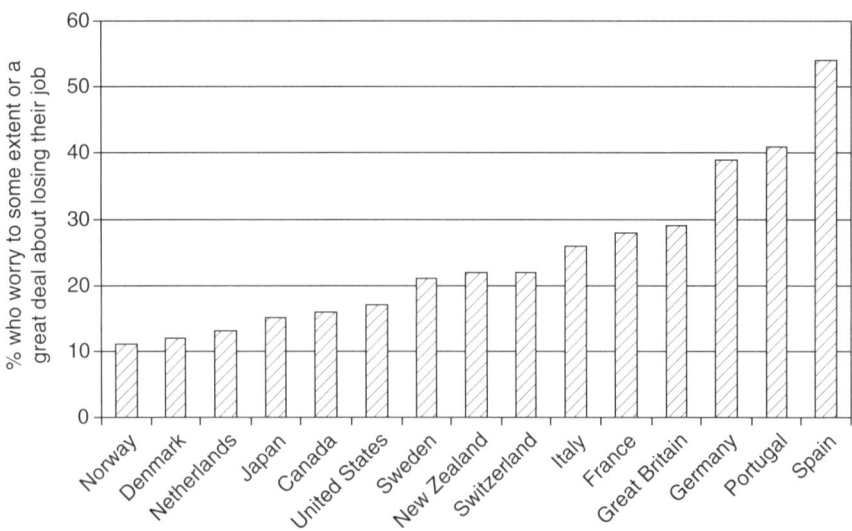

Figure 1   Workers' worries

Source: C.J. Anderson and Jonas Pontusson, 'Workers, Worries and Welfare States: Social Protection and Job Insecurity in 15 OECD Countries', *European Journal of Political Research* 46 (2007), p. 216.

compensation reduces worries about the income loss associated with unemployment.[16]

Two questions derive from this analysis, demonstrating how difficult it is for policy-makers to draw the correct conclusions: First, to the extent that the same policy instruments also affect unemployment levels, protective measures might increase security but reduce employment chances and thereby decrease security at the same time. The overall effect could be that security remains the same but at lower employment levels. Second, looking at the policy instruments which have a positive effect on job security perception, it is unclear whether they represent alternative pathways or work in combination with each other. Can some countries opt for stricter employment protection and others for active labour-market policies? And if we combine the two issues, could it be that low unemployment levels help workers to reduce insecurity in countries with more flexible labour markets, while higher spending on unemployment benefits and employment protection are the necessary consequence for reassuring workers in settings with high unemployment? And could it be that stronger employment protection is warranted in countries with higher levels of employment in manufacturing as compared to countries with a large service sector?

Income volatility and inequality

Currently, much less is known about income volatility. There is evidence that incomes in the US have become more volatile over recent years.[17] But in general we know more about income and wage inequality. Wage and income differentials among various groups of workers have widened in most countries. In particular, the very high-skilled have greatly benefited from their skill levels, while the low-paid have not been able to improve their wages.

Moreover, in order to make work pay,[18] the focus of social spending has changed from compensating primarily those with no market income to expanding coverage to those with low market incomes. These are the prime group of losers of globalisation, particularly the low-skilled and low-paid. Activation policies, which have spread beyond the liberal Anglo-Saxon countries to almost all advanced industrialised countries, have led to a whole array of subsidies for low-paid employment, either in the form of tax credits, in-work benefits or workfare. As displaced low-skilled workers do not find sufficient employment in the private sector but should not remain unemployed for too long, governments have experimented with a vast variety of forms of employment subsidies which target either employers, employees, or both. Recently, concepts of wage insurances have been suggested and implemented in the United States (and in different forms in Germany), which give in-work benefits to pre-defined groups in low-income brackets who have lost their jobs through off-shoring and accepted lower-paid employment.[19]

In-work benefits and wage subsidies have generally worked for improving employment levels for the low-skilled. They have topped up very low wages with benefits to lift them just above the poverty line. In almost all OECD countries there is now a growing share of the working population who cannot survive on the wages from full-time employment.

At the same time, poverty is related to income inequality. Countries with high levels of inequality are also countries with relatively high shares of people living in poverty.[20] In the past, the most important factor for keeping income inequality at bay was not taxation or redistribution but rather a low degree of wage inequality facilitated by labour-market institutions. There is a strong correlation between the degree of centralisation of wage-setting institutions and the compression of wages. Moreover, the rise of wage inequality in industrialised countries is directly connected with the demise of unionisation and the weakening of labour-market institutions.[21]

Therefore, the scepticism about and outright opposition to centralised wage-setting institutions and unionisation, as expressed by many governments – including some social democratic ones – might have been counter-productive with regard to income inequality. At the same time, centralised bargaining and unionisation cannot be copied or imported easily from one country to the next. But we might want to conclude that government in those countries where co-ordinated wage-bargaining structures still exist should develop approaches in which centralised bargaining institutions continue to deliver the benefits of the past: productivity-oriented wage settlements and a relatively compressed wage structure. Rather than encouraging further dispersion of wages and thereby incomes, flatter wage structures can help to keep widening income disparity at bay.

This is particularly important, since widening economic inequality increasingly causes worry not only among the low-skilled but also among people with middle-class incomes. The unskilled move between subsidised employment and no employment and have little to lose from further economic restructuring. It is the lower middle classes, the ones who have specialist medium-level skills, who are most at risk and who worry that they will end up in the low-income brackets after having lost their well-paid jobs in manufacturing industries. Collective agreements, which regulate pay for skills and trades, can help sustain a wage structure, which pays a premium for skills and prevents a market-driven polarisation of middle-class incomes.

Flexicurity

As of now, the most sophisticated policy approach, which aims to combine change, flexibility and the protection of workers, is encapsulated in the concept of 'flexicurity'. Flexicurity has been discussed within the European Union for the last decade or so and has recently moved high onto the agenda of the European Commission. The concept was endorsed by the European Council of Ministers in December 2007 and has informed the discussion on revitalising the Lisbon Agenda. In essence, it 'involves the deliberate combination of flexible and reliable contractual arrangements, comprehensive lifelong learning strategies, effective active labour market policies, and modern, adequate and sustainable social protection systems'.[22] Moreover, the EU Commission has realised and appreciated the role of social dialogue when engaging in reform policies and accepted the need for diverse policy agendas in different countries.

Positive examples of a combination of high levels of mobility and economic security are Denmark and Sweden. In Sweden, the Rhen–Meidner model had already realised in the 1950s that workers benefit from being able to move between jobs rather than fighting for the stability of existing workplaces. There, active labour-market policies were combined with early investment in education, good childcare facilities, centralised wage bargaining and a large public sector. Today, Denmark excels at achieving high growth rates, high employment levels and high degrees of worker mobility. Its model of success is worth studying and can definitely serve as an example of how open economies can sustain large welfare states and high degrees of egalitarianism.[23]

Flexicurity is certainly the model which can and should inform successful adjustment policies. The issue is not the combination of flexibility to adjust and the protection of the individual, which has also been recognised by the World Bank and a number of policy analysts.[24] The issue is rather which concrete policy conclusions should be drawn from the concept and from countries acting as role models with regard to the combination and appropriateness of certain policy instruments and the room for national adaptation.

Taking diversity seriously

Hence, we face a similar issue of general effects in highly diverse settings. We know that labour-market institutions and policies do make a difference in outcomes. Take again the example of the US and Europe. In North America, the effects of globalisation are generally associated with real wage stagnation or real wage losses for the lower strata of the labour market, due to a much more flexible labour market. In continental Europe, where stronger labour-market regulation and wage-bargaining institutions protect the wage structure more effectively, the low-skilled generally face long-term unemployment rather than lower wages.

While the role of national diversity in successful policies is increasingly recognised, it is still not sufficiently conceptualised. For instance, the OECD published its influential *Job Study* on the labour market in 1994 and advised a general decentralisation and deregulation approach, regardless of the institutional, economic or political context of the countries concerned.[25] Today, in the face of the continuing and re-emerging success of small and open European countries, which are based on regulated labour markets and centralised wage-setting institutions, the OECD has had to accept that there is more than one model which can produce high employment levels and good economic performance.[26] If anything, the Scandinavian countries provide the role model today for how to cope with the adverse effects of globalisation in the early twenty-first century.

But even here, it is still not clear how much of the institutional architecture is really understood and how much of current assessment is just ex-post rationalisation. Denmark, as well as the Netherlands, was in deep trouble in the 1980s due to several failed attempts to adjust to external shocks and closer monetary integration in the European Union. Similarly, Sweden in the 1990s was no showcase for dealing with globalisation. Today their institutions of training, wage-setting and social and family policy are seen as leading the way to adjustment.

Moreover, even if countries tried to follow the Scandinavian path of combining high welfare with high flexibility in the labour market, it is far from clear what the effects would be. If continental European governments were enthusiastically adopting 'flexicurity' policies, would they all end up looking like Denmark? How would they move towards a high-taxation regime in a global context, in which tax competition takes place? Or is there a danger that their welfare states would lose the benefits of the protection of their traditional institutions, without gaining the flexibility and the welfare provisions of a Scandinavian welfare state? Rigidities in labour markets can stem from many more sources than just the regulations arising from employment protection legislation. They can be rooted in training certifications, social transfers, business regulation and a lack of inter-regional mobility of workers.

In many countries, employment protection is interlinked with social protection in a rather complex way. In many – in particular southern European – countries, employment protection has been substituted for welfare provision. A call for a general decrease in employment protection in order to facilitate workers' mobility is therefore not a solution.[27] A lot depends on the labour-market institutions, the policies supporting labour turnover and workers' expectations of the consequences of job losses.

Similarly, education and training are highly country-specific. Countries with successful manufacturing industries, such as Germany, often have training systems which focus heavily on intensive and specific training at secondary level. While these training systems are highly successful in getting young people into work, they often do not provide sufficient general skills for workers to easily change professions at a later stage. Further training courses are few and difficult to combine with initial training. In the Anglo-Saxon countries, tertiary training, which usually provides more general skills at a higher level, is more developed.

Therefore, training regimes in continental countries should adapt towards providing more general training at a higher level, in particular for those who have started out with a lower degree. The funding of training courses later in life should be made available for those who work in industries that are exposed to foreign competition. Firms should be encouraged and asked to contribute to further training for all their employees in order to maintain and increase the employment opportunities of workers well before redundancies might arise.

At the same time, since globalisation deepens economic specialisation, governments should take care that firms have enough incentives to continue to invest in industry-specific skills. A brash move towards tertiary education at the expense of high-quality secondary education, as is often implied and recommended by comparative studies on education by the OECD, might weaken countries' competitive base without enabling them to compete at the level of high-quality services at which many tertiary education degrees are aimed.

Therefore, rather than rushing towards developing a 'one size fits all' policy agenda, governments should focus on establishing ways of improving tailor-made solutions for nationally specific problems when facing the various social and economic challenges presented by globalisation. Putting a premium on activation, skills and flexibility as guidelines for improving the employability of low- and medium-skilled workers who are facing job losses is, however, a general answer which does not easily translate into policy measures.

Therefore, national governments need to engage much more thoroughly in discussions on which schemes, developed elsewhere, might work most effectively in their own national contexts. Again, the Scandinavian countries could serve as a role model, where royal commissions and expert groups develop joint policy recommendations which are outside the realm of electoral competition. However, governments need to be aware that many of the role models which were celebrated yesterday have turned into problem cases today, and that this might happen to today's heroes. Policy analysis should be explicit in taking national contexts and complementarities into consideration.

The politics of economic security

Political support for better protection of working people in a globalised world can come from three sources: from the demand for social protection from middle-class earners, from a renewal of social partnership, and from corporate responsibility and accountability. These three sources can be employed to varying degrees depending on the political and institutional situations of the countries at hand.

While those most vulnerable to the detrimental effects of globalisation are the low-skilled, the politics of redistribution have traditionally been based on coalitions between the working and middle classes. Large welfare states provide welfare not just for the poor but for the majority of the electorate. Middle-class voters are only willing to pay for a large welfare state if they are beneficiaries too. Moreover, welfare states that focus too narrowly on poverty relief tend to be mean and lean. They can hardly muster the support for poor-relief programmes and will not be able to provide the benefits which are needed to help vulnerable workers maintain their ability to find good work.

The politics of welfare in globalised markets therefore must address middle-class concerns for employability, education and economic security. Their need for social protection generally depends on how specific workers' skill assets are and how easily they can move from one position to another.[28] High degrees of specific skill sets and regulated labour markets lead to higher demands for social protection than more general skill sets in flexible labour markets. This is what makes welfare reforms in many of the European countries so difficult. The restructuring of welfare programmes, subsidised employment, retraining and education should therefore take the distribution of skills into account. More generally, they should be targeted at the working population as a whole and not focus too narrowly on those who need help in order to sustain political support for expansive policies. Left-of-centre politics should have the common interests of middle- and low-income workers in mind when thinking of ways to reduce economic insecurity.

Besides, regulated economies and expansive welfare states have in the past relied heavily on the regulatory capacities of the social partners, particularly trade unions. Where capacities for self-regulation in the labour market are still in place, institutional support seems a good investment against a further widening of economic inequalities. Trade unions as labour-market experts could be encouraged to engage in training and retraining, as well as facilitating economic restructuring to a much larger extent, as the Scandinavian countries show. Rethinking the role of unions in labour-market regulation and servicing for vulnerable workers in a co-operative way can potentially be a fruitful strategy so long as ways of mutual co-operation are found. This requires some institutional support by governments. In many countries however, social partnership has deteriorated and disintegrated over the last decades, due in some cases to harsh exclusionary politics. In some cases, trade unions have concentrated too narrowly on the vested interests of labour-market insiders and have had little to offer to new groups on the labour market. It seems that the previous beneficial liaison between labour unions and labour parties needs a thorough restructuring in order to focus on the tasks at hand. Finally, global business has taken on a new role of assuming responsibility and accountability vis-à-vis communities. Corporate social responsibility is not just a fad but a living reality for many global firms these days. The reasons why firms engage in CSR are more mundane than the values espoused in company mission statements. However, businesses' increasing role of responsibility has become necessary in a global economy where important issues are no longer regulated by the state.

Companies increasingly have to consider whether their business strategy meets the wider expectations of the communities in which they operate. This is true not only for firms who have brand names to protect. They have to respond to consumers' expectations, which increasingly go beyond the mere quality of the product to also include a fair treatment of their workforce. Many firms are also dependent on political decisions, either in the context of regulation, or in the context of public–private partnerships and government contracts. Public procurement has become a field where firms are increasingly also judged on their record as a good corporate citizen. Asking firms for their policies on dealing with mass redundancies, their contribution to the skill base of their workforce and measures to increase the employability of their staff has become more and more common.

Policy-makers can tap into companies' responsibility strategies in several ways: they can raise the expectations on corporate behaviour with regard to how firms deal with mass redundancies in the context of off-shoring decisions. Firms can be held in part responsible for the employability of their workforce; they can be asked to train better and more and provide severance payments to those who lose their jobs. Firms can also be questioned as to how compatible cheap labour strategies are with passionate mission statements on fairness and values. Firms' strategies, as noted above, are not set in stone and are not uniformly hooked on cost reductions. Responsible restructuring can be expected from those firms who otherwise tend to take advantage of the institutional arbitrage the world economy provides them with.

Conclusions

The effects of globalisation do not just concern jobs. While increasing economic integration prompts firms to move jobs to developing countries, new employment might be created by the growing wealth of the south. Yet, in combination with technological progress and the rise of the service sector, the effects of globalisation are also about an increase in economic insecurity which primarily hits low-skilled workers and their families as well as those who have invested in specific and not easily transferable skills. Countries are affected by this development to various degrees and in various ways. Depending on their economic specialisation, their institutional legacy of labour-market institutions, and on their capacity to forge political coalitions for social protection, they have adopted different pathways of adjustment and are likely to continue to do so. Adjusting to change is the only way of dealing with the challenge of globalisation, which should not be equated with a passive acceptance of further trade liberalisation. Instead, governments have to identify their comparative strengths in terms of both their economic and their institutional assets, using them to the advantage of social and economic cohesion. Ultimately, they ought to increase their investment in human resources and calculate more clearly the costs of not doing so. Yet, investment in people's skills – be it general or specific skills – needs to be protected by social insurance and labour-market regulation in order to enable business models that are based on high productivity, thereby providing the economic security which workers and their families need in an era of global interconnectedness.

Notes

1 See M. Wolf, *Why Globalization Works* (New Haven and London: Yale University Press, 2004); Jagdish Bhagwati, *In Defense of Globalization* (Oxford: Oxford University Press, 2004); World Bank, *Global Economic Prospects: Managing the Next Wave of Globalization* (Washington, DC, 2007).

2 D. Rodrik, *Has Globalization Gone Too Far?* (Washington, DC: Institute for International Economics, 1997).

3 G. Garrett, *Partisan Politics in the Global Economy* (New York: Cambridge University Press, 1998).

4 http://www.worldpublicopinion.org/pipa/pdf/apr07/CCGA+_GlobTrade_arti-cle.pdf

5 Study released on 5 December 2007 by the German Marshall Fund of the United States, *Perspectives on Trade and Poverty Reduction: A Survey of Public Opinion: Key Findings Report 2007*: http://www.gmfus.org/economics/tpsurvey/index.cfm.

6 K.F. Scheve and M.J. Slaughter, 'A New Deal for Globalization', *Foreign Affairs* (July/August 2007); and Kenneth F. Scheve and Matthew J. Slaughter, 'Economic Insecurity and the Globalization of Production', *American Journal of Political Science* 48:4 (2004), pp. 662–74.

7 OECD, *Employment Outlook 2007. Summary in English* (Paris), p. 3.

8 S. Berger, *How We Compete: What Companies Around the World are Doing to Make it in Today's Global Environment* (New York and London: Currency Books, 2006).

9 OECD, *Employment Outlook 2007*, p. 108.

10 R. Freeman, 'Are Your Wages Set in Beijing?', *Journal of Economic Perspectives* 9:3 (1995), pp. 15–32; L.F. Katz and D.H. Autor, 'Changes in the Wage Structure and Earnings Inequality', in O.C. Ashenfelter and D. Card (eds), *Handbook of Labor Economics*, Vol. 3A (Amsterdam: Elsevier, 1999).

11 On the increase in economic insecurity see OECD, 'Is Job Insecurity on the Increase in OECD Countries?', *Employment Outlook 1997*; on the stability of job tenure rates see OECD, 'OECD Workers in the Global Economy: Increasingly Vulnerable?', *Employment Outlook 2007*.

12 Berger, *How We Compete*, p. 54.

13 According to a survey of works councils in German firms conducted by the German Trade Union Research Institute in 2007.

14 These are answers to a survey among workers on how much they worry about their jobs, which was conducted in 1997. C.J. Anderson and J. Pontusson, 'Workers, Worries and Welfare States: Social Protection and Job Insecurity in 15 OECD Countries', *European Journal of Political Research* 46 (2007), pp. 211–35.

15 OECD, *Employment Outlook 1997*; OECD, *Employment Outlook 2007*.

16 Anderson and Pontusson, 'Workers, Worries and Welfare States', p. 228.

17 J. Hacker, *The Great Risk Shift* (Oxford: Oxford University Press, 2006).

18 OECD, *Boosting Jobs and Incomes: Policy Lessons from Reassessing the OECD Jobs Strategy* (2006): http://www.oecd.org/dataoecd/47/53/36889821.pdf

19 L. Kletzer, 'A Prescription to Relieve Worker Anxiety', Policy Brief No. 01–2 (Washington, DC: Institute for International Economics, 2001).

20 R. Liddle and F. Lerais, 'Europe's Social Reality: A Consultation Paper from the Bureau of European Policy Advisers' (2007): http://ec.europa.eu/citizens_agenda/social_reality_stocktaking/docs/background_document_en.pdf

21 M. Wallerstein, 'Wage-Setting Institutions and Pay Inequality in Advanced Industrial Societies', *American Journal of Political Science* 43:3 (1999), pp. 649–80.

22 Commission of the European Communities, *Towards Common Principles of Flexicurity: More and Better Jobs Through Flexibility and Security*. Communication from the Council, the European Parliament, the European Economic and Social Committee and the Committee of the Regions (2007): http://ec.europa.eu/employment_social/employment_strategy/flexicurity%20media/flexicuritypublication_2007_en.pdf

23 There is by now a large literature on 'flexicurity' and the Danish model in particular. See T. Schulze-Cleven, B.C. Watson and J. Zysman, 'Innovation and Adaptability in a Digital Era: How Wealthy Nations Stay Wealthy', BRIE Working Paper 177 (24 May 2007).

24 World Bank, *Global Economic Prospects 2007*, pp. 128ff.; O. Blanchard, 'European Unemployment: The Evolution of Facts and Ideas', *Economic Policy* (January 2006), pp. 5–59.

25 OECD, *The Jobs Study* (Paris, 1994).

26 OECD, *Boosting Jobs and Incomes*.

27 The irony is that struggles over plant closures were traditionally much fiercer in countries with rather liberal and flexible labour markets than in countries with higher degrees of employment protection. Low levels of employment protection in themselves do not make workers more mobile, just as higher levels of employment protection do not make labour markets more sclerotic.

28 T. Iversen and T. Cusack, 'The Causes of Welfare State Expansion', *World Politics* 52 (2000), pp. 313–49.

13
The Progressive Challenge: Shared Prosperity

Gene Sperling

The issue of whether increased globalisation and the spread of new information technology will be viewed as strengthening or hollowing out the middle class may be the paramount economic question facing OECD nations, and in particular the United States. Indeed, around the world, the concerns of growing inequality within individual nations – even those with strong growth – is at the heart of much of the debate over the future of globalisation.

The challenge for progressives in this very challenging economic environment is to neither take lightly very real concerns about growing inequality nor simply to pull back on pro-market, pro-competition and pro-innovation policies that lead to dynamic growth. Rather, the goal for progressives must be to find the policies that succeed in fulfilling President John F. Kennedy's famous dictum: 'a rising tide lifts all the boats'.[1]

For many conservatives, the notion of a rising tide lifting all boats is not a test but an automatic assumption. These conservatives invoke the rising-tide argument to suggest that growth which helps the most affluent will trickle down and lift everyone else up. Some even argue – incorrectly – that Kennedy devised the metaphor to defend his decision to reduce the high marginal tax rates that existed at the time.

For progressives, the notion of a rising tide lifting all boats is not an automatic assumption, but rather an aspiration, test, and measure of success. Do the economic policies progressives propose and implement create both growth and shared prosperity? Indeed, in the United States, the eight years of the George W. Bush presidency were a stark example of how wide the disconnect can be between growth and shared prosperity.

The reality is that both those most concerned with supporting dynamic, open economies and those concerned with equity should aspire to what I call 'rising-tide economics'. Around the world we are witnessing growing resistance to economic dynamism, even where openness, innovation and trade are fostering growth, when too many people feel their boat is not rising, or is even sinking. In the US in particular, where job loss often leads to a loss of health care and where adjustment policies are weak and fragmented, the persistent fear of steep economic falls risks creating a popular backlash against economic openness and dynamism. Yet, it is a mistake for pro-growth progressives to see the policy response as means to the end of greater support for economic openness. The end for progressives must always be shared prosperity in and of itself that lifts incomes and opportunities for the middle class and those struggling to get in. The goal should be how to craft a collection of policies – including those related to globalisation – that can be best shaped to serve that fundamental progressive aspiration.

Such a set of policies must certainly include measures that deal with job creation through alternative energy, small-business development and research, together with broader, universal and smartly crafted help for workers and policies to ensure the rights of labour at home and among trading partners. Particularly important to building a stronger social compact in an increasingly dynamic global economy are policies ensuring the ability of workers to provide health care, higher education and pension savings for their families, without predicating that ability on each turn of the labour market.

On the other hand, those most concerned with social equity must also see the imperative of not turning our back on promoting competition and innovation that can spur economic growth – even with the inevitable dislocations that can result. In the US, growth unquestionably helps create conditions that make it easier to live up to America's credo that it can always make room for new minorities, immigrants and the working poor – without having to push anyone else out or down. Ethnic division can flourish more easily when individuals and communities sense that the economy is a zero-sum game, where one group's gains can come only through someone else losing out. To paraphrase Ben Franklin's revolutionary caution that 'we will hang together or hang apart' – if we do not grow together, we risk growing apart. Simply put, it is easier to have a melting pot if we also have a growing pot.

The New Productivity Decade: shared prosperity or growing inequality?

While many analysts often look at US trends over the last 30 years, it is intriguing to examine the period 1995–2007 – what I refer to as the 'New Productivity Decade', where the United States finally rose out of the productivity doldrums. The different faces presented by globalisation and the growth of information technology during this twelve-year period are striking. While productivity growth was mediocre, averaging 1.4 per cent between 1974 and 1995, between 1996 and 2007 the US witnessed resurgence in productivity growth, averaging 2.5 per cent. Thus, it is worth asking, has this surge, which coincided with the increased globalisation of the American economy and growth in information technology, lifted all boats? The answer is almost a tale of two cities.

During the New Productivity Decade, globalisation, investor confidence, the diffusion of information technology, and the end of the Cold War came together to spark efficiency and productivity in everything from inventory management to personal finances. During the first half of this decade, productivity – after languishing for twenty years at just over 1 per cent – took off in 1996, averaging 2.6 per cent over the next five years. It was a perfect example of a rising-tide-lifting-all-boats argument: as productivity grew 13 per cent overall from 1995 to 2000, median family income kept up, growing 11 per cent. From 1993 to 2000, every economic quintile showed income growth above 16 per cent, with the strongest growth (23.4 per cent) among the bottom 20 per cent of earners.

From 2001 to 2007, while productivity kept expanding at an average of 2.5 per cent per year, the story on shared prosperity could not have been more different. From 2000 to 2007, the typical working household saw its income fall by 3.7 per cent or $2,176. Hourly wages for non-management workers fell over the first four years of the recovery. Rising productivity and historic corporate profits even seemed predicated on disappointing wages: Goldman Sachs found that more than 40 per cent of record corporate profit growth of the second five years was due to the historically low share of national income going to labour. The contrast with the previous five years could not have been starker.

A significant difference between these two halves of the New Productivity Decade is that during the second half increasing globalisation and the growth in information technology dramatically expanded the capacity of workers from around the world to contest American middle-class service jobs. While jobs at the top and bottom of the income ladder requiring a physical presence or face-to-face collaboration were less affected, an increasing number of jobs seemed to be falling into what economists Lori Kletzer and Brad Jensen have called the 'tradeable services' category: white-collar service jobs capable of being performed in a vast number of global locations. As a result, tens of millions of traditionally middle-income service and manufacturing jobs faced downward wage pressure.

Comparing the economic evidence from both halves of the New Productivity Decade underscores the imperative for economic policies that are focused both on growth and on ensuring that its benefits are widely shared. Globalisation is making competition fiercer and the need for flexibility, innovation, top-notch human capital, and access to global supply chains ever greater. Yet global labour competition also raises the spectre of downward wage pressure and dislocation for an increasingly broad cross-section of the workforce.

A new economic reliance?

Many conservatives argue that concerns over the fate of middle-class incomes are overblown. And certainly in the 1980s many feared our middle class would be weakened by Japan's rise as an economic superpower, missing both its structural flaws as well as the rise of the internet. Yet, even with these caveats, the case for today's concerns over the weakening of middle-class wages and rising inequality in America seems compelling for several reasons.

First, the new global labour-market competition could be far more enduring. Competitors of the recent past like Japan and Korea represented 3 per cent of the global workforce, but competitors of today like China and India make up a whopping 40 per cent. While we have already seen evidence of these two new emerging giants running into their own skill shortages, the larger truth is that it could be a generation before either country approaches the limit of its potential low-cost labour pool. Also, price competition is fiercer today. Whereas manufacturing labour costs in Japan are 85 per cent of those in the US, and in South Korea 62 per cent of the US cost, in China they were measured as low as 3 per cent in the most recent 2004 data. According to the Harvard labour economist Richard Freeman, it could take more than fifty years for labour costs in China and India to reach parity with those in the United States.

Second, in recent years we have witnessed a broadening and even upskilling of economic anxiety. Twenty years ago, the sense that one's job could be contested by lower-wage labour was real and painful to many communities and millions of workers – but they tended to be located in manufacturing communities and regions. While the magnitude of off-shored and potentially off-shoreable jobs remains a hotly contested topic (with some such as former Federal Reserve Vice-Chair Alan Blinder projecting 42 million potentially off-shoreable US jobs, while others at the McKinsey Global Institute are projecting closer to 3 to 5 million), today the threat of outsourcing, the growing ability of tradeable service jobs to contest US jobs – or at least produce downward pressure on wages – is significant. This has spread economic anxiety to a larger swath of white-collar workers, including those with some college education. Indeed, even college-educated men – who saw their incomes go up $11,000 during the Clinton years – saw a $900 fall in income from 2001 to 2007.

Third, there is greater evidence of the middle class falling further behind those at the very top. Yet, today, the fact that many lower-wage jobs require a physical presence in the United States somewhat reduces the global labour-market competition for certain service and construction jobs. As top economists from Lawrence Summers to Paul Krugman have documented, those at the very top of the income distribution have received the lion's share of the recent economic gains. Krugman writes that 'the income of the top 0.01 per cent – people with incomes of more than $5 million in 2004 – has risen by a factor of 5'.[2] Summers points out that if national income in 2004 were distributed as it was in 1981, the top 1 per cent would have approximately $640 billion less in total income, and the bottom 80 per cent would have $637 billion more. That's the equivalent of an approximately $7,000 transfer from each household in the bottom 80 per cent, with each household in the top 1 per cent receiving approximately $560,000.

This evidence fits into what the Harvard labour economist Lawrence Katz describes as the new polarisation in the workforce. While Americans tend to think of inequality as the distance between the very top and the very bottom, these trends show the great movement in inequality between the top and the middle. Katz reports this 'upper tail' wage inequality (the wage gap between the 90th and 50th percentiles) as steadily and rapidly increasing. He points out a fact which should be especially worrisome for progressive policy-makers: 'Rising wage inequality was not offset and actually has been reinforced by changes in employee benefits (health insurance, pensions, sick days) and working conditions (e.g. work-place safety).'[3]

Fourth, the accounts and experiences of even higher-skilled service and manufacturing workers losing their jobs to overseas competition or seeing their wages stagnate show that what I have called 'economic reliance' – the unspoken social compact that hard work and a college education could buy anyone a modicum of economic security – is starting to deteriorate. The message coming even from President Clinton in the 1990s was that this economic reliance or economic compact was not broken; it only had to be updated and modernised for the high-tech economy by adding an element of lifelong learning and technological literacy. But the breakdown of this compact is of profound significance. When the hard-working parent who has sweated to send his or her child to a decent public college starts to question whether or not it will any longer buy that child a better life it challenges the unspoken economic assumptions on which that person has based much of his or her life. When one hears the line from a laid-off worker, 'I did everything I was supposed to do', one is hearing the pain not just of a lost job, but of someone who feels their economic reliance may have been built on outdated assumptions.

Supply-side blindness

The Bush White House and many conservative commentators have been highly resistant to recognising these trends out of a commitment to espousing the successes of supply-side economic ideology, whereby simply reducing marginal tax rates on income and investment for the most well-off will trickle down and produce shared prosperity for the working poor and middle class alike. With a strong vested interest in establishing that the tax cuts of 2001 and 2003 must be working, conservatives have been hesitant to recognise the extent to which even when the tide has been rising, it has not been lifting a high percentage of economic boats.

Spokespersons for the Bush administration often spoke of the great success of their policies and a booming economy, even while median household income of working-age families went down by $2,176 over seven years, poverty went up 5.7 million, job growth was historically weak for a recovery and there were 7.2 million more Americans without health insurance. Moreover, they showed a profound blindness towards the increased sense of risk and economic anxiety felt by working Americans. A 2006 Pew Research Center poll found that half of the respondents worried that their children would grow up to be worse off than they are, while 61 per cent of Americans think theirs or a friend's job may be at risk from globalisation.

While the Bush administration's rhetoric revealed an insensitivity if not blindness to rising economic anxiety, its economic policies were like a boxer leaning into a left hook – responding to that anxiety by imposing even more risk on the individual, from attempting to partially privatise social security to pushing incentives to move more Americans into an often callous individual health market. Taken together, these policies amount to what the Economic Policy Institute economist Jared Bernstein calls YOYO ('you're on your own') economics.

Indeed, the ideological insistence on smaller and smaller government prevents conservatives from embracing growth-maximising public policies that can help attract high-value jobs, encourage more risk-taking, and reduce the backlash against globalisation, precisely by mitigating the negative effects of job loss. Under the pretence of keeping the size of government down, conservatives refuse to see that a broader adjustment strategy might increase support for open markets and a dynamic economy. Entrepreneurial risk-taking has certainly been encouraged in the United States by the fact that the price of failure is at worst temporary bankruptcy, rather than debtor's prison. Yet, there is little recognition by supply-siders that smart expansions of public policies to help people adjust to job or even occupation loss can encourage more risk-taking in personal careers. As Yale economist Robert Shiller wrote, our current policies may deter personal career risk-taking, as such 'ventures they set out on, are all limited by the knowledge that economically we are on our own and must bear all of the losses we incur'.[4]

The 'rising tide, raise all boats' opportunity

The progressive response to supply-side economics cannot simply be its mirror image: policies so exclusively directed at redistribution and combating insecurity that they ignore private sector growth, upward mobility, innovation, savings and entrepreneurship. We shouldn't replace a focus on growth regardless of equity with a focus on equity regardless of growth. The answer lies neither in following the 1990s Clinton playbook word for word, nor in an overreaching reaction focused only on how to divide the current economic pie. Nations like the United States that do not have an aggressive strategy for encouraging investment and high-wage jobs on their shores risk seeing those opportunities go elsewhere. Yet, without bold and comprehensive policies to structure shared growth, there is a danger of the continuation of growth with the benefits going to a smaller and smaller sliver. The rise in insecurity and wage pressure certainly demands a stronger public commitment to the social compact, as well as greater scrutiny of trade deals than there was in the 1990s.

Yet becoming more sensitive to the potential downsides of globalisation should not cause us to forget the benefits of an open economy, especially when it is combined with broader job, education and adjustment policies as well as a greater commitment to a more level playing field for collective bargaining and labour rights, at home and among trading partners. Catherine Mann, at the Peterson Institute for International Economics, finds that the globalisation of IT hardware in the 1990s reduced prices for IT in the US by 10 to 30 per cent, contributing significantly to the spread of such technology and productivity gains. And while there are legitimate concerns today about the wage pressure coming from greater engagement with China and India, for our children a major economic imperative may be to create jobs by being able to export to those exploding middle classes – as per capita income in India and urban China is projected to triple in the coming twenty years.

Progressive politicians must also ensure that their words and policies communicate that they are more than just the folks who are there for you when something bad happens in your life. They must also be the people who share in Americans' upward aspirations. Perhaps the most important thing in life is to have friends and advocates who are there for you in bad times. But most people also want friends to share their dreams and upward aspirations. Americans want a firmer floor to limit falls in the global economy. But they also want affirmative and optimistic policies designed to show how they can share in and contribute to a growing economy through increasing their savings so that they can retire someday with a nest egg, afford higher education, start their own business, or find a job with a cutting-edge Fortune 500 Company or small business.

We need a stronger social compact with stronger policies ensuring that American workers are empowered directly with the tools for access to higher education for themselves and their children, with health care, and with matching saving incentives that are not simply contingent on individual employers or what is offered on the job and which are thus not lost or dramatically set back with each career and job transition. These are critical aspects of our social compact. In our increasingly dynamic labour market there should be greater efforts to ensure that workers who work hard and play by the rules should not be denied those fundamental aspects of both economic security and upward aspiration as a result of the whims of global labour-market competition.

The following six sections are designed to offer a sense of the specific policies that would form a strategy to both raise the tide and lift all boats in the United States. Some of the proposals may also be relevant in the context of other OECD countries.

1. A progressive compact on trade

One of the greatest challenges and most controversial issues in laying out a progressive pro-growth economic agenda concerns international trade. In the United States, while progressives were united in support behind the efforts of the Clinton administration to include enforceable labour standards in trade agreements and strengthen the International Labour Organisation (ILO), there was often intense disagreement over the degree to which President Clinton should have supported specific trade agreements that did not reflect his broader reform agenda – either because he inherited it from the previous administration or because of the limitations inherent in seeking to pass any legislation with a conservative Republican Congress for the last six years of his presidency.

Yet looking forward, there is room for a new consensus among progressives. There is growing recognition by nearly everyone that the wage inequality we have seen in the second half of the New Productivity Decade requires a stronger social compact both at home and abroad and less of an automatic assumption that market openings will strengthen, not strain, America's middle class. In the US, this means a more ambitious agenda to spur job creation, pass universal health care, strengthen collective bargaining, increase the pool of skilled workers, and strengthen re-employment assistance. Among trading partners, it demands a stronger commitment to enforcing trade agreements, preventing currency manipulation from countries like China, better labour standards and partnerships to strengthen safety nets, a 'decent work' agenda as championed by the International Labour Organisation and the Center for American Progress, a commitment to universal basic education, and an ILO with more funding and enforcement powers to monitor labour rights. A commitment to decent working conditions abroad is not about shielding the US from all low-wage competition. Instead, it is about ensuring that low-wage competition is not based on extreme exploitation offensive to basic human rights, such as child labour, sweat shops, bonded labour, or the killing or jailing of labour leaders. Thea Lee, policy director and chief international economist at the AFL-CIO, rightly noted this distinction when she explained that the union's claims against China were not about the country's 'right to compete in the global economy on the basis of low wages', but about the 'incremental cost advantage that comes from the brutal and undemocratic repression of workers' human rights'.[5]

The question facing policy-makers now is how to proceed. Some promote moving forward – even without progress on a broad new social compact – with the notion that more trade is always better than less. Others call for a complete pause on even a new and improved development round until that ideal social compact is in place, even if that takes several years. Neither approach is wholly right. A business-as-usual strategy ignores the negative evidence of rising inequality and insecurity, as well as the large holes in our labour rights and adjustment policies. On the other hand, a blanket pause on all trade agreements would in the meantime reinforce Bushian unilateralism, unduly limit diplomatic and economic progress, and send a negative signal to poor nations seeking to use trade to reduce extreme poverty.

Rather, the US should impose a 'staged progress test' on trade policies, based on a case-by-case analysis of the importance of the trade opening and the degree to which it is promoting the interest of workers and the amount of progress being made towards a richer social compact, both in the United States and abroad. By these measures, there is a principled reason why some progressives opposed CAFTA – where labour standards were seen as being weakened – and voted for the trade deal with Peru, where Democratic leaders achieved consensus on the enforceable labour standards implemented in the Jordan agreement.

Rising-tide economics also should include a 'raising all boats' analysis that identifies and addresses the downside risks of a trade agreement to vulnerable workers on all sides. Such an analysis should not be used to raise the goal posts so high that no trade deal is ever good enough, but it should also not seek to mask in any way the downsides of such agreements or the degree to which we face cost-sharing crises where the burden of such policies is unfairly concentrated on select communities and workers.

2. Smart job creation

Adjustment assistance for laid-off workers is the pre-nup of public policy – it is the protection you are promised in the case of devastating news. It should be no surprise that most people would rather figure out how to save their marriage or their job than focus on the counselling or assistance after things go south. Unfortunately, what people most want from government – a plan to save specific jobs or to pinpoint exactly where new ones are coming from – is where government is not the most competent. After all, it was not long ago that the US government was convinced that one of the fastest-growing occupations in the new economy would be travel agents.

So what can the government do to save and create jobs? In the 1990s, with booming job creation, we focused on laying the foundation for job creation with smart long-term investments. This is what former Treasury Secretary Lawrence Summers and I used to joke was a public investment 'Field of Dreams' strategy: If we build the right research facilities, have the right pre-schools and lifelong learning programs, and spread the reach of the Internet, middle-class jobs would come. Implicit in that vision was that the 'next big thing' would drive virtuous economic cycles of growth and job creation in ways we couldn't imagine at the time. This public investment strategy to lay the foundation for future private sector jobs and innovation should remain a cornerstone of progressive economic policy. Today, however, when a large percentage of workers think the nation is going in the wrong direction and are worrying about their jobs, a universal pre-kindergarten or research agenda – however good long-term policy – is understandably not the most comforting response.

The challenge for progressives today is to continue their 'field of dreams' focus on vital long-term investments in education and modern infrastructure, but also to be more aggressive in devising policies that answer the 'where are the new jobs coming from' question without falling into the trap of 'picking winners' or overly relying on large public-works programmes.

First, progressives should focus on policies to make the United States a magnet for good jobs. These days, many corporations see themselves as international firms, with little preference about what is performed where, as long as it improves the bottom line. But while these CEOs may feel that their fiduciary duty to shareholders should make them indifferent about where productive investment and high-value jobs are located, it should matter to American policy-makers. We shouldn't assume that what is good for GM or Intel is good for American jobs; rather, we should look for the intersection of a company's bottom line with the interests of the workers, wages and standard of living of America's citizens, and devise policy accordingly.

Second, there is more that can be done to compete for lower-skilled jobs through non-protectionist means – that should include an 'insourcing agenda'. For example, there is no reason why there could not be more policy incentives to help poor rural and urban parts of the United States – with lower labour costs – compete for the call-centre and back-office jobs that are increasingly outsourced to lower-wage nations. Wages in rural areas are often low enough to be price-competitive with many outsourcing options; average wages in rural America are 30 to 40 per cent lower than in urban areas.

Moreover, Deloitte and Touche has found that 38 per cent of companies find hidden costs when they outsource, including quality control, training and increased travel costs. But America is falling behind in rural broadband infrastructure, which limits our ability to 'insource'. While 67 per cent of suburban households have Internet access, only 52 per cent of rural households are online – and only one in five rural Internet users have broadband access. Investments in rural broadband would go a long way towards helping rural areas compete with low-cost call centres and back-office jobs abroad.

Finally, and most importantly, we need an investment strategy targeted towards the innovation jobs of the future. Progressives must draw a distinction between the narrower 'picking winners and losers' approach associated with industrial policy and strategies that encourage more high-value added jobs in areas where we know America must be competitive. Yet, at the very time we are facing such a strong competitive threat, the Bush administration did not for three years provide a single inflation-adjusted dollar of increase to the National Institutes of Health (NIH) – by far America's largest pool of research dollars. In the budget agreement finally passed in January 2008, the NIH received an increase of less than one per cent – barely one-quarter of the amount needed to keep up with inflation, according to the Associated Press. As I wrote in an op-ed in the *Washington Post* in July 2007, this policy discourages new scientists and entrepreneurship, and threatens to reduce research-related jobs on US shores.

With the strength of its university system and capacity to create high-return 'clusters' of research parks, universities and pools of entre- preneurs, the United States should adopt the opposite strategy and engage in an all-out battle to make the country a magnet for research jobs.

The effort to spur the US towards a low-carbon economy offers signif- icant opportunities for smart policies to foster job creation. This effort does not require the government to pick a single winning technology or oil alternative, nor does it rely simply on an energy-based public jobs initiative. What does make sense, however, is to put forth a national strategy that invests both in the incentives and jobs involved in spreading existing low-carbon practices, and in the broader research in which private companies may currently be under-investing due to their inability to capture what may be risky or speculative investments. Furthermore, as the Center for American Progress has proposed, a national strategy should invest in a series of new and expanded tax incentives to develop new job-creating technologies to achieve the goal of 25 per cent renewable sources by 2025. Another idea that deserves to be expanded is an Energy-Darpa – which would encourage the type of blue-sky research that led DARPA to help fund projects that sparked the creation of Google, as well as the development of the Internet and the personal computer.

3. Balancing job security and flexibility

A central goal for rising-tide economics is to increase economic secur- ity while preserving the flexibility in the US labour markets to help keep unemployment to a minimum. This requires progress on five fronts.

Universal security – regardless of the reason for job loss: This requires broadening adjustment-assistance spending and making it universal and non-contingent on how your job was lost. Currently, the United States spends only 0.5 per cent of GDP on adjustment assistance – half as much as the United Kingdom, and one-sixth as much as Germany and Denmark, according to the McKinsey Global Institute. An ambi- tious adjustment-assistance strategy that offers this security must be universal, so that the focus to determine eligibility is not on how jobs were lost, but rather on how benefits best spur re-employment.

We must end for good the notion that eligibility for any adjustment policy is conditioned on how you lost your job. From an equity stance, such distinctions make no sense. And in the global economy, the distinctions between a job lost due to trade or technology or changes in consumer tastes or poor management will become murkier and murkier.

User-friendly one-stop: In addition to being universal, adjustment assistance must be user-friendly. If Costco can provide one-stop shopping for life's day-to-day necessities, then the government should be able to have a single toll-free number and one-stop centres that handle all re-employment issues, from unemployment insurance to training to expanded benefits like mortgage assistance and 'entrepreneurial training' – for instance, learning how to start your own business, as has been piloted in Washington, Massachusetts and North Carolina. Only if adjustment assistance succeeds on universality and simplicity will it ever be able to make a major impact on the growing economic anxiety.

Beyond the business cycle: We need to throw out the notion that longer assistance should be tied only to times of national economic stress. In a global economy where entire job classifications may come under threat even in solid national economic times, basing the scope of things like unemployment insurance on the state of the overall economy is a relic of the past. Policy should also recognise that the length of job loss may be determined more by the fall one's community has taken or when specific job classifications come under threat than by whether the overall economy is hurting.

Pro-search incentives: In designing adjustment assistance, we should strive to combine the flexibility and relatively low unemployment rates of US markets with the greater protection afforded by European nations. The goal for us is to have a broader, more universal and simpler system that avoids the disincentives for employers to hire new employees or for workers to get back into the job market. One example is a wage insurance programme. Unions are right to say wage insurance is not a cure-all and should not be a substitute for examining broader issues. But when done right, it can both limit falls while avoiding negative incentives to search for work. A 50 per cent wage-insurance programme would reduce the depth of economic falls: If a worker making $20 an hour were forced to take a new job at $10 an hour, wage insurance would cover 50 per cent – or $5 an hour – for a period of years, which could be extended for those in their fifties who may have trouble starting new careers. Yet, because wage insurance is triggered only by finding a new job, it cannot be accused of replicating European disincentives to get back into the workforce. This deserves serious expansion beyond the very small pilot passed in 2002.

Level playing field for unions: Moreover, the antagonistic view of too many businesses in the United States to organised labour is unfortunately limiting the potential for unions to play a larger role in ensuring that adjustments for workers are smooth, as well as looking for new pre-emptive policies to help those laid off before they are caught in a downward spiral. Critics of unions argue that they will be too demanding and force wage requests that will make competition and job creation less, not more, likely. But employers should let the market decide rather than turning increasingly to using abusive tactics on organisers. Just as some corporate managers have taken steps that have hurt the competitiveness of their companies, there may be some unions which will make unrealistic wage- and work-rule demands. Just as the market punishes management who do not stay on the cutting edge, so workers reject organised labour leaders who do not adjust to market realities. Yet, if policies that restore a level playing field and combat the abusive tactics that prevent labour organising help the unions to prove themselves a creative partner with workers and employers in saving jobs when possible – but smoothing transitions when necessary – they could find new strength by taking the lead in both ensuring layoffs and wage cuts are a last, not first, option, and in reducing economic anxiety by smoothing adjustments as opposed to blocking change.

Pre-emptive policies: Finally, progressives must do more to create adjustment policies that are 'pre-emptive', meaning that they provide options for workers to get assistance and for localities to seek economic diversification before predictable mass layoffs occur. The Clinton administration used tax incentives for investment and job creation as incentives for poor communities to devise strategies for their economic future. These included Empowerment Zones, Community Development Banks and New Market Tax Credits. Building on the model of the Empowerment Zones, progressives should consider championing 'Dynamic Adjustment Zones' offering new business investment incentives and wage credits to communities based not just on poverty levels, but also on the danger of suffering due to massive layoffs or relocation of their major factories or service providers.

With a pre-emptive approach, a Dynamic Adjustment Zones process might inspire different stakeholders from a vulnerable community – business leaders, union representatives, elected officials, local investors and non-profits – to start work on an economic diversification strategy two years before economic devastation hits, instead of two months after. The same must be true for training policies. More initiatives should be passed that give workers the ability to search and train for new jobs – when they face job threats but before they have felt the sting of a pink slip.

4. The pro-growth rationale for a more inclusive labour force

Early college intervention for poor youths: The moral and values case for addressing the shame of youth poverty – 34 per cent for African-American children – is reason enough to have a bold effort to attack child poverty. Yet it also threatens economic growth because it reduces the supply of workers with the skills that can help attract jobs. For decades, the US has relied on a healthy increase in the educated population to help foster economic growth. In the past two decades alone, the pool of workers aged twenty-five to sixty-four grew 44 per cent, but in the next two decades we will see zero net increase in the pool of native-born workers, while minorities and traditionally disadvantaged groups who usually have lower education levels will make up a larger share of the American workforce. Over the past two decades, the share of workers with at least a high school degree grew by 19 per cent; over the next two decades it will grow by only 4 per cent. Since neither massive new immigration nor increased fertility rates are predicted, the US will need to increase its pool of highly skilled workers among the currently projected workforce or face a growing labour shortage.

Tackling these moral and economic concerns begins early. America needs to expand and transform the pre-kindergarten programmes Head Start and Early Head Start into a truly comprehensive education and childcare initiative that offers all children aged nought to five from modest- and low-income families access to quality infant, toddler and pre-school programmes. Launching such an effort might cost $20–30 billion annually, but that is only 25 per cent of what recent tax cuts for the most affluent 1 per cent of Americans will cost each year. These expenses are well worth the cost when we keep in mind the critical skills that the US workforce will need in the coming decades.

Starting young is not enough; we must ensure that disadvantaged youth remain in the academic pipeline. An appealing model is Gaining Early Awareness and Readiness for Undergraduate Programs, or GEAR UP, an innovative programme that President Clinton started in the late 1990s which reaches out to disadvantaged children at young ages and stays engaged with them through high school. It is an approach that experts like Steven Zwerling of the Ford Foundation, who has spent years analysing anti-dropout and mentoring initiatives, find has proven successful at increasing the pool of college-ready young people from disadvantaged backgrounds. This is a programme and idea that is ripe for expansion. With additional public support, we should not shy away from asking colleges themselves to lead this effort. One idea would be for a group of top universities, particularly in the Ivy League, to start a High Hopes Coalition that any state or private college could join. Each school would agree not only to institute new long-term early intervention programmes in their communities, but also that any participating student who performs well enough to gain admission would be given free tuition to any school in the coalition.

Greater inclusion for those with disabilities: The under-employment of people with disabilities is a critical, if underappreciated, problem in America's ageing society. People with disabilities work at just half the rate of those without disabilities; in 2006, just 37.5 per cent of working-aged disabled Americans worked, compared to 74.4 per cent of working-aged Americans without disabilities. Among college graduates, the numbers aren't heartening; 54 per cent of college graduates with disabilities are employed, compared to 82 per cent of college graduates without disabilities. Empowering these individuals will become more important as the workforce ages. The United Nations predicts that the share of the population over sixty years of age in North America will grow from 16.7 per cent of the population in 2005 to 27.3 per cent of the population by 2050. According to Gregg Vanderheiden of the Trace Center at the University of Wisconsin, the share of people between the ages of fifty-five and sixty-four with functional limitations is more than five times that of the group between twenty-five and thirty-four.

While the US population is ageing faster than ever, we now have access to an unprecedented range of rehabilitative technologies that can help people work – but all too often at a considerable cost. Ensuring that all significantly disabled Americans have access to rehabilitative technologies is a cost that can easily be justified on both moral and economic grounds.

5. A PRA progressive wealth creation agenda

In addition to traditional progressive goals of equality of opportunity and income, twenty-first-century progressives must also be concerned with equality of wealth. Part of the disturbing story on economic inequality in recent years has been the trend towards winner-take-all and loser-lose-all outcomes, as documented by leading economists such as Paul Krugman, Elizabeth Warren, Jacob Hacker, Edward Wolff and the *Los Angeles Times*' Peter Gosselin. Largely restoring the top two upper-income-tax rates of the 1990s and placing a limit on the amount of yearly investment gains subject to significantly lower rates would go a long way to promoting equity in wealth.

But progressives cannot fall into the trap of only having policies that promote 'work over wealth'. They need a smart strategy for spreading wealth creation and savings. One way to do that is to start with righting the 'upside-down' system for savings. Of the more than $200 billion in tax incentives offered for each year for savings, only 10 per cent goes to the bottom 60 per cent of Americans. This upside-down system is a disgrace from both an equity and a growth perspective. Two ideas which could promote wealth creation are a universal 401(k) and a flat 30 per cent tax incentive for savings. The universal 401(k) would be offered to every working family and include matching tax credits and even greater incentives for the working poor. A refundable 30 per cent flat credit would mean that both the highest-paid executive and the lowest-income workers at a firm would get 30 per cent savings incentives. If such a plan were funded by freezing the estate tax at a $7 million-per-couple exemption (denying a further estate tax cut to only the wealthiest three-tenths of 1 per cent of estates), progressives could spread wealth-creation opportunities by offering effective savings incentives to over 50 million households.

6. The quadruple win of universal health care

A final, critical element of a rising-tide economic agenda is universal health care. Like poverty, the moral case alone should be enough to justify the US ending its unfortunate place as the only major indus-trial nation that allows so many of its citizens to go to sleep knowing that they are only one pink slip or one illness away from economic devastation.

First, rising costs are squeezing middle-class families. In nominal terms, premiums for family coverage have increased 78 per cent since 2001, while wages have risen 19 per cent and inflation has gone up 17 per cent over the same period. The average premium for family cover-age in 2007 was $12,106, and workers on average now pay $3,281 out of their pay cheques to cover their share of the cost of family policy. In designing a new system, cost reduction is the first place to start. By increasing preventative care, transitioning to an electronic medical records system, reducing unnecessary procedures and reigning in malpractice and insurance costs, responsible experts estimate that we could lower national health spending by at least $120 billion a year.

Businesses could achieve $25 billion in annual savings, and families could save $2,200 per year, according to the Business Roundtable. By improving certification and training and providing financial incen-tives to guard against medical errors, quality of care will improve while costs are contained. A universal coverage system would still require substantial investment, but by reducing health costs and requiring employers and workers to pay their fair share, the progressive goal of universal health coverage is achievable.

Second, health costs are hurting the competitiveness of American businesses. In a world where labour-intensive industries have to compete with workers in China and India, and high-skill industries compete with European businesses with lower health-care costs, it is increasingly difficult for businesses to provide coverage for all of their employees. The costs of health care are severely compromising the competitiveness of US manufacturing firms; it is a well-known, if unfortunate, fact that General Motors spends more on health care than on steel, giving the company labour costs at least $20 an hour higher than foreign competitors. Small businesses, especially, face nearly insurmountable health costs. Small businesses are the little engines of growth powering the economy. From 1990 to 2003, firms with fewer than 20 workers accounted for 79.5 per cent of net new jobs, despite accounting for less than 18.4 per cent of all jobs in 2003. According to the National Federation of Independent Business, as of 2006, 60 per cent of businesses employing 3 to 199 people offered employee health insurance, but only 48 per cent of those employing 3 to 9 did so, a number that has declined over the last five years. Because small businesses are so vital to the economy, any health reform plan should avoid placing burdens on such entrepreneurs. Tax credits to incentivise health coverage for small businesses would get the double benefit of increasing both health coverage and American competitiveness.

Third, health reform is key to alleviating much of the economic anxiety American families are feeling. As costs have increased and coverage dropped, health insurance has become one of the greatest sources of anxiety among American families. Since its first survey in 2004, the Kaiser Family Foundation Health Security Watch has consistently found that more Americans are worried about their health-care costs than about losing their job, paying their rent or mortgage, losing money on the stock market, or being the victim of a terrorist attack. Even in the middle of the subprime mortgage crisis, the August 2008 Kaiser poll found that while 14 per cent of Americans thought making rent or mortgage payments was a 'serious' problem, 24 per cent thought affording the medical care they need was 'serious'. In recent polls, half of those with health insurance say they are somewhat or very worried about losing their coverage.

Fourth, controlling health-care costs is a key component of dealing with the long-term entitlement challenges that the federal government faces. While many major fiscal debates in Washington over the last five years have centred on social security, many budget experts argue that this issue pales in comparison to America's real long-term budget buster – Medicare, the government insurance programme for the elderly. Medicare will soon be the largest strain on the federal budget, projected as it is to rise from 3 per cent of gross domestic product today to a whopping 11 per cent by 2080. A damaging misconception is the notion that what is driving this fiscal challenge is Medicare's excessive generosity. Not so.

First, to state the obvious, Medicare costs will rise under any scenario because of an ageing society. But, most fundamentally, the per-person costs of Medicare are rising because health-care costs for our entire society are rising faster than both the rate of inflation and of economic growth. This leads to an important but often underappreciated truth: the most effective way to control the spiralling costs of Medicare and Medicaid is not taking a meat-axe to these programmes but rather finding ways to lower health-care cost inflation. A universal health care programme that focuses on reducing costs through prevention, reducing cost-shifting, catastrophic care management, and eliminating the cost from companies seeking to deny coverage based on health conditions, is the most effective way to achieve this.

Conclusion: moving beyond trade-offs

The great progressive economist Arthur Okun entitled one of his most famous books *Equality and Efficiency: The Big Trade-Off*. Yet it is increasingly clear that with a careful eye on both raising the tide and lifting all boats, policies that most fit progressive values can be crafted to also be among the wisest pro-growth strategies. Policies that provide first chances to children born into the most disadvantaged environments, new chances at jobs from investments in alternative energy, and second chances to workers dislocated in the global economy clearly promote progressive aspirations of dignity and security for hard-working families and help create a nation where life opportunities are not denied as a result of the accident of birth.

The search for rising-tide economic solutions should be invigorated by the knowledge that there are two ways for a nation to grow apart. One is to have growth whose spoils are seen as rigged for the privileged and not flowing to a growing and inclusive middle class. The other is to have a stagnant economic pie, where expanding opportunity for one segment of society is seen as leaving a smaller slice for everyone else. During this time of global competition and technological change, progressives have an obligation to do all they can to ensure we are growing together – not apart.

Notes

1   President John F. Kennedy first used the line in a speech delivered in Colorado following the approval of the Fryingpan – Arkansas Reclamation Project, August 17, 1962.

2   P. Krugman, 'Whining Over Discontent', *New York Times*, 8 September 2006.

3   L. Katz, 'Globalization, Growth and Social Equity: American and European Perspectives', Presentation to Center for American Progress and Policy Network Conference, Washington, DC, 1 October 2007.

4   R.J. Shiller, *The New Financial Order: Risk in the 21st Century* (Princeton: Princeton University Press, 2003), p. 10.

5   Testimony of Thea M. Lee, Policy Director, American Federation of Labor and Congress of Industrial Organizations Before the Committee on International Relations Subcommittee on Africa, Global Human Rights, and International Operations, On Human Rights in China: Improving or Deteriorating Conditions?, 19 April 2006, p. 4: http://www.aflcio.org/issues/jobseconomy/manufacturing/iuc/upload/lee_04192006.pdf

Index